CQ's Vital Issues Series

Welfare Reform

Ann Chih Lin, editor

Kristin S. Seefeldt, author

CQ PRESS

A Division of Congressional Quarterly Inc.

WASHINGTON, D.C.

CQ Press

A Division of Congressional Quarterly Inc.

1255 22nd St. N.W., Suite 400

Washington, D.C. 20037

(202) 822-1475; (800) 638-1710

www.cqpress.com

Printed in the United States of America

06 05 04 03 02   5 4 3 2 1

Grateful acknowledgment is made to the following for granting permission to reprint material: CQ Press, *The CQ Researcher* (August 3, 2001): "Welfare Reform," by Sarah Glazer; the Brookings Institution for Table 1-1 and "Should the government encourage welfare recipients to marry?" by Wade F. Horn (p. 36).

Cover design: Debra Naylor

⊗ The paper used in this publication meets the minimum requirements of the American National Standard for Information Sciences—Permanence of Paper for Printed Library Materials, ANSI Z39.48-1992.

Library of Congress Cataloging-in-Publication Data

Seefeldt, Kristin S.
    Welfare reform / Ann Chih Lin, editor; Kristin S. Seefeldt, author.
        p. cm. -- (CQ's vital issues series)
    Includes bibliographical references and index.
    ISBN 1-56802-660-9 (cloth : alk. paper) -- ISBN 1-56802-659-5 (pbk. : alk. paper)
    1. Public welfare--United States. 2. Welfare recipients--United States. 3. United States--Social policy. I. Lin, Ann Chih. II. Title. III. Series.
  HV95 .S4 2002
  361.973--dc21

                                                    2001008381

Contents

Preface

CQ Press is pleased to present CQ's Vital Issues Series, a new reference collection that provides unparalleled, unbiased analyses of controversial topics debated at local, state, and federal levels. The series covers all sides of issues equally, delving into the topics that dominate the media, shape election-year politics, and confront the American public. Each book includes an issue from *The CQ Researcher* that introduces the subject; in-depth explanations of relevant politics, policy, and political actors; analyses of major for-profit and nonprofit business interests; and discussion of international reaction to how the United States handles the issue. In addition, each volume features extensive appendixes to aid in further research. Titles in the series include *Welfare Reform, Capital Punishment,* and *Immigration.* We believe CQ's Vital Issues Series is an exceptional research tool, and we would like your feedback. Please send your comments to VIfeedback@cqpress.com.

Introduction

As I write this introduction barely three weeks after the tragedies of September 11, 2001, the political landscape of a year ago seems as different, and distant, as the moon's. In autumn 2000 domestic political issues were in the ascendancy. Only one presidential debate dealt with foreign policy in any detail, and "security" meant programs for the elderly rather than protection from terrorist attacks. The economy was showing signs of a slowdown, but times were still easy in America. When we sat transfixed by the news, it was the collapse of ballot boxes that caught our attention. Some comics wondered, as weeks went by without a decision from the November election, if we would be better off without a new president.

Today I write in a country where issues other than criminal investigation and economic downturn have all but vanished from the political agenda. Our grief over the deaths of thousands, admiration for heroic rescue workers, and anger at the perpetrators have pushed aside, for the moment, much partisan rhetoric and debate. Was it really only this spring when a "bill of rights" referred to patients and their HMOs? Were competing versions of education legislation, just months ago, the subjects of congressional compromise and recriminations?

Yet in some ways our national tragedy has confirmed the continuing relevance of the public policy issues with which we inaugurate CQ Press's new Vital Issues Series. Capital punishment, welfare reform, and immigration: all are issues at the core of our national sense of justice, our definition of who is part of our country, and our understanding of rights and responsibilities. As we try to understand the crimes that led to such a massive loss of life, will our evaluations of the death penalty change? As we see Muslims and Arab immigrants targeted indiscriminately, will we think about immigration policy differently? As we struggle through layoffs and economic retrenchment, hard times that hurt everyone but affect the poor the most, will our view of the legacy of welfare reform change?

These questions deserve careful thought and thorough knowledge. The volumes in CQ's Vital Issues Series seek to provide the answers. They gather together a clear summary of the various dimensions of each of these important issues; a comprehensive look at the politics and policy developments of the past decade; a discussion of the various business, nonprofit, and political actors who influence the debate; and a view of the international context of U.S. policy. For those new to the subject, a Vital Issues book provides the necessary background in a readable and accessible format. For readers already acquainted with the debates, a Vital Issues volume is a useful reference for facts on various aspects of the issues, for an analysis of how those aspects fit together, and for further sources of information.

Each book in the series follows a format designed to make research and understanding as easy as possible. The first chapter of each book, "Issues, Viewpoints, and Trends," is a lively, succinct, and balanced account of the current policy debate. Reprinted from *The CQ Researcher*, this section is a primer for the novice. The second chapter, "Politics and Policy," presents a thorough look at policymaking and implementation: What have been the major developments of the past decade? How have debates at the level of policy formulation been translated into policy on the ground? This section pays particular attention to variations at the state and local levels: a Vital Issues book gives readers the story not only from Washington, D.C., but also from around the country, with an account of innovations and a summary, where appropriate, of each state's experience.

The third chapter, "Businesses and Nonprofit Organizations," explains the specific role that business and nonprofit organizations play in shaping—and continuing to shape—policy developments. Sketches of important organizations and their contributions are included, along with contact information and Web addresses. The final chapter, "International Implications," draws attention to the international context of our policy debates. Americans tend to forget that policies affect and are affected by events and policies in other countries and ignore the experience of other nations in struggling with similar problems. One of the distinctive contributions of CQ's Vital Issues Series is that it summarizes this international context, reporting accurately—but simply—the major worldwide trends, comparisons, and reactions that Americans need to know to make good policy at home.

As debates over capital punishment, immigration, and welfare reform recur—and they loom just over the horizon—we may find ourselves, more self-consciously than before, speaking both as interested individuals with differing points of view and as citizens with a responsibility to our common life. We hope that CQ's Vital Issues Series will provide readers with the information and perspective necessary to have these conversations. Whether you are a student, a journalist, an activist, or a concerned citizen, this series is for you. Let us know if we have been successful.

Ann Chih Lin
University of Michigan

1   Issues, Viewpoints, and Trends

The CQ Researcher Welfare Reform Update

The destitution among children and single mothers that liberals predicted when welfare was overhauled in 1996 has not come to pass. Conservatives credit the sweeping welfare reforms with a historic rise in employment among former welfare mothers. But many remain in poverty. When welfare reform comes up for reauthorization in Congress in 2002, Republicans will argue for trimming funding, since half as many people are on welfare. But Democrats will argue for generous funding to help those still unable to work and to assist new workers with child care and other work expenses. More aid may be forthcoming, now that welfare mothers have become the "working poor"—a group the American public is far more willing to help.

The Issues

After more than five years on welfare, Connie Rounds, the divorced mother of two teenagers, went to work as an aide at a residential facility for the elderly in Oregon. It was 1998, and she was paid $6.30 an hour.[1]

When Rounds's boss required her to work overtime, her income went over the monthly eligibility limit for Medicaid and state health insurance, a major disaster for Rounds, who is in her forties and suffers from chronic health problems.

Losing health insurance saddled Rounds with more than $3,000 in medical bills, which she must pay from a monthly income that has no room for luxuries. After her old car gave out, Rounds purchased a better used car, which put her over the

---

This article was written by Sarah Glazer for *The CQ Researcher* (August 3, 2001): 601–632.

eligibility limit for food stamps.* For several months, Rounds had to choose between buying the daily pain killers that enabled her to work or paying for basic expenses such as car insurance, the electric bill for her trailer, and food.

Although her income has gone up $1.60 an hour since she started working,
Rounds and her family are no better off financially than when she first left welfare
because her increased wages make her ineligible for health insurance and food
stamps.[2]

When Rounds first left welfare, she only worked half-time. One of her teenage
daughters was doing poorly in school, smoking, and staying out late. About a year
ago, Rounds began working thirty-two hours a week to boost her income, but she
worried about losing time she could spend with her daughter. The extra hours also
kept Rounds continually exhausted and strapped for time to complete a recertifica-
tion course she needed to qualify for a higher-paying job as a licensed practical
nurse.

Looking back, Rounds feels lucky that welfare enabled her to stay home with her
children when they were young. That is something her coworkers are not able to
do under the tougher work requirements that came with the sweeping welfare reforms passed in 1996. Citing a coworker whose milk dried up because she had to
work when her nursing baby was three months old, Rounds says, "Working full-
time is too hard when you are a single parent."[3]

When Congress passed the welfare reform bill, conservatives had high hopes for
breaking what they saw as a culture of dependence on welfare while liberals predicted destitute children in the streets. Now, five years later, the liberals' dire pre-
dictions of vastly increased poverty have not come to pass. But experts disagree
whether the dramatic behavioral changes touted by reform advocates are the result
of a newfound work ethic triggered by the law or were the result of the booming
economy.

Moreover, the complex process of leaving welfare has raised new issues. As
Rounds's story illustrates, the average $6.75 per hour wage earned by former wel-
fare mothers is so low that many are no better off than when they were on welfare.[4]
And if a welfare mother loses welfare-associated benefits, like health insurance and
food stamps, she can end up even worse off. Not only that, long working hours—

---

* Last October Congress raised the cap on how much cars owned by food stamp recipients
could be worth without disqualifying them from the program.

coupled with obstacles to obtaining child-care subsidies promised when the law was passed—often result in children and teens being left unsupervised.

Studies have found that teens with parents in early welfare-to-work programs did worse in school and had more behavior problems than adolescents in other welfare households, perhaps because working parents have less time to monitor their teens' behavior and may saddle them with more responsibilities at home.[5] By contrast, studies of elementary children have found either positive or neutral effects on children's behavior and school performance, which some researchers attribute to the boost in pride a working mother passes on to her young children.[6]

The landmark 1996 law—officially the Personal Responsibility and Work Opportunity Reconciliation Act (PRWORA)—ended the open-ended entitlement to cash benefits, guaranteed to single mothers under the old welfare system. Now no one can receive a monthly welfare check for more than five years in a lifetime, except in hardship cases as defined by the states. However, states were allowed to impose even earlier deadlines, and some did so. The law also required welfare recipients to work, or be involved in activities leading to work, within two years after receiving welfare.

Federal welfare funding to the states, which had been based on the welfare population in each state, was converted to a single block grant of $16.5 billion annually over six years to be distributed to all the states. Because the block grant expires in October 2002, Congress is expected to revisit many of these issues when lawmakers reauthorize the program sometime in 2002.

Nationally, welfare reform has had dramatic effects: welfare rolls have declined by more than half since their peak in 1994; more poor, single mothers are working than ever before; single-parent families are seeing their earnings rise and child poverty is at its lowest level ever.

But plenty of problems remain, in addition to low wages and lost health benefits:

- About half the welfare recipients who left welfare in 1996 and 1997 had lower household incomes in the year they left—more than $50 a month lower—than their last months on the rolls, according to a study based on a national sample of more than 30,000 households.[7]
- Some welfare recipients have lower net earnings than they had on welfare because they do not keep their job for the entire year, or they lose food stamps and Medicaid, sometimes erroneously, when they leave the welfare rolls.

Welfare Rolls Have Been Declining

The nation's welfare rolls have dropped by more than half from their peak of 14.2 million recipients in 1994—two years before the 1996 welfare reform bill passed. Conservatives tend to credit the law's toughened time limits and work requirements, which many states had already enacted on a trial basis. Liberals generally credit a strong economy that provided a wealth of low-wage jobs. Economists credit both factors.

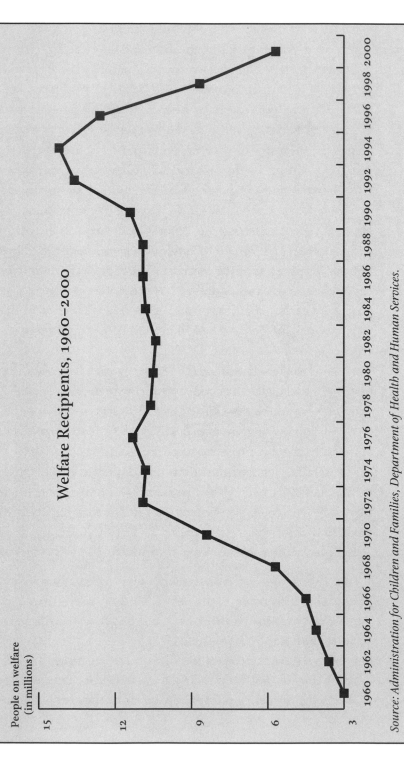

People on welfare
(in millions)

Welfare Recipients, 1960–2000

Source: Administration for Children and Families, Department of Health and Human Services.

- Up to a third of those who left welfare for low-wage jobs were back on welfare within a year, largely because of the lack of steady work and the difficulty of keeping a job while maintaining a patchwork of child-care arrangements.[8]
- About 40 percent of former recipients who have left the welfare rolls are not working, leaving welfare officials scratching their heads as to how they are surviving.

Nevertheless, champions of welfare reform say the law's success should be judged by the dramatic number of recipients who have gone to work, not by how many are still in poverty.

"Welfare reform is about altering the culture of poverty, not reducing poverty," argued journalist Mickey Kaus, a long-time critic of welfare, at a recent Brookings Institution forum.[9] Rather than achieve "equal income" for the poor, he writes, the aim is to provide "equal respect . . . the respect our society reserves for workers, even if they gain not a cent of income."[10]

"We're showing that—at least in a good economy—we can promote work," boasts Ron Haskins, a senior fellow at Brookings who helped write the 1996 law as former chief welfare adviser to Republicans on the House Ways and Means Committee. "We've had a huge impact," he says, noting that never-married mothers are now more likely to be working than receiving welfare a reversal from the years before reform.

Some reform advocates say that even if former welfare recipients are worse off in the short-term, the long-term dismantling of a system that encouraged an urban underclass of idle, unmarried mothers is worth it, citing the leveling off in the 1990s of births to unmarried mothers.

Skeptics doubt it was the welfare law that caused out-of-wedlock births to level off, noting that the percent of single-mother births leveled off in 1994—more than two years before the law was enacted. But reformers point out that during the early 1990s—when the unwed-births began declining—many states already were experimenting with time limits and work requirements for welfare recipients.

Even so, the huge increases in homelessness, foster care, and hunger that liberals predicted would follow welfare reform have not materialized, admits Christopher Jencks, a sociologist at Harvard University's John F. Kennedy School of Government, who opposed the reforms when they passed. "It's hard to argue there's an increase in material hardship through this period," he concedes. "That's telling me that the gloom-and-doom set—of whom I number myself—overdid it a bit."

Nevertheless, say welfare reform critics, the largest economic expansion in decades has been far more influential in getting welfare recipients into the workforce than any cultural conversion to the work ethic. Contrary to the popular stereotype, critics argue that many welfare moms had prior work experience, only used welfare between jobs, and would have left the welfare rolls even without welfare reform.

"I do not think these welfare mothers were as out-to-lunch as conservatives think," Jencks says. He says the welfare rolls shrank so rapidly because state welfare offices discouraged new applicants from coming onto the rolls by requiring them to seek employment first.

Many experts worry about what will happen if there is a recession. Typically, a 1 percent rise in unemployment translates into a five percent rise in the welfare rolls for single mothers and a ten to fifteen percent rise for married couples, notes economist Rebecca Blank, dean of the Gerald R. Ford School of Public Policy at the University of Michigan. And, if families that lose their jobs come knocking at the welfare office doors, they may be turned away if they have reached their five-year time limit. Furthermore, many will not qualify for unemployment insurance because they only had part-time jobs or will not have worked long enough.

An economic downturn could be devastating to poor children, who compose about two-thirds of the welfare caseload, notes Ann Segal, former deputy assistant secretary for policy initiatives in the Health and Human Services Department under President Bill Clinton. "What happens when the time limits come and Mom cannot find a job?" asks Segal, who now studies children's issues for the David and Lucile Packard Foundation in Los Altos, California. "I cannot believe the country would write off that number of children. It's a scary thought to me."

Conservatives say state and federal governments have not "written off" anybody. Instead, they have more than doubled the $30 billion per year they spent on the old welfare program at its peak. Total aid to the working poor increased to about $65 billion by 1999, primarily through state and federal earned-income tax credits (EITC)—tax refunds only available to low-income working families. A mother with two children leaving welfare and earning $10,000 a year can supplement her income by $4,000 in cash from the tax credit and by more than $2,000 in food stamps, bringing her total income to $16,000—lifting her above the official poverty line. But in most states that income is still marginal. A child-care crisis, broken-down car, or ailing family member could cause a newly working parent to lose that first job. "They're one disaster away from destitution," Blank says.

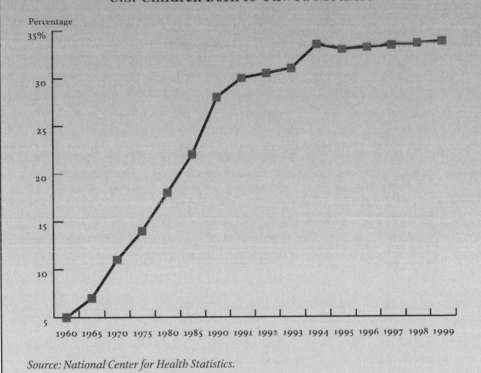

Out-of-Wedlock Births Stopped Rising

The steady rise in out-of-wedlock births flattened out in 1994, but experts are unsure what role the 1996 welfare reform bill or earlier state reforms played. Some experts suggest that increased use of the contraceptive Depo Provera and concern about AIDS and other sexually transmitted diseases played the key role.

U.S. Children Born to Unwed Mothers

Source: National Center for Health Statistics.

When refunding for welfare reform comes up for debate in 2002, Congress is expected to clash over how much federal money states should continue to receive for welfare. Democrats are expected to push for more exemptions from the time limits, while Republicans are likely to seek measures encouraging marriage and discouraging out-of-wedlock births—two goals of the 1996 law that the administration of George W. Bush strongly supports.

As lawmakers and policy experts debate the law, here are some of the issues they will tackle:

Did welfare reform move recipients off the welfare rolls and into employment?

After years of steady increases, the nation's welfare rolls have dropped by more than half from their peak of 5.1 million families in 1994. But the downward trend began more than two years before the 1996 federal welfare reform bill passed and several years before most states implemented those reforms. Does the welfare reform bill deserve the credit?

Conservatives tend to credit the law's toughened time limits and work requirements for transforming welfare recipients' attitudes toward work. Liberals generally give more weight to the strong economy, which provided a flood of low-wage jobs and the lowest unemployment rate in twenty-five years. Economists credit a mixture of both factors.

The employment rate among never-married mothers, who typically have little education or work experience and spent the most time on welfare, shot up to 65 percent in 1999, compared with 49 percent in 1996.[11] New York University politics Professor Lawrence M. Mead III, who has long criticized welfare's failure to emphasize work, cites those statistics as evidence of the success of the welfare reform program, called Temporary Assistance for Needy Families (TANF). "It's the first large increase in work levels since the 1960s," he says. "A key part of that story is eliminating the welfare entitlement and requiring adults to function. There's no denying the success of TANF."

Ironically, most people left the rolls long before time limits actually begin to kick in this fall, which Mead attributes to the word getting out on the street that the deadlines were approaching.

"You make it no longer acceptable to be dependent, and a lot of people get the message," Mead says. "Now the caseworkers are saying, 'The clock is ticking. You should bank your hours because you're really going to need them.' " By "banking hours," recipients conserve their lifetime limit of five years of welfare eligibility for a future emergency, such as a health problem or getting laid off or fired.

But sociologist Jencks says conservatives are wrong to think the law somehow transformed welfare mothers from idlers into workers for the first time. "Even without welfare reform, nearly half the single mothers on the rolls in 1994 would have left by 1999 simply because their children grew older, they found work, or they got married," he says. However, he concedes that without welfare reform most of the mothers who left welfare would have been replaced by other mothers who had just had their first baby, split up with their husband, or lost their job.[12]

Welfare reform made its biggest difference in state welfare offices, which tended to open fewer new cases. In some states, caseworkers handed newspaper "Help Wanted" sections to applicants, telling them to return after making thirty calls, Jencks says. A lot of mothers never came back, he thinks, and word of mouth probably discouraged other mothers from applying.

Moreover, work is not foreign to most welfare mothers, he contends. According to survey data, 60 percent of all welfare recipients had worked in the previous two years. *Making Ends Meet,* a study of 214 welfare-reliant women in four cities, found that mothers had an average of five years of job experience. But the mothers who were on welfare had concluded that returning to the kinds of jobs they had in the past would not make them better off or that the job might vanish and leave them without income to support their small children. Many had plans to return to work when their children were older.[13]

Critics of welfare reform say the economy has been so strong in recent years that it is hard to know what the law's effect would have been in its absence. After 1996, the nation experienced its lowest unemployment rate in twenty-five years: The annual rate fell from 6.9 percent in 1993 to 4 percent in 2000. During this longest-running expansion in U.S. history, real hourly wages for the lowest-paid workers (adjusted for inflation) began to rise after falling for two consecutive decades.[14]

Mark Greenberg, a senior attorney at the liberal Center for Law and Social Policy who opposed welfare reform, worries about what will happen in a recession. "The way the welfare system has worked during a strong economy gives us very little information about what the picture will be in a deteriorating economy," he says.

Experts from both camps agree that a large chunk of the declining caseloads is attributable to recently passed laws that make work pay, such as expanding the EITC. The credit, available only to low-wage workers with children, can have as much value as a $2 per-hour raise. Some call the EITC the government's largest antipoverty program.

Other policies that helped the working poor include health insurance for low-income children not receiving welfare, increased spending on child-care subsidies, and increased earned-income "disregards," which permit welfare recipients to keep more of their earnings while remaining on welfare.[15]

In a recent summary of economic studies, Douglas J. Besharov, a resident scholar at the conservative American Enterprise Institute (AEI), concluded that aid to the working poor explained 30 percent to 45 percent of the caseload decline. He thinks welfare reform accounted for another 30 percent to 45 percent of the drop and credits the healthy economy with 15 percent to 25 percent of it.[16]

Conservatives like Haskins say that if the booming economy were mainly or even solely responsible for the dropping welfare rolls, past economic booms should have produced similar reductions, but they did not. Instead, caseloads rose even in the best labor markets. During economic expansion in the 1980s, when the American economy added twenty million jobs, welfare rolls still grew by nearly half a million families, notes Haskins, of Brookings.[17] Similarly, caseloads continued to rise by 700,000 families between December 1991 and March 1994, the first couple of years of the most recent recovery, even as the economy added six million jobs.

Welfare rolls did not begin their sustained decline until 1994, when more than half the states implemented work-requirement programs that predated the 1996 reforms. In the 1990s, Haskins argues, it was the new welfare-assistance deadlines and tougher work requirements that pushed families into the job market.

A report just released by the conservative Manhattan Institute in New York City concludes that TANF accounts for more than half the decline in welfare participation and more than sixty percent of the rise in employment among single mothers. By contrast, a report by two Baruch College economists finds that the booming economy of the 1990s explains less than twenty percent of either trend.[18]

Many economists argue that it was both the booming economy and the harder line coming from welfare offices. In 1999 the Council of Economic Advisers (CEA) estimated that welfare reform accounted for one-third of the caseload reduction from 1996 to 1998, and the robust economy for about ten percent.

By contrast, from 1993 to 1996, when unemployment was dropping even more sharply, most of the decline was due to the strong labor market, the CEA concluded. Tough new state work requirements during that period accounted for only about ten percent of the drop, the CEA said. Increases in state and federal minimum wages also accounted for about ten percent of the caseload decline, the CEA said.[19]

"The bottom line is we could not have had the dramatic decline in caseloads if we had not had the biggest social policy change in decades," says the University of Michigan's Blank, a former CEA member under President Clinton, who counts

How Much Is Welfare Worth?

The monthly welfare benefit for a single parent with two children in 2001 ranged from a low of $120 per month in Mississippi to a high of $923 in Alaska, according to Pamela Loprest, a welfare expert and senior research associate at the Urban Institute. Pennsylvania, which lies in the middle of the TANF (Temporary Assistance for Needy Families) benefits range, paid $403 per month. The monthly food stamp grant for a single mother with two children and no work income added approximately $330. Only about a quarter of TANF recipients received a government housing subsidy. Ron Haskins of the Brookings Institution estimated the annual value of Medicaid insurance at about $4,000. But liberal experts are reluctant to place a dollar value on Medicaid because it does not add dollars to a family's income that can be spent on something else like food. Also, its value is highly dependent on the health of an individual family.

herself as one of the early liberal skeptics of welfare reform. She says the reforms were more successful than she expected because "states have been more serious than I expected in . . . changing their bureaucracies."

Are welfare recipients and their children better off after they leave the rolls?

Much of the reauthorization debate in 2002 will no doubt center on whether those leaving welfare are better off than they were while receiving benefits. No one disputes that as the caseload declined, so did overall child poverty. By 1999, child poverty had fallen to its lowest rate since the government started measuring it in 1979—to 19.6 percent of all children (fourteen million children), compared with the peak of 26.3 percent in 1993.[20] Black child poverty declined more in 1997 and 1999 than in any previous year, reaching its lowest level ever in 1999.[21]

But, these numbers do not tell the story of those at the bottom of the income scale. Welfare-reform critic Wendell E. Primus, director of income security at the Center on Budget and Policy Priorities, stresses that the decline in poverty has not been as steep as the drop in the welfare caseload. Deep poverty—defined as having an income below fifty percent of the poverty level—has, in fact, been growing.[22]

Female-headed families appear to be leaving welfare because they can earn more money now than before, Primus points out. Earnings have risen for the bottom 40 percent of these families, and annual earnings for the bottom 20 percent increased nearly eighty-two percent from 1993 to 1999. Earnings for the next lowest twenty percent rose almost 100 percent.[23]

Despite the higher incomes, those leaving welfare more recently appear to be having a harder time making ends meet in some respects. According to a recent study by the Urban Institute, a liberal-leaning Washington-based think tank, about a third of those who left welfare in both 1997 and 1999 say they have had to skip or scrimp on meals in the past year. The study also found that the most recent welfare-leavers tend to have more health problems than those who left earlier.

Furthermore, rising housing costs appear to be causing trouble for the most recent welfare graduates. A significantly higher percentage of those who left welfare in 1999 have housing worries. Forty-six percent were unable to pay mortgage, rent, or utility bills in the past year, compared with 39 percent of those who left welfare in 1997. The study suggested that this could reflect rising housing costs driven up by tight housing markets.[24]

In addition, many of those who left welfare earliest may have been less capable of working than more recent leavers. Many left welfare not to work, but because their benefits were terminated when they failed to meet welfare reform's work requirements or because health problems prevented them from working.[25]

Furthermore, critics of reform say that once work expenses like child care and transportation are factored in, many families are only marginally better off when they leave welfare, and some are actually worse off. For instance, the poorest two-fifths of families headed by single mothers increased their average earnings by about $2,783 per family between 1995 and 1999, but their disposable incomes increased only $643 after inflation and work expenses were factored in, according to Primus.

Moreover, those at the very bottom of the income ladder—700,000 families—appear to be worse off, he says. The average disposable income of the poorest one-fifth of single mothers fell 3 percent in real terms from 1995 to 1999, he notes.

Primus also notes that while some working families leaving welfare are making higher incomes on paper, their net earnings are less. For instance, some do not continue to receive Medicaid and food stamps for which they are eligible, or their rising incomes make them ineligible for such supports. Or they fail to work a full year, either because their jobs are unstable or their lives are too chaotic.

The Urban Institute found after researching welfare families in twelve states that many families leaving welfare are eligible for food stamps but are not receiving

Wisconsin's 'Workfare' Experiment: Miracle or Mirage?

Policy-makers have long flocked to Wisconsin to figure out how the state managed to cut its welfare rolls more than any other urban state in the nation.[1] Wisconsin has reduced its monthly caseload by more than 93 percent since 1987, when it began its first experiments with a work-based system.[2]

"Welfare is gone in Wisconsin," says Demetra Smith Nightingale, director of the Welfare and Training Research program at the Urban Institute in Washington, D.C., who has surveyed research on the state's welfare experiment. About 85 percent of Wisconsin's welfare cases are now concentrated in Milwaukee, a heavily black and Hispanic city that is one of the most depressed in the nation.[3]

Wisconsin abolished the welfare entitlement check altogether in 1997 and replaced it with a new program called Wisconsin Works, or W-2. It requires virtually everyone to work and pays a cash subsidy only to those in government jobs or treatment programs. Almost everyone has to work—including the disabled, drug abusers, and mothers with young children.[4]

Then-Gov. Tommy G. Thompson, who oversaw the creation of the program before being tapped by President Bush as secretary of Health and Human Services, calls his state's program "the standard for welfare reform in America." Conservatives have hailed the state's tough work policies and the influence of conservative theorist Charles Murray, who has argued that traditional welfare created a culture of nonwork among the poor.[5]

But what often gets overlooked in the political compromise brokered between a Republican governor and Democratic legislators is financial help for low-income workers on a scale so generous that it has been compared with a European welfare state.[6]

Wisconsin subsidizes child care and health care for all working families with incomes up to 165 percent of poverty (not just former welfare recipients), adds a state tax credit on top of the federal earned-income tax credit, and has massively increased health insurance for children.

"They're more progressive on the services side while tougher on the work side" than any other state, Nightingale says.

"W-2 redefined who the government helped," says Milwaukee Director of Administration David Riemer, one of the Democratic architects of the program. "The old AFDC [Aid

1. Lawrence M. Mead, "The Politics of Welfare Reform in Wisconsin," *Polity,* summer 2000.
2. Tommy G. Thompson, "Welfare Reform's Next Step," *Brookings Review,* summer 2001, 2–3.
3. Amy L. Sherman, "The Lessons of W-2," *Public Interest,* summer 2000, 36.
4. Ibid.
5. Mead, *Politics of Welfare Reform.*
6. Ibid.

to Families with Dependent Children] system was very narrow: It took the poorest of single parents and ignored all above the poverty line and ignored people with no kids. W-2 created a de facto entitlement to child care and health care for the entire working poor."

In his 1988 book *The Prisoners of Welfare: Liberating America's Poor from Unemployment and Low Wages*, Riemer argued for replacing government aid with government jobs as a progressive goal. Today, he contends that Wisconsin's program approaches the liberal ideal of providing a guaranteed minimum income for the working poor.

"The key to political success in Wisconsin was a concordat where the Democrats abandoned the idea of entitlement to welfare and the Republicans abandoned the idea of downsizing government," says Lawrence M. Mead, a professor of politics at New York University, who is writing a book on the Wisconsin experience. "They junked the old system and created a new one that is simultaneously very severe and very generous. It says, 'You have got to work, but if you work, we will help you in all these ways.'"

However, only a small proportion of the working poor take advantage of all the generous supports, according to Lois Quinn, senior research scientist at the University of Wisconsin-Milwaukee Employment and Training Institute, which has been studying W-2. Child-care subsidies, for example, reach less than one-quarter of the eligible children in Milwaukee, according to the institute. "There's been a dramatic increase in child care, but it's not serving the majority of working poor families. And it's not going to, because it would break the bank," says Quinn, who doubts the legislature would support the funding if all eligible families claimed it.

Although the legislature initially passed what looked like massive increases in spending for the poor, the welfare caseload plunged so dramatically that the program quickly became self-financing, Mead says.[7]

"Gov. Thompson went out in a burst of glory because he had these programs that looked like they served the entire working poor," Quinn says, "but the price tag, had it been utilized, would have been very expensive."

One reason more eligible parents don't take advantage of the child-care subsidies is that many of them—especially former welfare mothers—rely on informal babysitting arrangements with neighbors and relatives, which often do not qualify for subsidies.

Wisconsin's child-care subsidies go only to licensed or certified day care. Few qualified centers stay open on nights and weekends, when many former welfare mothers work in fast food, retail, and nursing homes. They "need you on the weekend and maybe Tuesday night because Becky can't come in. Informal care is about the only thing that works for that," Quinn says. Only twenty-four licensed child-care providers with 458 slots were open after

---

7. Ibid.

7 p.m. in Milwaukee's central city, according to an institute study conducted from 1996 to 1999.[8]

Moreover, former welfare recipients have a hard time keeping steady work. The Urban Institute reported that while at least 75 percent of former recipients work some of each year after they leave the rolls, less than half are continuously employed.[9] And a study by the University of Wisconsin-Madison found that more than 60 percent of those who left welfare in 1995 and 1997 remained in poverty.[10]

In addition, as Wisconsin gets down to a welfare population that may be hard to employ, people are hitting the twenty-four-month point without getting jobs. "What does it mean for the safety net?" Nightingale asks.

Riemer contends that as a result of W-2, Milwaukee's low-income population is better off. Some data bear out his contention. In nine Milwaukee neighborhoods with the highest concentrations of former welfare families, incomes have risen since the advent of W-2, and the number of single parents filing income taxes continues to increase, according to Quinn.

But, Quinn notes, "The largest [income] increases came before welfare reform in Milwaukee County, likely due to the economy" in Wisconsin, which has been blessed with a low unemployment rate following W-2. Currently, Quinn reports, the number of working poor families is declining in Milwaukee. But the number of near-poor (earning incomes at 100 to 125 percent of poverty) is growing. "The big challenge," she says, "will be moving beyond that."

---

8. John Pawasarat and Lois M. Quinn, "Impact of Welfare Reform on Child Care Subsidies in Milwaukee County, 1996–1999," October 1999, University of Wisconsin-Milwaukee Employment and Training Institute. Accessed at www.uwm.edu/Dept/ETI.

9. Demetra Smith Nightingale and Kelly S. Mikelson, *An Overview of Research Related to Wisconsin Works (W-2)*, Urban Institute, March 2000. Accessed at http://urban.org/welfare/wisc_works.html.

10. Maria Cancian et al., *Before and After TANF: The Economic Well-Being of Women Leaving Welfare*, May 2000, Institute for Research on Poverty, University of Wisconsin-Madison.

them. Families leaving welfare often lose both their Medicaid and food stamps, either because they do not know they are still eligible or because claiming them requires repeated in-person visits to a welfare office during work hours.[26]

A recent University of Wisconsin study found that less than a third of the mothers who left welfare for work in that state had higher incomes a year later, and more than 60 percent remained in poverty because the loss of food stamps and other benefits outweighed their increased earnings.[27] "The glass is half-full," says Maria Cancian, lead author of the study and a professor of public affairs and social work at the University of Wisconsin-Madison. "You've seen big increases in employment and earnings. But these women are not [earning] incomes to bring children out of poverty."

Even with higher wages, many of these women rarely reach above $10 an hour, Cancian says. Many have sporadic employment because either the job does not last a full year or personal crises force them to quit before the year is out. Other studies show that about twenty percent of mothers leaving welfare go through long periods without work, and many more are sporadically unemployed.[28]

Still another study found that about half of the women who left welfare remained below the poverty level eighteen to twenty-one months later, primarily because only a minority got good-quality jobs with benefits, reliable hours, and decent wages, says Sandra Morgen, director of the University of Oregon's Center for the Study of Women in Society, which conducted the study for Oregon state.[29] "What we've done in most states is force people into a problematic labor force," she says.

In addition, small raises frequently cause these mothers to become ineligible for food stamps and Medicaid. Because state-required copayments for child care are based on income, a small wage increase can also jack up the copayment so high that mothers are forced to "pull the kid out of decent child care and stick him with grandma or the boyfriend," she adds.

The study also raised serious concerns about the poor quality of child care that former welfare mothers can afford and the precarious, patched-together arrangements many moms rely upon. If one thing goes wrong in that complicated structure, Morgen says, it can lead to job loss. "We have families who wake up at 5:30 a.m. to take a sleeping kid to Aunt Lola, who gets the kid to school; someone else picks the kid up and later takes the kid somewhere else," she says. "The kid may have three different child-care arrangements, and if any one of them gets screwed up, it can send the whole system out of whack." In addition, for many women, child care becomes unaffordable in the summer when children need all-day care.

"An awful lot of families want to work and think they're better off. But a significant percentage—who do not want to be working and think their kids need them—think they're worse off," Morgen says.

But welfare-reform advocates say that even if newly working mothers are poor, it is better than being on the dole because it boosts their self-esteem, creates a better role model for their children and gives them a first step toward a better job.

Welfare critic Mead concedes that, "over several years, if people keep working, they usually do escape poverty. But it's a long and painful climb."

The University of Michigan's Blank suggests that even if a former welfare mother loses her first job, she may persist in looking for a second job because she will have figured out how to cope with child care and transportation.

Robert Rector, a senior research fellow at the conservative Heritage Foundation, disputes the idea that a family's income determines a child's well being. "The worst thing about welfare is that it destroyed the marital and work ethic and damaged children's life prospects," Rector says. "A child in a working single-mother household will do better than where the mother is collecting a welfare check."

But the research on children of working mothers remains equivocal. About half the studies find significant improvements in children's behavior or academic achievement, while the other half find no effects.[30]

Another puzzle is the so-called "missing 40 percent." When Congress takes a close look at welfare funding in 2002, it will no doubt look at the large percentage of women who do not go to work after leaving welfare, according to a recent analysis by AEI scholar Besharov. Studies suggest that some have other forms of government aid or are getting help from family members, friends, or boyfriends.

But Harvard's Jencks thinks the nonworking welfare-leavers may be the one-third or more of welfare recipients who are unemployable because of poor job skills, mental health issues, or drug problems. Democrats are expected to question whether this unemployable population will need more assistance to stay out of dire poverty after their five-year limits expire. If they are unable to exploit a social network, Jencks suggests, this population will be worse off after the time limits hit.

Background

Widows' Relief

The original aim of cash welfare in the 1930s was to enable widows to stay home and raise their children. In 1935 Congress passed the Aid to Dependent Children bill. The goal, as stated in a report to President Franklin D. Roosevelt, was to "release from the wage-earning role the person whose natural function is to give her children the physical and affectionate guardianship necessary . . . but more affirmatively to rear [her children] into citizens capable of contributing to society."[31]

But in the 1970s, when the single-mother population rose dramatically and became dominated by divorced, separated, and never-married women, Americans became increasingly hostile to aid for single mothers. In the 1930s, single mothers

Chronology

1930s *During President Franklin D. Roosevelt's administration, widows are classed with the disabled as unable to work.*

1935 Congress passes Aid to Dependent Children to help widows with children.

1936 Less than 1 percent of families with children are on welfare.

1960s *Welfare rolls surge, welfare-rights movement reduces welfare's stigma, divorce and illegitimate birthrates rise.*

1962 Welfare program is renamed Aid to Families with Dependent Children (AFDC).

1964 President Lyndon B. Johnson declares "war on poverty," establishing antipoverty programs.

1970s *As the U.S. economy slows, Congress begins tightening eligibility for welfare and requiring more AFDC parents to take jobs or enroll in job training.*

1971 Congress requires all AFDC parents to register for work or job training unless they have children under age six.

1974 The earned-income tax credit is enacted to provide tax refunds for the working poor.

1980s *The federal government starts granting waivers to states to experiment with welfare-to-work programs.*

JULY 31, 1981 Congress cuts cash benefits for the working poor and allows states to require welfare recipients to work.

OCTOBER 31, 1988 President Ronald Reagan signs the Family Support Act requiring states to implement education, job training, and placement programs for welfare recipients.

1990s *Most states are allowed to experiment with work requirements and penalties. Congress passes major welfare-reform bill. Poverty and unemployment drop to historic lows.*

1992 Democratic presidential candidate Bill Clinton promises to "end welfare as we know it."

1993 Newly elected President Clinton raises the amount paid to poor working families under the earned-income tax credit.

1994 Welfare rolls reach peak of 5.1 million families.

1995 Republican majority takes over Congress and begins debating ways to reform welfare.

1996 President Clinton signs the landmark welfare-reform law on Aug. 26 removing the open-ended entitlement to welfare and converting the program to a block grant to states. Congress raises the minimum wage from $4.25 to $4.75 an hour.

SEPTEMBER 1, 1997 The minimum wage is increased again to $5.15 an hour. Falling welfare caseloads enable states to begin amassing a $5 billion surplus in unspent federal welfare funds.

1998 Child poverty drops to its lowest level since 1989.

1999 Employment of never-married single mothers rises to all-time high of 65 percent.

2000s *Amid historic lows in welfare cases and unemployment, Congress prepares to debate welfare-reform reauthorization.*

SEPTEMBER 2000 Welfare caseload drops to 2.2 million families, a 50 percent decrease from its 1994 peak. Jobless rate drops to historic low of 4 percent.

OCTOBER 2001 Five-year time limit on welfare benefits begins to kick in.

OCTOBER 1, 2002 Congress must reauthorize welfare-reform legislation.

were grouped with the aged and disabled as citizens who should not be asked to work, and most married mothers did not work at the time. By the 1990s, work had become the norm for U.S. mothers.

Polls consistently show that two-thirds or more of Americans support policies to help "the poor" who cannot help themselves, especially children and the disabled. But the same number also say they do not support "welfare."[32] Polls also show that Americans have traditionally opposed government aid for the able-bodied.[33] As the public increasingly perceived single mothers as fully capable of working, opposition seemed to mount in tandem with growing welfare rolls.

For nearly sixty years, it seemed that welfare rolls could only grow, regardless of the economy's health. Except for a few brief declines, the rolls grew from 147,000

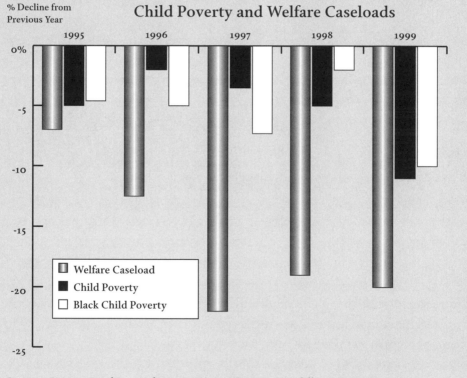

Child Poverty and Welfare Caseloads Declined

Child poverty and welfare caseloads both declined after passage of the 1996 welfare-reform law. By 1999, child poverty was at its lowest rate since the government started measuring it in 1979—19.6 percent of all children (fourteen million children), compared with the peak of 26.3 percent in 1993. Black child poverty reached its lowest level ever in 1999. However, welfare-reform critics say that the decline in poverty has not been as steep as the drop in caseloads.

% Decline from Previous Year

Child Poverty and Welfare Caseloads

1995   1996   1997   1998   1999

0%
-5
-10
-15
-20
-25

Legend:
- Welfare Caseload
- Child Poverty
- Black Child Poverty

Sources: Congressional Research Service; Census Bureau; Wendell E. Primus, Center on Budget and Policy Priorities, "TANF Reauthorization," National Governors Association Briefing, June 6, 2001, Washington, D.C.

families in 1936 to about five million in 1994—from less than one percent of the families with children to about fifteen percent.

After President Lyndon B. Johnson declared war on poverty in 1964, the rolls surged 230 percent from 1963 to 1973. The rise largely reflected two factors, according to the AEI's Besharov: administrative changes that made it easier for income-eligible families to get benefits, and the welfare-rights movement, which removed some of the stigma of being on welfare.[34] But this period also saw a rise in divorce and concern about the decline of traditional families.

After remaining roughly steady for the next fifteen years, the welfare rolls shot up thirty-four percent between 1989 and 1994. Fears that welfare was discouraging work and encouraging illegitimate births resurfaced with new urgency during this period. Much of the caseload rise was due to the major economic downturn of the late 1980s and early 1990s, according to Besharov. But there were other important influences: a spike in out-of-wedlock births, government efforts to get single mothers to sign up for Medicaid—and therefore also for welfare benefits—and an increase in child-only welfare cases, perhaps resulting from the crack epidemic that rendered addicted parents incapable of caring for their children.[35]

Since the 1970s, welfare policy has been "a tug-of-war between those trying to protect children and families from penury and those who believe that welfare dependency is even worse for families than poverty is," writes Gordon Berlin, senior vice president at the Manpower Demonstration Research Corporation, and author of numerous welfare studies.[36] But until the 1990s, he notes, neither side gained much of an edge in changing welfare.

Until the early 1970s, most changes in the program—renamed Aid to Families with Dependent Children (AFDC) in 1962—tended to expand eligibility and liberalize benefits. Grants grew slightly during the 1970s and 1980s, but not enough to keep up with inflation.

Beginning around 1972, as the economy slowed and poverty increased, public resentment grew against the tax burden needed to support large federal antipoverty programs. Efforts to reform welfare over the next twenty years revolved around reducing benefits, tightening eligibility, and requiring more AFDC parents to take jobs or enroll in job training.

But none of the changes dramatically affected welfare caseloads. In a last-ditch effort Congress passed the Family Support Act of 1988, requiring states to place most mothers with children over age three in education, work, or training.

The public's dissatisfaction with welfare stemmed partly from the growing size and costs of AFDC and partly from resentment that it was supporting a large proportion of unwed mothers, most of whom were assumed to be African Americans. In fact, more whites than blacks received AFDC.[37] In addition, by the 1990s it had become more common for mothers to work than to stay home—a reversal from the societal position of mothers in 1935.

'I'm Grateful I'm Not on Welfare Today' Job-Training Graduate Says

When New York City's welfare office told Gregory Cannon he would have to clean city buildings to work off his $34 weekly welfare check, he bought crack cocaine with the bus fare they gave him. Today Cannon is drug free and working, thanks to Binding Together Inc. (BTI), a job-training program for former welfare recipients.

"I had plenty of jobs where I told off the boss and walked away," he says. "At Binding Together, I learned to get along with people. BTI gave me what [New York City's Work Experience Program] did not—pride and dignity."

Binding Together mainly serves the hard-to-employ. About seventy-five percent of its trainees have prison records, and many were drug users. But in the past two years, clients have had multiple problems—including lower literacy levels, untreated mental health problems, and less experience living a sober life, according to Program Director Angelia Holloway.

Because New York state limits how long an individual can receive welfare assistance—including time spent in drug treatment—many people now arrive at the program with much shorter periods of sobriety under their belt—as little as three months compared with eighteen months previously. Thus, they still have to learn basic skills like getting along with co-workers and arriving at work on time. The program is also finding higher rates of depression and learning disabilities. The average reading level has dropped—from eighth grade to about a fifth-grade level. The program is also getting an increasing number of women navigating their first job for whom child care is a major logistical issue.

Nationally, some welfare experts expect to see more such problems as the country's welfare caseload shrinks to a hard core of people who have little work experience and multiple health and substance-abuse problems.

As a result, BTI does a lot more counseling and handholding to get people ready for work, Holloway says. Constance Hayes, age forty, who came to BTI directly from a drug-treatment program, says she was "still in a shell" when she first arrived. "Since I've been here," she says, "I am able to open up and socialize better with people. BTI taught me I can live in a productive way and can get money." She is counting on BTI to find her a copying job for about $8 an hour.

Several recent BTI graduates say they were motivated to find job training because they could barely make ends meet on welfare, and they knew their time limits on welfare assistance were approaching.

Desiree Dennis, age thirty-nine, the mother of five, had been on public assistance for more than seven years when New York City assigned her a "workfare" job cleaning highways. She found the work "disgusting and degrading" and decided to find a job-training program. She recently started working as a copier operator at a print shop next door to Binding Together.

Yet at the $8 hourly wages typically paid to copy operators, some mothers are not much better off than on welfare. Joann Gonzalez, age twenty-five, who was on public assistance for almost eight years, decided to get job training because she couldn't support her two children on the $390 per month she received from workfare for collecting trash in city offices. "I just decided to get up and start working because public assistance wasn't giving me enough money to live off," she says.

Gonzalez had not looked for work when her children were younger, she says, because she had no job experience and lacked a high school diploma. After training at BTI, she got work in January as a copy operator. She makes $220 a week, working from 2 to 10 p.m. That sum is quickly gobbled up by the $150 she pays to her babysitter and her $75 contribution to her subsidized rent. "I can't live off $220," she says. "Besides the rent and the light bill, you've got expenses for the kids: clothes, school pictures, notebooks." But her husband recently moved back in with her, which makes the job viable. He picks the kids up at 9 p.m. from the babysitter when he gets home from his job.

Graduates generally agree there should be time limits on welfare.

Vanessa Ratliff, age forty, a mother of three, described herself as a "dedicated and sincere" cocaine user since high school. Today she works at BTI. "I'm grateful I'm not on welfare today," she says. "I was on it for a good twenty years, and it was OK with me. It shouldn't be that way, where I should be comfortable on it for twenty years."

Welfare Reform

On the presidential campaign trail in 1992, Democratic candidate Clinton promised to "end welfare as we know it." After the election, his administration granted waivers from federal welfare regulations to many states, allowing them to experiment with toughening work requirements and imposing time limits on benefits. Both approaches became cornerstones of the Republican-backed 1996 welfare reform law.

The changes ultimately adopted were based more on a Republican plan than on an administration bill. Both bills imposed time limits on benefits, but the Clinton proposal included an entitlement to a public job afterward, and that was not in the final bill. The Republican bill changed the program from one in which all recipients were entitled to a benefit under AFDC—and states received open-ended funds

as their caseloads grew—to a capped block grant, which gave states an incentive to
cut caseloads because they would get to keep any unspent money.

It was largely this change—and the fear that states would not have either the
money or the incentive to support welfare recipients adequately—that led to several high-profile resignations of welfare policy-makers from Clinton's Department
of Health and Human Services (HHS), including Primus.

TANF was seen as a cut in federal funding because states would get funding
based on their 1995 caseloads, recalls Greenberg, of the Center for Law and Social
Policy. "Our question was: How will states manage with fixed funding and rising
caseloads? But caseloads had begun falling in 1994, so TANF resulted in a significant increase in funding to the states," he says. "If you compare TANF to AFDC in
1997, the states had an additional $4.7 billion."

The result was more positive than Greenberg had expected, he says, because the
states used the extra money to support families leaving the welfare rolls with additional child-care subsidies, child health insurance, and other assistance, ameliorating the dire situation foreseen under low wages.

A recent study in Cleveland, Los Angeles, Miami-Dade, and Philadelphia concluded that "the worst fears" of welfare reform's critics—that states would slash
benefits and services—"have not materialized." On the contrary, the study found,
states are actually keeping some people longer on the rolls because they are per-
mitting working people to both earn money and receive cash assistance. Under the
old rules, a mother would be cut from the rolls once her caseworker discovered she
had a job that earned significant income.[38]

The Working Poor

The massive increases in aid to the working poor initiated by Clinton and passed
by the Republican Congress also helped prevent the grim forecast of the bill's
opponents. Such subsidies now exceed the amount spent on the old AFDC
program.

The most important support is the EITC, available only to working parents. Between 1993 and 1999, the income supplement for a single mother of two more than
doubled from $1,700 to about $3,900 per year.[39]

Clinton also pushed through a two-stage increase in the minimum wage—from
$4.25 to $4.75 an hour in 1996 to the current $5.15 an hour in 1997. In addition, real
hourly wages for the lowest-paid workers began to rise after falling for two consec-

utive decades.[40] The prospects for welfare-leavers also brightened during this period as the annual unemployment rate fell from 6.9 percent in 1993 to four percent in 2000, its lowest rate ever.

Child care and Medicaid subsidies also expanded to record highs. Between 1996 and 1999, millions more children have become eligible for health insurance through the Medicaid program, and child-care subsidies have been expanded, essentially becoming an entitlement for families leaving welfare. Total annual federal and state child-care expenditures rose from $8 billion to more than $12 billion from 1993 to 1999, Besharov calculates, providing subsidies for more than 1 million additional children.[41]

However, advocates for the poor say child-care subsidies often buy poor quality care and that only a fraction of the eligible low-income families take advantage of them.

Current Situation
Reauthorizing TANF

Because the states' TANF block grant of $16.5 billion annually for six years expires in October 2002, the welfare-reform law must be reauthorized before then. Some hearings were held in 2001, but serious legislative action is not expected until early 2002.

The size of the block grant is the biggest issue to be resolved. Because the grant was established before caseloads plummeted, several states have had large unspent surpluses. In 1999 federal lawmakers were shocked to learn not only that there was an unprecedented $7.4 billion in federal welfare funds sitting unspent, left over from fiscal 1997 and 1998, but also that some states had used their surpluses for nonwelfare uses such as reducing middle-class taxes.[42]

Since then, much of the surplus has melted away, with only about four percent remaining unobligated, says Gretchen Odegard, legislative director for human services at the National Governors' Association (NGA). Moreover, many states are holding their surpluses in reserve in case of an economic downturn. Others are using them to provide child care and transportation for the newly working poor.

"Those structures are in place," Odegard says. "They're the reason the funding needs to continue. The governors will fight reductions in funding."

While Republican lawmakers are likely to argue that the unspent surpluses indicate that federal welfare assistance should be cut, Democrats will argue that states

Are Welfare Time Limits Unfair?

Two of the most controversial provisions of the 1996 welfare reform law were its five-year time limit on benefits and financial penalties for families not complying with the work requirements.

So far it is hard to gauge the effects of the time limits, since most families have left the rolls before their time limits kick in. Many families, however, will be affected starting October 2001 and in subsequent years.

Although time limits are unlikely to be challenged, Democrats are expected to push for provisions to soften the limits' effects.

A recent University of Michigan study found high rates of depression and physical health problems among Michigan welfare recipients. Moreover, the women who reported the problems tended to work fewer months out of the year. High school dropouts and those with little work experience tended to have trouble keeping a job.[1]

Democrats will point to such studies to argue that a high proportion of welfare recipients may not be able to start working before the time limits hit and that exceptions should be made for hardship cases.

But Republicans can be expected to resist. Ron Haskins, former chief welfare adviser to Republicans on the House Ways and Means Committee when they were crafting the welfare reform bill and currently a senior fellow at the Brookings Institution, notes that current law permits states to exempt twenty percent of their caseload from the time limit. "There's no evidence that any state will press up against the time limit," he says. Moreover, he points out that a surprisingly high proportion of women with mental health and other problems manage to work at least part of the year, suggesting they may not have insuperable barriers to work.

The changes Democrats are expected to propose include:

• Stopping the clock on the five-year time limit for welfare recipients who are working but still receiving TANF (Temporary Assistance for Needy Families) benefits. Under some state policies, recipients continue to receive reduced welfare benefits while working to encourage their transition to working. Democrats will argue that such recipients should not be penalized by lifetime welfare limits while they are making the transition toward self-sufficiency and that states should have the option of subsidizing low wages.

---

1. Mary Corcoran et al., University of Michigan Program on Poverty and Social Welfare Policy, "Predictors of Work Among TANF Recipients: Do Health, Mental Health and Domestic Violence Problems Limit Employment?" Unpublished paper for Brookings Institution press briefing, May 21, 2001.

- Changing the basis for the twenty percent hardship exemption. Under the law, states are currently permitted to exempt twenty percent of their welfare caseload from the time limits. Few states have actually defined who will count under the twenty percent. Democrats will argue that the twenty percent should be based on the higher caseloads states had at the time of welfare reform's passage, not today's drastically reduced caseloads. Such a recalculation would permit a higher number of recipients to be exempted from the time limits.

- Loosening restrictions on training and education. Under current law, welfare recipients are permitted to enroll in vocational education for a maximum of one year under the federal work requirement. Democrats will argue that welfare recipients should be allowed to extend their education for longer than that and for a wider array of educational programs, such as college and English classes, before facing sanctions for not participating in work.

Advocates working with the poor at the community level say they are opposed to the entire concept of time limits. "Poverty does not have time limits, so helping people should not have time limits," says Don Friedman, senior policy analyst with the Community Food Resource Center, a social service agency in New York City. "It is inhumane and outrageous to arbitrarily decide someone isn't entitled to assistance."

Friedman claims that, in practice, the time-limit exemptions are not helping the people they should. For example, New York City requires even people with serious disabilities to come into its offices to be reevaluated to see if they are exempt from the time limits. "I predict ten percent of the caseload will be sanctioned for nonparticipation because they cannot understand the rules or they cannot make it in," he says.

For Nancy Nay, who suffers from sickle cell anemia and cancer, it is not clear that she can be defined as one of the twenty percent of hardship cases, because the number of slots keeps shrinking as the caseload declines, the *New York Times* recently reported.[2]

Federal law also allows states to exempt welfare mothers who are coping with domestic violence. But in New York, which opted for such a provision, more than half the women were never screened for domestic violence, and of those who said they were victims fewer than half were referred for help, according to Marcellene Hearn, an attorney at the NOW Legal Defense and Education Fund.

"Many states have adopted laws that are pretty good" for welfare recipients who are victims of domestic violence, Hearn says, but "caseworkers are just not following through."

---

2. Nina Bernstein, "As Welfare Deadline Looms, Answers Don't Seem So Easy," *New York Times*, June 25, 2001, A1.

should keep the money as a contingency fund for leaner times or for child care and health insurance for the working poor.

Time limits are another major issue to be debated. Democrats and liberals are expected to propose more generous exemptions from TANF's five-year time limit for former recipients working part-time or completing their education and job training, as well as those considered the hardest-to-employ. Some studies suggest that many who are still on welfare are currently unemployable due to multiple problems, including drug or alcohol addiction, depression, disabled children, and lack of work experience.[43]

States already are permitted to exempt up to 20 percent of their caseloads. So far, few states have defined who will be eligible for exemptions. According to on-going research, a significant number of people who do not qualify for disability benefits, such as people undergoing treatment for cancer, cannot meet existing work requirements.[44]

Republicans are expected to argue that the 20 percent exemption should be sufficient to take care of problem cases.

Work Requirements

TANF required welfare recipients to work—or take up to twelve months of vocational education—within two years of receiving benefits. States were required to have half of their recipients involved in such activities by 2002.

Because caseloads have fallen so dramatically—more than 50 percent in some states—states have been able to meet those targets without having to create the kinds of extensive work programs envisioned by the bill. Republicans, led by HHS Secretary Tommy G. Thompson, argue that states should not be released from the requirement to establish good work or work-plus-training programs.

Democrats will argue that the bill should have a broader definition of what qualifies as work, including a broader definition of what kind of education is allowed. Republicans are likely to argue that only work works, pointing to past failures of government-funded job-training programs.

Democrats also would like to see the law include an explicit new goal: reducing poverty. The law should not just aim to get a welfare recipient the first job available, but a well-paying job, they will contend.

Most states have allowed welfare recipients to keep most of their earnings from a job—up to a certain salary—without losing supplemental cash support.[45]

Table 1-1 Temporary Assistance for Needy Families (TANF) Provisions
for Reauthorization
(Major funding provisions of the current program, which Congress must
reauthorize by October 1, 2002.)

Provision	Description	Funding	In Baseline?
Basic TANF block grant to states	To help needy children, reduce nonmarital births and other purposes	$16.5 billion annually, FY1996–FY2002	Yes
Illegitimacy bonus for up to five states	To reward greatest reductions in out-of-wedlock birth rates	$100 million annually, FY1999–FY2002	Yes
Performance bonuses	To reward high performance by states	$1 billion for FY1999–FY2003	Yes
Population and poverty adjustor for seventeen states	Grants for states with high population growth and low welfare spending	Up to a total of $800 million for FY1998–FY2001	No
Contingency fund	Matching grants for needy states	$2 billion for FY1997–FY2001	No
Native Americans	Grants for tribes	$7.6 million annually, FY1997–FY2002	Yes
Territories	Grants for TANF, foster care and other programs	About $116 million, FY1997–FY2002	Yes
Loan fund	Interest-bearing loans for state welfare programs	Total amount of loans may not exceed $1.7 billion	N/A
Medicaid for families leaving welfare	Federal payments for up to twelve months of Medicaid	About $0.5 billion per year	Yes
Additional Medicaid costs	Funds to compensate for computing Medicaid eligibility	$500 million total	No

Table 1-1 *continued*

Provision	Description	Funding	In Baseline?
Research by Census Bureau	To study impact of TANF on poor families	$10 million annually, FY1996–FY2002	No
Research by Dept. of HHS	Funds to study costs/benefits of TANF	$15 million annually, FY1997–FY2002	No

Note: If a TANF provision is in the baseline, then Congress will not need to find a funding mechanism (either a tax increase or a program cut) to reauthorize the provision. If funding is not in the baseline, Congress must find a funding mechanism.

Source: Brookings Institution.

Democrats will argue that recipients who are in the transition between welfare and work should not have to risk hitting their five-year time limit on assistance and becoming ineligible for benefits if they need them in the future.

There is also a growing momentum in both parties in Congress to let welfare mothers keep a larger share of child-support payments paid by absent fathers. Under current law, the state and federal governments retain all of a father's child-support payments while mothers are on welfare and about half the payments on overdue child support after mothers leave welfare. The provision has discouraged some unwed mothers from cooperating with state and federal agencies trying to find so-called "deadbeat dads," because often the father is paying some support to the mother unofficially.

Both conservative and liberal advocacy groups argue that families should get more of these collections in order to benefit the children involved.

Noncustodial fathers of children on welfare often do not pay child-support regularly because they are unemployed or employed in low-wage jobs. Helping such fathers get good-paying jobs is high on the agenda of several progressive groups, who point out that most federal employment efforts have so far been aimed only at mothers.

TANF at a Glance

The 1996 welfare-reform law replaced the old AFDC (Aid for Families with Dependent Children) program with the radically different TANF program (Temporary Assistance for Needy Families). TANF's five key provisions are:

1. The individual entitlement to benefits provided by AFDC was repealed. The right to cash welfare was replaced by a system of mutual responsibilities in which cash benefits are conditioned on attempts to prepare for self-support.

2. The funding mechanism of open ended federal payments for every person added to the welfare rolls by states was replaced by a block grant with a fixed amount of funding for each state for six years. States were given far more discretion than under AFDC law, to spend funds for purposes other than cash assistance, such as transportation, wages subsidies, pregnancy prevention, and family formation.

3. States were required to place an escalating percentage of their caseload in work programs.

4. Financial sanctions were placed both on states and individuals who fail to meet the work standards. In the case of individuals, states must reduce the cash TANF benefit and sometimes the food stamp benefit of adults who fail to meet the work requirements designed by states. Similarly, the federal government will reduce the block grant of states that fail to meet the percentage work requirement. This requirement stipulates that states must have fifty percent of their caseload involved in work programs for a minimum of thirty hours per week by 2002.

5. States are generally not allowed to use federal dollars to pay the benefits of families who have been on welfare for more than five years.

Unwed Mothers

Promoting marriage and reducing out-of-wedlock pregnancies ranked among the 1996 law's key goals. The virtual disappearance of married families from many poor, urban neighborhoods worries the administration, according to HHS Secretary Thompson, who pushed through one of the earliest welfare-to-work experiments as governor of Wisconsin. "The nation has clearly had major success in rolling back the culture of not working," he wrote in a recent article, "but the incidence of single-parent families, especially those formed by births outside of marriage, is still too high." [46]

Any proposals delving into the private arena of marriage, however, will be viewed as government intrusion and likely will face strong opposition from the National Organization for Women (NOW) and other progressive groups. It is not clear what proposals might be offered, other than exhorting the states to try harder to reduce unmarried births and possibly setting aside a fixed pot of money to encourage state experiments.

Although many states have used federal funds—provided under the 1996 law—to prevent teen pregnancy, congressional Republicans are disappointed at how little states have done to promote marriage. Lawmakers are expected to discuss whether states should be offered federal money to encourage more marriage. Rector of the Heritage Foundation proposes paying a $1,000 annual bonus over five years to reward at-risk women who wait to have a child until they are age twenty and married—as long as they remain married and off welfare for five years.

Most states have been leery of plunging into this controversial territory, although West Virginia adds a $100 marriage incentive to the monthly cash welfare benefit of any family that includes a legally married man and women living together.[47]

Timothy Case of the NOW Legal Defense and Education Fund condemns both West Virginia's approach and Rector's proposal as "rank discrimination against families where parents are unmarried." In addition, he says, "The government should not try to coerce people into marrying. Marrying or not marrying is a private decision."

Rector argues that welfare currently creates a "profound [financial] antimarriage incentive," even though mothers are no longer required to be unmarried in order to qualify for benefits. As long as a man earning $7–$8 an hour does not marry the woman he loves who is on welfare, she keeps her benefits. Once they marry, his income gets counted, pushing the wife over the income eligibility line and forcing her to lose almost all benefits, Rector observes.

Eloise Anderson, former director of social services for California's welfare system, argues that the married family environment prepares a child for citizenship and adulthood "better than any other social arrangement." She is among those who have proposed that unmarried couples be urged to consider marriage in the hospital as soon as their child is born.[48]

Wade Horn, President Bush's new assistant secretary of HHS for children and families, actively supports government programs advocating marriage. He points out that most children born in single-parent families will experience poverty be-

Child-Care Aid Goes Unused

Most former welfare recipients who are working do not receive the child-care subsidies they are eligible to receive. In many parts of the country, subsidies go to less than one-third of the former recipients, according to a study by the liberal Center for Law and Social Policy (CLASP).[1]

Study coauthor Mark Greenberg, a senior CLASP attorney, says 40 percent are simply unaware that they could get child-care assistance. When families leave welfare, the state welfare office may not know that they have gone to work and may not get an opportunity to inform parents face to face that the aid is available. Meanwhile, parents still on welfare are actually more likely to receive child-care subsidies, probably because they have greater contact with government offices.

Many parents do not apply for the subsidy because states usually do not pay for the kind of informal, unlicensed care that many welfare recipients must rely upon to cover their night and weekend work shifts, when few child-care centers are open. By contrast, families that are receiving the subsidies are more likely to use organized, center-based care than those using a neighbor or relative. Still other families may be overwhelmed by the administrative and paperwork hassles of applying for the aid.

The child-care subsidy, which varies from state to state, may not be high enough to provide a mother with the child care of her choice. The federal government requires each state to pay a day-care subsidy high enough to meet the fees at 75 percent of that state's child-care providers, based on the most recent market survey. But only 23 percent of the states meet this requirement, Greenberg says.

According to the Department of Health and Human Services, only 12 percent of the 15 million eligible low-income children benefit from the major source of federal child-care funds, the $13.9 billion, six-year Child Care and Development Block Grant. Another study, of low-income workers in Santa Clara, Calif., showed that a third of the parents were unable to work because they could not afford child care, while another third reduced their work hours.[2]

---

1. Rachel Schumacher and Mark Greenberg, "Child Care After Leaving Welfare: Early Evidence from State Studies," October 1999. Accessed at www.clasp.org.
2. Linda Giannarelli and James Barsimantov, "Child Care Expenses of America's Families," December 2000, Urban Institute. Accessed at www.urban.org. Spending was $3.45 billion in 2000. See U.S. Department of Health and Human Services, "Fact Sheet: Administration for Children and Families Child Care Development Fund," January 23, 2001. Accessed at www.acf.dhhs.gov, and HHS press release, "New Statistics Show Only Small Percentage of Eligible Families Receive Child Care Help," Dec. 6, 2000.

The child-care block grant is underutilized because it does not provide enough federal funding to cover all the eligible families, so there are few state outreach or information programs aimed at getting more families signed up for benefits, Greenberg says. "Why have a big outreach campaign if you cannot respond to the need?" he asks.

About twenty percent of federal welfare funds, called Temporary Assistance for Needy Families (TANF), now goes to paying for child care, Greenberg says. Much of that comes from surpluses of federal welfare money realized by the states after their caseloads declined dramatically following reform efforts. But the number of children benefiting from the child-care subsidy has not increased as fast as the number of mothers leaving welfare to go to work.

If Republicans succeed in cutting TANF during the welfare-reform reauthorization in 2002, it could have a "huge impact on the child-care system," Greenberg says.

fore they turn eleven and that fatherless children are more likely to fail at school, engage in early sexual activity, and develop drug and alcohol problems.[49]

In hospital interviews conducted in a national survey, 80 percent of unwed couples reported being "romantically involved" at the "magic moment" of their child's birth.[50] Usually it is the father's poverty or unemployment that prevents them from marrying, says study coauthor Sara S. McClanahan, a professor of sociology and public affairs at Princeton University's Woodrow Wilson School of Public and International Affairs. "I do not think signing them up for marriage will solve the problem. They're just going to split up," unless the husband's unemployment and the couple's lack of parenting and relationship skills are addressed, she says.

Other welfare experts worry that such policies could have dire consequences if the father is physically abusive. It is also not clear that marriage produces better futures for children or if the kinds of couples who decide to get married already have the kinds of relationship and parenting skills that are better for children.

AEI's Besharov suggests that increased use of the long-acting contraceptive Depo Provera and concern about AIDS probably has had a larger influence on curbing out-of-wedlock births than any changes in welfare policy. It is too early to say, many agree, whether welfare reform can affect sexual behavior.

Outlook

Decline Tapering Off?

Many welfare experts are concerned that as welfare rolls fall the population of re-cipients will be composed increasingly of those who are harder to employ. But sta-tistics paint a mixed picture.

For example, it now appears that less than 10 percent of the welfare population has a drug abuse problem, far lower than the twenty-five percent assumed during the welfare-reform debate, notes Peter Reuter, a visiting scholar at the Urban Insti-tute. And, he adds, it is not clear that addiction should keep welfare recipients from working. "Most people who have substance abuse problems who are not on welfare are employed," Reuter says. "They find jobs and on the whole keep them."

Moreover, Urban Institute studies have found that 1999 welfare recipients were no more disadvantaged than those on the rolls two years earlier.[51] One reason may be that those least able to work have been among the first forced off the rolls by work requirements, while those with jobs sometimes are permitted to stay on the rolls under new state rules.

However, some employers and job-training companies say they are now seeing a less educated, more troubled population, with higher levels of depression among former welfare recipients undergoing job training or entering the workforce.

"Businesses we work with say they are having a more difficult time finding work-ready applicants [among former welfare recipients] than two or three years ago," says Dorian Friedman, vice president for policy at the Welfare to Work Part-nership in Washington, D.C. The partnership is comprised of employers commit-ted to hiring ex-welfare recipients.

At CVS drugstores, which have hired some 12,000 former welfare recipients, newer applicants have lower literacy levels and are more likely to have prison records, notes Wendy Ardagna, who specialized in working with former welfare recipients at CVS and is now on loan to the Welfare to Work Partnership.

Nevertheless, companies will continue to be interested in hiring former welfare recipients because they foresee a shortage of entry-level workers at least through 2020, according to Ardagna. Former long-time welfare recipients may have trouble getting promotions and more pay, she says, because of their low level of educa-tion—frequently no more than an eighth-grade reading level, even among the most hard-working employees.

Should the government encourage welfare recipients to marry?

YES

Wade F. Horn
Assistant Secretary for Children and Families,
Department of Health and Human Services
From the *Brookings Review*, summer 2001

Marriage is in trouble, especially in low-income communities. It is no accident that communities with lower marriage rates have higher rates of social pathology. Unfortunately, [federal and state governments] have been reluctant even to mention the word, let alone do something to encourage it. Public policy . . . needs to show that [society] values marriage by rewarding those who choose it. . . .

Congress should make clear that the intent of the 1996 [welfare reform] law was to promote marriage, not cohabitation or visits by nonresident parents. . . .

Second, states should be required to indicate how they will use Temporary Assistance for Needy Families (TANF) funds to encourage marriage. Anyone who has ever spent any time in a state welfare office can attest to the . . . not-so-subtle message that marriage is neither expected nor valued.

Third, Congress should reduce the financial disincentives for marriage [by requiring states] to eliminate the antimarriage rules . . . in the old [welfare] program. The law that established the TANF block grant to states allowed, but did not require, states to eliminate the old rules. Congress should also reduce or eliminate financial penalties for marriage in other programs, like the earned-income tax credit.

Fourth, Congress should implement marriage incentives, [such as] suspending collection of child-support arrearages if the biological parents get married . . . and requiring states to provide a cash bonus to single welfare mothers who marry the child's father.

Fifth, Congress should fund programs that enhance the marital and parenting skills of high-risk families. Many men and women lack [such skills] because they grew up in broken homes without positive role models [or] . . . had inadequate or abusive parents themselves. Congress should provide resources to religious and civic groups offering meaningful premarital education. . . .

Finally, [Congress should] earmark some TANF funds for a broad-based public awareness campaign to publicize the importance of marriage and the skills necessary to form and sustain healthy marriages.

When it comes to promoting healthy, mutually satisfying marriages, doing nothing has not worked. Perhaps doing something might.

Should the government encourage welfare recipients to marry?

NO

Jacqueline K. Payne, policy attorney,
and **Martha Davis,** legal director,
NOW Legal Defense and Education Fund
Testimony submitted to House Ways and Means Human
Resources Subcommittee hearing, June 28, 2001

Marriage is not the solution for everyone, nor is it the solution to poverty. Our country consists of diverse family structures: those in which parents are married, single, remarried, gay and lesbian, foster and adoptive. These families . . . deserve to be valued and respected as they are.

Marriage is a constitutionally protected choice. The Supreme Court has long recognized an individual's right to privacy regarding decisions to marry and reproduce as "one of the basic civil rights of man, fundamental to our very existence and survival" (*Skinner v. Oklahoma*). Significantly, this constitutional right equally protects the choice not to marry. This right of privacy protects an individual from substantial governmental intrusion into this private decision. Marriage promotion mandates in [proposed] bills essentially coerce economically vulnerable individuals to trade in their fundamental right to privacy regarding marital decisions in exchange for receiving job and life-skills training. . . .

Supportive services should be made available to all families, regardless of their marital status or family composition, including services to help improve employment opportunities, budget finances, promote nonviolent behavior, improve relationships, and provide financial support to children. Where parents choose to engage in an intimate relationship, resources should be available to help ensure that it is a safe, loving, and healthy one.

Promotion of marriage requirements endangers lives. Violence against women both makes women poor and keeps them poor. Over fifty percent of homeless women and children cite domestic violence as the reason they are homeless. Many depend on welfare to provide an escape from the abuse. [Studies] demonstrate that a significant proportion of the welfare caseload—consistently between fifteen percent and twenty-five percent—consists of current victims of serious domestic violence. . . .

Where the very lives of these women and children are at stake, we cannot afford to encourage the involvement of [abusive] fathers without taking every reasonable precaution, and without recognizing that in some cases father involvement is not appropriate.

Political Consensus?

Both liberals and conservatives say they detect an increased willingness among legislators and voters to improve the lot of the working poor, who enjoy much greater support in national polls than nonworking welfare recipients.

"If you redefine single moms as working, the public's willingness to support them increases," says Harvard's Jencks, who argues for raising the minimum wage and increasing child-care subsidies.[52]

By transforming so much of the welfare population into the working poor, conservatives may have handed liberals the kind of consensus they need to get more government help for workers.

As evidence, welfare critic Mead of New York University notes that some provisions in the tax-cut bill signed in 2001 by President Bush were aimed at helping the working poor. The bill increased by $88 billion over ten years the tax refunds that low-income families with children will receive.[53]

A similar consensus is gathering in the states, where governors will fight to keep the programs they established to subsidize health insurance and child care.

Many experts think the consensus will spill over to the reauthorization of the food stamp program, which also comes up for review in 2002. Advocates for the hungry would like to see it made easier for the working poor to receive food stamps and for restrictions on working families to be relaxed.[54]

In a supreme political irony, Mead foresees enlarged support for improving job quality through an increased minimum wage and other prolabor measures traditionally associated with the political left—as a result of welfare reform's conversion of welfare mothers to workers.

"Now we are going back to the 'me too' politics of the 1950s and 1960s, where Republicans were competing with Democrats to do good things for ordinary people," Mead predicts. "We're going to see child care and all kinds of things coming from Washington to help out all those struggling workers.

"But," he points out, "if they had not become workers it would never have happened."

For More Information

Brookings Institution, 1775 Massachusetts Ave., N.W., Washington, D.C. 20036; (202) 797-6105; www.brookings.edu/wrb. This think tank's Welfare and Beyond project sponsors forums and issues reports on controversial issues relating to welfare reform and the upcoming reauthorization bill.

Center on Budget and Policy Priorities, 820 First St., N.E., Suite 510, Washington, D.C. 20002; (202) 408-1080; www.cbpp.org. This nonpartisan research group analyzes government policies affecting low-income Americans and has been in the forefront in arguing that the poorest families are worse off after welfare reform.

Center for Community Change/National Campaign for Jobs and Income Support, 1000 Wisconsin Ave., N.W., Washington, D.C. 20007; www.communitychange.org. The center and the National Campaign represent grass-roots welfare-rights advocates across the country and have released reports critical of state welfare-reform efforts.

Center on Law and Social Policy, 1616 P St., N.W., Washington, D.C. 20036; (202) 328-5140; www.clasp.org. CLASP is a research and advocacy organization for the poor that provides analyses of many welfare-related issues from a perspective that is critical of welfare reform.

Heritage Foundation, 214 Massachusetts Ave., N.E., Washington, D.C. 20002; (202) 546-4400; www.heritage.org. This conservative think tank has been a vocal critic of welfare and a supporter of policies to encourage marriage in welfare-prone communities.

House Human Resources Subcommittee, House Ways and Means Committee, U.S. House of Representatives; www.house.gov/ways_means/humres.htm#HumanResourcesHearings. This subcommittee has primary jurisdiction over welfare in the House. Its Web site includes links to hearing documents and witness testimony.

Joint Center for Poverty Research, Northwestern University/University of Chicago, 2046 Sheridan Rd., Evanston, Ill. 60208; (773) 271-0611; www.jcpr.org. The center summarizes its own and others' research on welfare reform in its newsletter.

Manpower Demonstration Research Corp. (MDRC), 16 E. 34th St., New York, N.Y. 10016; (212) 532-3200; www.mdrc.org. This nonprofit, nonpartisan research organization has a reputation for objective, influential studies of welfare and welfare reform.

Senate Finance Committee, U.S. Senate; www.senate.gov/~finance/. The committee with primary jurisdiction over welfare reform in the Senate is expected to hold hearings on welfare reform as the reauthorization deadline approaches.

Urban Institute, 2100 M St., N.W., Washington, D.C. 20037; (202) 833-7200; www.urban.org. This nonpartisan think tank has issued numerous influential reports regarding welfare reform.

U.S. Department of Health and Human Services, Administration for Children and Families (ACF), 901 D St., S.W., Washington, D.C. 20447; (202) 401-9215; www.acf.dhhs.gov. ACF is the federal agency with primary jurisdiction over temporary aid to needy families. Its welfare reform Web site includes links to HHS policy documents and data.

Notes

1. Connie Rounds is a fictitious name used in the following report to protect the confidentiality of the person interviewed by the study authors. Center for the Study of Women in Society Welfare Research Team, University of Oregon, "Oregon Families Who Left Temporary Assistance for Needy Families (TANF) or Food Stamps: A Study of Economic and Family Well-Being from 1998 to 2000, January 2001," Vol. II, 65–68.

2. Ibid.

3. Ibid., 67. For background on the 1996 law, see Christopher Conte, "Welfare, Work, and the States," *The CQ Researcher,* Dec. 6, 1996, 1057–1080.

4. Ron Haskins et al., *Welfare Reform: An Overview of Effects to Date,* January 2001, Policy Brief No. 1, Brookings Institution.

5. Tamar Lewin, "Surprising Result in Welfare-to-Work Studies," *New York Times,* July 31, 2001, A16.

6. Pamela Morris et al., "Welfare Reform's Effects on Children," *Poverty Research News,* Joint Center for Poverty Research, July–August 2001, 5–9. Accessed at www.jcpr.org.

7. Richard Bavier, "An Early Look at Welfare Reform in the Survey of Income and Program Participation," *Monthly Labor Review,* forthcoming.

8. Ibid.

9. Kaus spoke at a Brookings Institution forum on May 17, 2001, in Washington, D.C.: "Beyond Welfare Reform—Next Steps for Combating Poverty in the U.S." Accessed at www.brook.edu/com/transcripts/20010517/htm

10. Mickey Kaus, "Further Steps toward the Work-Ethic State," *Brookings Review*, summer 2001, 43–47.

11. Ron Haskins, "Giving Is Not Enough," *Brookings Review*, summer 2001, 13–15.

12. Christopher Jencks and Joseph Swingle, "Without a Net," *The Prospect Online*, Jan. 3, 2000. Accessed at www.prospect.org.

13. Kathryn Edin and Laura Lein, *Making Ends Meet: How Single Mothers Survive Welfare and Low-Wage Work* (1997), 63–64. National Survey data cited in Edin is from the Panel Study of Income Dynamics.

14. Wendell Primus, "What Next for Welfare Reform? A Vision for Assisting Families," *Brookings Review*, summer 2001, 17–19.

15. Ibid.

16. Douglas J. Besharov and Peter Germanis, "Welfare Reform—Four Years Later," *Public Interest*, summer 2000, 17–35.

17. Haskins, "Giving Is Not Enough."

18. June E. O'Neill and M. Anne Hill, *Gaining Ground? Measuring the Impact of Welfare Reform on Welfare and Work*, July 2001, The Manhattan Institute. Accessed at www.manhattan-institute.org

19. The White House, "The Effects of Welfare Policy and the Economic Expansion on Welfare Caseloads: An Update," Council of Economic Advisers, August 3, 1999. Accessed at http://clinton4.nara.gov/WH/EOP/CEA/html/welfare/.

20. Wendell E. Primus, Center on Budget and Policy Priorities, "TANF Reauthorization," NGA Briefing, June 6, 2001, Washington, D.C. According to Primus, counting the additional income received by low-income families from tax and government benefits, the percentage of children in poverty is even lower (12.9 percent in 1999, compared to 20 percent in 1993).

21. Ibid.

22. Ibid.

23. Haskins et al., *Welfare Reform*, 5.

24. Pamela Loprest, "How are Families that Left Welfare Doing? A Comparison of Early and Recent Welfare Leavers," Urban Institute, April 2001, 5–6.

25. Ibid., 6.

26. Ron Haskins, Isabel Sawhill and Kent Weaver, "Welfare Reform Reauthorization: An Overview of Problems and Issues," *Welfare Reform and Beyond Policy Brief No. 2*, January 2001, Brookings Institution.

27. Maria Cancian et al., "Before and After TANF: The Economic Well-Being of Women Leaving Welfare," Institute for Research on Poverty, *Special Report No. 17*, May 2000.

28. Haskins et al., *Welfare Reform Reauthorization*, 4.

29. Center for the Study of Women in Society, "Oregon Families."

30. Haskins et al., *Welfare Reform*, 6–7.

31. "Report of the Committee on Economic Security," January 1935, cited in John E. Hansan and Robert Morris, eds., *Welfare Reform*, 1996–2000 (1999), 6.

32. Gordon Berlin, "Tug-of-War," *Brookings Review*, summer 2001, 35.

33. Ibid., 9–10.

34. Besharov and Germanis, *Welfare Reform*, 18.

35. Ibid., 18–19.

36. Berlin, "Tug-of-War."

37. In 1992, 38.9 percent of families receiving AFDC were white, 37 percent were black, and 17.8 percent were Hispanic. See Hansan and Morris, *Welfare Reform*, 9.

38. Manpower Demonstration Research Corporation, "Big Cities and Welfare Reform: Early Implementation and Ethnographic Findings from the Project on Devolution and Urban Change," April 1999. Accessed at www.mdrc.org.

39. Besharov and Germanis, *Welfare Reform*, 24.

40. The hourly wage rate for the 20th percentile rose from $6.58 in 1993 to $7.13 in 2000 for female workers. See Primus, "TANF Reauthorization."

41. Besharov and Germanis, *Welfare Reform*.

42. For background, see Kathy Koch, "Child Poverty," *The CQ Researcher*, April 7, 2000, 295.

43. Haskins, *Welfare Reform Reauthorization*, 4.

44. Berlin, "Tug-of-War," 38.

45. Ibid.

46. Tommy G. Thompson, "Welfare Reform's Next Step," *Brookings Review*, summer 2001, 2–3.

47. See testimony of Theodora Ooms, senior policy analyst, Center for Law and Social Policy, before the House Committee on Ways and Means Subcommittee on Human Resources, May 22, 2001. Accessed at www.clasp.org/marriagepolicy/toomstestimony.htm.

48. Anderson quote is from the May 17 Brookings forum. Accessed at www.brook.edu/com/transcripts/20010517.htm.

49. Wade F. Horn and Isabel V. Sawhill, *Making Room for Daddy: Fathers, Marriage, and Welfare Reform,* Brookings Institution, written for the New World of Welfare Conference, February 2001, 2.

50. This analysis comes from a new study "Fragile Families and Child Well-Being," which will follow 3,600 children born to unmarried parents and 1,100 children born to married parents in twenty cities. Information about the study is accessed at http://opr.princeton.edu/circw/ff.

51. See Sheila R. Zedlewski and Donald W. Alderson, "Before and After Reform: How Have Families on Welfare Changed?" Urban Institute, April 2001.

52. "A National Survey of American Attitudes Towards Low-Wage Workers and Welfare Reform," April 27–30, 2000, by Lake Snell Perry and Associates. Accessed at http://www.jff.org/pdfs%20and%20downloads/FinalSurvey Data.pdf.

53. See Robert Greenstein, *The Changes the New Tax Law Makes in Refundable Tax Credits for Low-Income Working Families,* Center on Budget and Policy Priorities, June 18, 2001. Accessed at http://www.cbpp.org/6-14-01tax.htm.

54. See Kathy Koch, "Hunger in America," *The CQ Researcher,* Dec. 22, 2000, 1048–1051.

Bibliography

Books

Edin, Kathryn, and Laura Lein. *Making Ends Meet.* New York: Russell Sage Foundation, 1997.

Hundreds of interviews convince the authors that poor single mothers are usually worse off once they leave welfare for low-wage jobs.

Articles

Besharov, Douglas J., and Peter Germanis. "Welfare Reform—Four Years Later." *Public Interest* (summer 2000), 17–35.

Besharov, a scholar at the American Enterprise Institute, and Germanis, assistant director of the University of Maryland's Welfare Reform Academy, largely credit falling welfare rolls to the good economy and government supports to the working poor.

Boo, Katherine. "After Welfare." *New Yorker,* April 9, 2001, 93–107.

The profile of this single mother who made it off welfare by working two full-time jobs has raised questions about whether children and teens are better off when their mothers are in the workforce.

Haskins, Ron. "Giving Is Not Enough." *Brookings Review* (summer 2001), 12–15.

Haskins, a principal aide to House Republicans in the crafting of the welfare reform bill, argues that the 1996 law produced the reductions in the caseload and record high-employment levels among single mothers.

Primus, Wendell. "What Next for Welfare Reform?" *Brookings Review* (summer 2001), 16–19.

Primus, who resigned in protest from the Clinton administration over the 1996 welfare reform law and is now at the liberal Center for Budget and Policy Priorities, argues that the reauthorization bill should shift its focus from reducing caseloads to reducing poverty.

Sawhill, Isabel. "From Welfare to Work." *Brookings Review* (summer 2001), 4–8.

In this special issue devoted to welfare reform, the senior Brookings Institution fellow summarizes the broad range of views on welfare reform.

Sherman, Amy L. "The Lessons of W-2." *The Public Interest* (summer 2000) 36–48.

This positive report assesses Wisconsin's work-based welfare experience, which reduced welfare caseloads by more than eighty percent.

Reports and Studies

Boushey, Heather, and Bethney Gundersen. "When Work Just Isn't Enough: Measuring Hardships Faced by Families after Moving from Welfare to Work." *Economic Policy Institute*, June 2001. Accessed at http://epinet.org

Families who have left welfare experience levels of hardship similar to other poor families.

Center for the Study of Women in Society, Welfare Research Team, University of Oregon. "Oregon Families Who Left Temporary Assistance for Needy Families (TANF) or Food Stamps: A Study of Economic and Family Well-Being from 1998 to 2000." January 2001.

About half the women had incomes below the poverty level a year and a half after leaving welfare. Volume 2 contains individual profiles of women interviewed.

Haskins, Ron, Isabel Sawhill, and Kent Weaver. "Welfare Reform: An Overview of Effects to Date." Policy Brief No. 1, Brookings Institution, January 2001.

A former architect of the welfare-reform bill and a liberal economist summarize the effects of the 1996 welfare reform law.

Haskins, Ron, Isabel Sawhill, and Kent Weaver. "Welfare Reform Reauthorization: An Overview of Problems and Issues." Policy Brief No. 2, Brookings Institution, January 2001.

A good summary of issues likely to be debated in Congress during the welfare-reform bill's reauthorization.

Horn, Wade F., and Isabel V. Sawhill. "Making Room for Daddy: Fathers, Marriage, and Welfare Reform." Brookings Institution, February 2001.

Horn, President Bush's new assistant secretary for children and families, and Brookings scholar Sawhill argue that public policy must help "bring fathers back into the family picture."

Loprest, Pamela. "How are Families that Left Welfare Doing? A Comparison of Early and Recent Welfare Leavers." Urban Institute, April 2001.

This report finds little evidence that recent welfare leavers are less capable of working than those who left several years earlier.

Rector, Robert. "Issues 2000, Welfare: Broadening the Reform." Heritage Foundation.

A scholar at the conservative foundation argues that the welfare system "bribed individuals" into having children out of wedlock.

THE NEXT STEP: ADDITIONAL INFORMATION

Child Care

Chavez, Stephanie, and Martha Groves. "Child-Care Report Stirs Emotions." *Los Angeles Times,* **April 20, 2001, B1.**
For some parents, this was just the kind of news that added anxiety to an already hectic morning: a national study saying that the child you are about to drop off at day care may be more disobedient and aggressive in kindergarten the more time he spends in day care.

Deerin, Meghan Mutchler. "Shedding Light on the Day-Care Doom and Gloom." *Chicago Tribune,* **July 15, 2001, C1.**
A recent study about the negative effects of day care on children may have panicked parents for no good reason, according to some of the study's own researchers.

Dionne, E. J. Jr. "Day Care Culture War." *Washington Post,* **April 27, 2001, A23.**
In public debates on matters relating to families, children, and sex, our culture has become thoroughly dysfunctional. The culture-war approach to child care, teen pregnancy, and many other issues is exactly wrong.

Garrison, Jessica. "Researchers in Child-Care Study Clash Over Findings." *Los Angeles Times,* **April 26, 2001, A1.**
A week after a high-profile study cast a negative light on child care, researchers—including the study's lead statistician—are sharply questioning whether their controversial work has been misrepresented.

Goo, Sara Kehaulani. "Despite Boom, Many Families Struggling." *Washington Post,* **July 24, 2001, A6.**
Despite the economic boom of the late 1990s, four million working-class American families wonder whether they will have enough money to meet basic expenses at the end of the month, according to a study to be released today.

Greenhouse, Steven. "Child Care, the Perk of Tomorrow?" *New York Times,* **May 13, 2001, A14.**
Ford has broken ground in several cities as part of an ambitious plan to create dozens of centers to provide child care, summer camps, and tutoring, as well as activities for teenagers and retirees.

Hendrix, Anastasia. "High Staff Turnover Imperils Child Care, Researcher Says." *San Francisco Chronicle,* **April 29, 2001, A8.**

Marcy Whitebook, a senior researcher at the Institute of Industrial Relations at the University of California at Berkeley, spent six years, from 1994 to 2000, studying seventy-five child-care centers in San Mateo, Santa Clara, and Santa Cruz—the most extensive and long-term study of its kind.

Kleiman, Carol. "Creative Options in Child Care Reduce Stress." *Chicago Tribune,* **June 26, 2001, N1.**

Two years ago, Abbott Laboratories, the giant global health-care company based in North Chicago, Ill., found an astonishing fact: its 15,000 employees in Lake County had some 5,000 children under age fifteen. And many of the parents reported they experienced stress because of the lack of quality, affordable child care in their community.

Waxman, Pearl L. "Child Care Question Centers on Quality; Need Is Clear; Know-How Is the Issue." *Washington Post,* **May 31, 2001, T5.**

We have known for a long time that the standards in too many child care settings are not considered to be ideal. Salaries for child-care staff are pitifully low, and turnover is too high.

Child Poverty

Dionne, E. J. Jr. "Putting Poor Children Before Politics." *Washington Post,* **February 16, 1999, A17.**

Bill Bradley, the presidential candidate and former senator, ticked off a list of problems going unaddressed in the country, including child poverty.

Ellis, Virginia. "Poverty Rate Among State's Children Rises Sharply." *Los Angeles Times,* **July 10, 1998, A1.**

The number of young children living in poverty in California climbed dramatically over the last two decades, leaving nearly one in three impoverished by 1996, according to a study.

Goozner, Merrill. "Welfare Reform a 2-Edged Sword for Kids, Study Concludes." *Chicago Tribune,* **December 22, 1999, N12.**

The plight of children who remain on welfare is getting worse, even as a steadily improving economy has continued to reduce child poverty, a study shows.

Healy, Melissa. "U.S. Children's Poverty Level Is Down 17% Since 1993." *Los Angeles Times,* **August 11, 2000, A18.**

The number of children living in poverty has declined significantly since 1993, partly reversing an increase that began two decades ago, according to a Columbia University study.

Hong, Peter Y. "Youths Face New Challenges." *Los Angeles Times,* **October 19, 2000, A3.**
California's adolescent population is increasing at more than twice the rate of the overall population, and the rapidly growing number of youths face pervasive poverty, poor health care, and a higher chance of incarceration than they would almost anywhere else in the nation, according to a study.

Russakoff, Dale. "Report Paints Brighter Picture of Children's Lives." *Washington Post,* **July 14, 2000, A1.**
The federal government's most comprehensive gauge of children's well being shows child poverty, child mortality, teenage pregnancy, and juvenile violence at their lowest rates in twenty years, officials announced.

Sengupta, Somini. "How Many Poor Children Is Too Many?" *New York Times,* **July 8, 2001, A3.**
As policy-makers evaluate what welfare reform has wrought, the question emerges: Is this the best the United States can do? Must so many children in the nation grow up poor?

Sherlock, Barbara. "State Law May Help Nation's Homeless." *Chicago Tribune,* **September 6, 1999, D1.**
The Illinois Education for Homeless Children Act, which was enacted four years ago, ensures that homeless children can have immediate enrollment, stay in their school of origin, and have transportation. Rep. Judy Biggert, R-Hinsdale, has included the majority of those provisions into legislation she is drafting to help the homeless.

Employment Rate

Neikirk, William. "Economy Still Shaky Despite Jobless Dip." *Chicago Tribune,* **June 2, 2001, N1.**
The unemployment rate fell slightly last month to 4.4 percent of the workforce, the government reported, but analysts warned of heavier joblessness ahead in an economy skirting near the edge of a recession despite lower interest rates and the prospect of tax rebates.

Pearlstein, Steve, and John M. Berry. "Layoffs Renew Recession Fears; April Job Loss Biggest in Decade." *Washington Post,* **May 5, 2001, A1.**
The U.S. economy shed nearly a quarter-million jobs during April, the government reported yesterday, all but dashing hopes that the economic slowdown that began last summer had nearly run its course.

Rosenblatt, Robert A. "Jobless Rate Rises to 4.5% as Economic Slide Persists." *Los Angeles Times,* July 7, 2001, A1.

The nation's jobless rate climbed to 4.5 percent during June, up from 4.4 percent, as the sputtering economy suffered a sharp decline in manufacturing employment, the Labor Department reported.

Silverstein, Stuart. "State's Jobless Rate Edges Up in April Economy." *Los Angeles Times,* May 12, 2001, C1.

California's unemployment rate edged up to 4.8 percent in April, marking the first time in six years that joblessness statewide climbed two consecutive months and providing strong evidence of a cooling economy.

Sinton, Peter. "Job Losses Highest Since 1991 Recession." *San Francisco Chronicle,* July 7, 2001, A1.

The nation's businesses cut 271,000 jobs in the second quarter, including 114,000 last month, the government said yesterday.

Sinton, Peter, and Sam Zuckerman. "Jobless Rate Jumps." *San Francisco Chronicle,* May 4, 2001, A1.

The U.S. economy hemorrhaged more jobs in April than any month in the past decade, the Labor Department said today.

Uchitelle, Louis. "Broad Job Losses Last Month Show Slump Is Lingering." *New York Times,* July 7, 2001, A1.

The nation's employers cut 114,000 jobs in June, mostly in manufacturing but in other sectors as well, the Labor Department said yesterday, throwing cold water on recent reports suggesting that the economy was beginning to recover.

Uchitelle, Louis. "U.S. Jobless Rate Hit 4.5% in April; 223,000 Jobs Lost." *New York Times,* May 5, 2001, A1.

The American job-creation machine went into reverse in April as companies shed employees across much of the weak economy. The workforce fell last month by an estimated 223,000 jobs on top of a loss of 53,000 jobs the previous month, the Labor Department reported yesterday.

Encouraging Marriage

Horn, Wade. "Wedding Bell Blues." *Brookings Review,* July 1, 2000, 39.

Even though a specific goal of welfare reform is promoting marriage, few states have enacted any policies to do so and most seem reluctant to take any steps to achieve the goal.

Horn, Wade F. "Marketing Marriage for Fathers." *Chicago Tribune,* June 16, 1999, N19.
In many inner-city communities, it seems, it is easier to find a vegetable garden than a responsible and involved father. Indeed, entire communities can rightly be termed fatherless.

Milbank, Dana. "A Marriage of Family and Policy; Bush Gives Government a Leading Social Role." *Washington Post,* April 15, 2001, A1.
The administration is devising proposals to strengthen American families, using grants to promote "responsible fatherhood," marriage counseling to prevent divorce, character education for children, and tax credits to promote two-parent homes and adoption.

Pear, Robert. "Human Services Nominee's Focus on Married Fatherhood Draws Both Praise and Fire." *New York Times,* June 7, 2001, A24.
Wade Horn's nomination to a top position in the Department of Health and Human Services has drawn fire from feminists because he says the government should aggressively promote marriage, especially for low-income families.

Peterson, Jonathan. "Marriage Would Be Job 1 for Bush Nominee to HHS Cabinet." *Los Angeles Times,* May 18, 2001, A8.
Twelve years ago, during a bout with cancer, a psychologist named Wade F. Horn vowed to devote whatever future he had left to being the best father he could be "forever and always." These days, Horn awaits his Senate confirmation for a job that will give him a rare opportunity to turn his personal goals into national priorities.

"Push to Help Families Thrive Comes Under Attack." *USA Today,* June 15, 2001, A13.
Today's debate: promoting fatherhood. Our view: When policies drive families apart, why not change them?

Rauch, Jonathan. "The National Divide Centers on 'I Do'." *Los Angeles Times,* May 29, 2001, B11.
In the debate over the reauthorization of the landmark 1996 welfare law, conservatives are talking about marriage. Liberals and many moderates believe that marriage is a good thing, but they worry that every federal dollar spent on "promarriage" initiatives is one less federal dollar for other antipoverty and profamily measures such as efforts to prevent teenage pregnancy.

Wildermuth, John. "The Marriage Movement/Bush Espouses Benefits of Matrimony/Unmarried Moms Fear Being Singled Out." *San Francisco Chronicle,* June 24, 2001, A4.
Addressing the National Summit on Fatherhood earlier this month, Bush talked about spending $64 million next year for local programs that would include parenting- and mar-

riage-skills training. Over five years, the president would commit $315 million to government efforts designed to strengthen American families.

Impacts

Besharov, Douglas J. "Welfare Reform — Four Years Later." *Public Interest,* July 1, 2000, 17.
Four years ago this August, a Republican Congress pushed a reluctant President Clinton to sign a bill that ended welfare as we had known it. But since the 1996 welfare-reform act expires on September 30, 2002, its eventual fate is not yet clear. Much will depend on how the law's impact is viewed.

Gerstenzang, James. "Clinton Touts Welfare-to-Work Progress." *Los Angeles Times,* August 4, 1999, A18.
President Clinton extolled a substantial drop in the nation's welfare rolls, even as some Democratic critics and policy analysts complained that onetime welfare families are still suffering.

Groark, Virginia. "64% Who Leave Welfare Stay Poor, Study Says." *Chicago Tribune,* January 21, 2000, M6.
Sixty-four percent of Illinois residents leaving welfare rolls for work are living in poverty and struggling to pay for groceries, housing, and utilities, according to a study.

Loprest, Pamela. "Long Ride from Welfare to Work." *Washington Post,* August 30, 1999, A19.
Three years after the passage of welfare-reform legislation, everyone wants to know if it is a success. On one hand, caseloads have declined precipitously, and many who left welfare are working. On the other, many former welfare families continue to struggle.

Wallis, Jim. "A Look at Welfare Reform." *San Francisco Chronicle,* March 2, 1999, A19.
To hear the politicians talk about it, you would think the 1996 welfare-reform law has been an unmitigated success. In his State of the Union address, President Clinton listed it as one of the signature achievements of his presidency, noting that the welfare rolls are smaller today than they have been in thirty years.

Wolf, Richard. "Poverty Report May Boost Welfare Reform." *USA Today,* October 1, 1999, A3.
For three years, the rap against welfare reform has been that although it cuts caseloads, it does not pare poverty. But a report by the Census Bureau offers the strongest sign to date that families leaving welfare for work may be escaping poverty as well.

Bernstein, Nina. "As Welfare Deadline Looms, Answers Don't Seem So Easy." *New York Times,* June 25, 2001, A1.

The letter from New York City to welfare veterans is blunt. "Your time limits for cash assistance will be expiring this year. We have scheduled an appointment for you to be seen so you can discuss how you plan to manage your household expenses." The notice went to Angel Martinez, one of two working parents in a family of five who were getting by on low wages and their small cash aid supplement.

Cimons, Marlene. "Welfare Plan Gives Families Surer Footing, Study Says." *Los Angeles Times,* June 1, 2000, A1.

In a comprehensive study that tracked the lives of 14,000 families, a research firm reported dramatic results for one approach to freeing welfare recipients from the cycle of poverty.

Kornbluh, Karen, and Felicia Kornbluh. "Redirect the Rebate." *Los Angeles Times,* July 8, 2001, M5.

What is wrong with this picture? Later this year, U.S. states will cut off support to millions of poor children and their mothers who, if they are lucky, have a job but cannot afford child care and, if they are not, may have no income at all.

Liu, Caitlin. "Activists Call for End to Welfare Limits." *Los Angeles Times,* August 19, 1999, B3.

Throwing down fistfuls of wristwatches and stomping until some cracked, more than 100 welfare recipients and activists rallied in Los Angeles to "stop the clock" ticking away for millions of poor people in America facing federally mandated expiration dates for financial aid.

Meckler, Laura. "Welfare Rules Pushing Some Right to the Limit." *Los Angeles Times,* July 15, 2001, A1.

Under time limits, one of the central features of the 1996 welfare overhaul, even the poorest families must leave welfare after a set period of time, whether or not they have a job or a plan to support their families.

Mistrano, Sam. "Welfare Clock Will Run Out Before Job Supply Catches Up." *Los Angeles Times,* July 16, 1999, B7.

As the coordinator of a network of 1,000 community-based social service agencies in Los Angeles County, here is what I see: welfare reform is failing in every respect.

Rivera, Carla. "Welfare Time Limit Boosts Hunger and Homelessness, 2 Studies Find." *Los Angeles Times,* **April 28, 1999, B1.**

Los Angeles County's imposition of time limits on general relief welfare benefits has done little to help recipients find work and instead has plunged many of them into greater homelessness, two surveys found.

Sengupta, Somini. "Living on Welfare: A Clock Is Ticking." *New York Times,* **April 29, 2001, A1.**

When welfare changes came to the Catskill Mountains, the clock began ticking on Jennifer Mosher's lifetime entitlement to a welfare check. Since then, Ms. Mosher, twenty-three years old, a single mother of two, has learned to drive, inherited a clunker of a car, and held down a part-time job at a supermarket twenty-five miles away. If nothing changes, she will reach her five-year lifetime limit on cash benefits by the end of this year.

Wolf, Richard. "Surprise Benefits in Welfare Reform; Marriage Rates, Incomes Rise." *USA Today,* **June 1, 2000, A3.**

For the first time, researchers in Minnesota have found that moving people from welfare to work can boost marriage rates, reduce domestic violence, and help children succeed in school.

Wisconsin Experience

Goldstein, Amy. "Ready to Tackle 'Disneyland East', Welfare Reform Pioneer Thompson Is Critic of Federal Role." *Washington Post,* **December 30, 2000, A1.**

Gov. Tommy G. Thompson, R-Wis., is poised to lead a federal bureaucracy he has long disdained as an obstacle to the welfare innovations he championed for his state.

Rubin, Bonnie Miller. "Q&A. Tommy Thompson, Health and Human Services Secretary; Taking on Welfare at National Level." *Chicago Tribune,* **July 22, 2001, C4.**

It has been six months since Wisconsin's Tommy Thompson left the governor's job, where he burnished his reputation as the architect of welfare reform, to be the secretary of Health and Human Services.

Simon, Stephanie. "Thompson's Welfare Reforms Cut Rolls but Also Safety Net." *Los Angeles Times,* **January 12, 2001, A1.**

Wisconsin's welfare program is the most severe in the nation: work, or you do not get a cent.

2 | Politics and Policy

In the United States today, the term "welfare" is most often associated with programs (primarily cash assistance) to assist low-income families, usually those headed by a single mother with children. Since its inception in the 1930s as Aid to Dependent Children (ADC), welfare has been overhauled numerous times. Over the course of its six decades in existence, the focus of the program has shifted away from the primary goal of helping children to one of stressing the responsibilities of their parents. The current debate over welfare has become highly charged and hotly argued, with policy discussions touching on issues ranging from welfare recipients' employment prospects to their behavior and moral values.

This chapter provides details on the passage and implementation of the latest round of welfare reform, the Personal Responsibility and Work Opportunity Reconciliation Act (PRWORA) of 1996. After a brief history of past welfare reforms and recent political debates that lead up to PRWORA, this chapter provides overviews of the various current policies—such as time limits, sanctions, earned income disregards, family caps, and cash benefits—that illustrate the complexity of the policy choices available to states under PRWORA. The chapter concludes with a discussion of several issues that may shape the welfare debate in the future—namely, the treatment of immigrants, caseloads declines, family formation policies, and the involvement of faith-based organizations in the welfare system.

Welfare and Welfare Reform: 1930s–1990s

When President Franklin D. Roosevelt included the ADC program in the Social Security Act of 1935, the program was a modest one, designed to support needy widows and their children. However, amendments to the Social Security Act in 1939 made widows and surviving children eligible for a husband's Social Security benefits upon his death. This had the effect of removing most widows from the ADC program.[1] Over time the program, which underwent a name change to the Aid to Families with Dependent Children (AFDC) in 1962, became one that primarily served single parents and their children.

From the 1970s to the 1990s, the characteristics of the typical single parent on AFDC also changed. In 1969 just over 40 percent of single mothers receiving AFDC were divorced, while slightly more than 25 percent of mothers had never been married. By 1992 30 percent of AFDC families were headed by a divorced mother, but more than 50 percent were headed by never-married mothers.[2] Those who studied welfare viewed this shift as important for two main reasons. First, analyses showed that families headed by never-married mothers tended to spend more time receiving assistance on AFDC than families headed by a divorced or widowed mother.[3] During this time period, as the AFDC caseload became made up of families with longer welfare "spells," and as the number of recipients increased, welfare expenditures grew. Second, some critics and politicians believed that AFDC allowed never-married women the option of relying on government instead of a husband for financial support. If true, this could cause an increase in out-of-wedlock births.

As the characteristics of clients served by AFDC changed over the years, so too did the focus of the program. Originally, AFDC was an income-support program. Its main purpose was to provide cash benefits to help low income families with living expenses. Eligibility for AFDC benefits hinged primarily on "deprivation": the loss of financial resources because of the absence, illness, disability, unemployment, or death or one or both parents. As such, AFDC was structured as a "means tested" program, in that families qualified for the program if their income and other assets were below a predetermined threshold for their household size. States were allowed to set these thresholds, called "need standards." For example, in 1996 a single parent with two children living in California could qualify for AFDC benefits if his or her income and other resources were less than $730 in the month in which he or she applied. However, if this same parent lived in New York City, his or her family's resources would have had to have been below $577 to qualify for aid.[4] AFDC was an open-ended entitlement program, meaning that all eligible individuals could receive benefits, and the federal government would pay the majority of costs. Few welfare recipients were employed. Having a job usually resulted in loss of benefits, and the costs associated with working (for example, child care and transportation) often did not make employment worthwhile.

But from the 1960s through the 1980s, the focus of AFDC began to change. Policymakers and politicians introduced reforms to promote training and work in an attempt to bring welfare recipients into the labor market. These efforts culminated with bipartisan support for and ultimate passage of the Family Support Act (FSA) of 1988. The centerpiece of the FSA was the Job Opportunities and Basic Skills (JOBS) program. JOBS attempted to address unemployment of welfare recipients by encouraging participation in education and training programs, with the ultimate goal of moving recipients from welfare to self-sufficiency.

Problems with the Family Support Act and JOBS

In the early 1990s, states were in the midst of implementing FSA and JOBS. Through JOBS, AFDC recipients could participate in education and training programs—including attending college, receiving assistance with finding employment, and gaining work-related skills through placement in community service jobs. The philosophy of FSA, which operated through JOBS, was that by acquiring education and skills, welfare recipients could move off the welfare rolls by finding employment at wages that would sustain them and their families.

Almost as soon as FSA became operational, state welfare officials and others in the policy community began finding flaws with the new law, in particular with JOBS. An often-mentioned shortcoming of JOBS was that many welfare recipients were not required to participate in the program to receive benefits. Although JOBS sought to promote getting clients off welfare through education and attainment of work skills, a significant proportion of welfare recipients were not required to participate. Recipients could be exempted because of the ages of their children, their health conditions, and other factors such as distance from education and training providers. In addition, many state and local program administrators complained that JOBS lacked "teeth." If recipients did not go to assigned activities, their family could lose a portion of their monthly benefit. Many program officials believed this financial penalty was too small to matter.

Other concerns about JOBS stemmed from fiscal provisions in the enacting legislation. Funding for both AFDC and JOBS was a mix of federal and state funds. The proportion of state funding for both programs, called "matching" funds, varied based on a state's relative wealth. Whereas states were mandated to pay their share of AFDC benefit costs, the same was not true for JOBS funding. In order to receive the *full* amount of federal funds available to them, states had to contribute their full "match." However, they could receive some proportion of federal funds if they matched state funds at a lower level.

During the economic downturn of the late 1980s and early 1990s, most states could not budget for their full state obligation. This meant that they were unable to obtain the maximum amount of federal funds available to them. As a result, most state JOBS programs did not have adequate funding to provide a full array of services, in particular child care for recipients participating in education, training, and other programs.

In the early 1990s states also began to complain about immigrant use of public welfare programs. Although not directly related to JOBS, immigrants who received welfare were perceived by many politicians as an additional drain on their state budgets. This was especially true in the states of California, Florida, New York, and Texas where there is a large immigrant population. The proportion of adult AFDC recipients who were legal immigrants nearly doubled between 1983 and 1993 (from 5.5 to 9.3 percent), while legal immigrants made up 30 percent of those receiving disability payments through the Supplemental Security Income (SSI) program.[5]

Candidate Clinton and "Ending Welfare as We Know It"

Tapping into many of these concerns, Bill Clinton, then governor of Arkansas, made welfare reform one of his top political priorities in his 1992 campaign for the presidency. During his campaign he pledged to "end welfare as we know it," primarily through:

- Increasing participation in education and training programs
- Expanding tax credits for the working poor
- Limiting benefit receipt to two years unless adults were working or performing community service.

As a governor, Clinton had been involved in shaping the FSA as well as in experiments in Arkansas to change the welfare system. Focusing part of his campaign on welfare reform was a natural extension of his work as governor. The potency of welfare reform as a campaign issue may have been another reason why Clinton advocated change. In the early 1990s welfare caseloads were at an all-time high and growing, with more than 4.7 million families receiving AFDC in 1992.[6] Public opinion polls showed great dissatisfaction with the current AFDC system, with the majority of those polled believing that most recipients would never leave welfare.[7]

Clinton campaign advisers viewed welfare reform as an issue that could reshape the Democratic Party and bring new voters into the fold.

Part of Clinton's strategy was to use welfare reform as a vehicle to show a "new" side to the Democratic Party, one that was not beholden to liberal groups such as labor unions, minorities, and feminists.[8] Although Clinton's proposals to expand education and tax credits reflected traditional liberal values, limiting recipients' time on welfare was an idea typically embraced by those with more conservative views. Paradoxically, welfare time limits were first introduced by liberal Harvard economist David Ellwood. But the rhetoric used to promote this idea, and other reforms, had its origins in more conservative camps. For example, Clinton spoke of "personal responsibility" and the need to promote work, two themes echoed by conservative scholars such as Lawrence Mead. In the early 1990s Mead published *The New Politics of Poverty,* the main thesis of which is that welfare dependency is rooted in "behavioral" problems of the poor—including nonwork. Mead believed that welfare recipients must be "obligated" to work and take responsibility for their lives in order to break dependency. He wrote:

> There is a culture of poverty that discourages work, but the poor will work more regularly if government enforces the work norm. Antipoverty policies aimed at barriers or the self-interest of the poor have failed to raise work levels, while work requirements linked to welfare may succeed.[9]

This approach to welfare reform is often labeled as "paternalistic" because of its focus on promoting government's role in regulating and overseeing the conduct of welfare recipients in order to achieve certain ends (for example, work). Increasingly, states were taking paternalistic approaches in their welfare reform policies so that adopting certain aspects of this paternalism put Clinton in line with many of his peers.

State Experimentation in the 1990s

Even while Clinton was campaigning to reform welfare, many states were experimenting with their systems. Under Section 1115 of the Social Security Act, states were allowed to request waivers from federal regulations to test new rules and policies. During the administration of George Bush (1989–1993), ten states[10] were granted waivers to broaden the categories of recipients required to participate in JOBS and toughen penalties for failure to meet program requirements. California was one such state, and its welfare program in the county of Riverside became well-known for its strict stance on participation in JOBS along with an emphasis on moving recipients quickly into employment (rather than having them participate in longer-term education and training programs).

Other states used the "waiver" feature of federal law to experiment with alternative approaches to serving welfare recipients. Florida, for example, became the first state to test the effects of time-limiting welfare benefits. Wisconsin was perhaps the most ambitious in its attempts to alter the welfare system. The state obtained numerous waivers, many of which were designed to alter recipients' behavior by making eligibility for benefits conditional on certain expectations for adults and even children receiving AFDC.

After Clinton entered the White House in 1993, the number of states submitting waiver applications to the U.S. Department of Health and Human Services (HHS), which manages the federal welfare program, increased. The politicization of welfare by Clinton and plans to reform welfare by his administration fueled the pressure from states to change the system. By May 1995 forty states had submitted various waiver requests to experiment with policies, such as disallowing further benefit increases to families when another child was born (commonly referred to as "family caps") and imposing tougher penalties (sanctions) for noncompliance, including termination of benefits.[11] More states were drawn to the notion of limiting the time period for receiving benefits, and seventeen states received permission from HHS to implement time limits in some or all parts of their states.[12]

In addition, states were moving away from the education and training philosophy of JOBS and implementing "work first" programs instead. These programs required recipients to search for employment either in conjunction with or in place of participating in education and training. Arkansas, under Gov. Clinton, implemented work first programs in areas of the state in the 1980s. The success of the Riverside, California, program in moving recipients into employment spurred this change, along with the shifting political and public opinion surrounding the welfare system.

As one former government official noted, use of waivers in states such as California and Wisconsin:

> . . . rapidly created a bandwagon effect in other states. Not only did waiver requests appear to offer political opportunities to claim credit, they offered evidence that a governor was trying to do something about a welfare system that

Clinton's Welfare Reform Plan

In 1994 President Bill Clinton unveiled his welfare reform plan that would require welfare recipients to work within two years of accepting their benefits. To ease the transition to work, the government would spend more on job training and child care. Those who still could not find work were to be placed in federally subsidized jobs.

To control costs—Clinton promised he would not seek new taxes to pay for his plan—the administration proposed applying the plan only to people born after 1971. Even at that, the Clinton plan would have cost $9.3 billion more than the existing welfare system over its first five years.

The president did not find much support in Congress in 1994 for his recommendations. Liberals were cool to the idea of a two-year limit, and to a proposal that would let states limit benefit increases to parents who had more children while on welfare. Republicans denounced the White House plan even more strenuously, complaining that it would cover only part of the welfare caseload, provide too much flexibility in administering time limits, do little to discourage out-of-wedlock births, and, unlike their own plan, continue to provide welfare assistance to immigrants. With midterm elections coming up, no action was taken on the bill during the remainder of the 103rd Congress.

Source: Excerpted from: Christopher Conte, "Welfare, Work and the States," *CQ Researcher*, December 6, 1996, 1071.

was almost universally regarded as broken, insulating them from charges by political opponents that they were indifferent to the welfare mess.[13]

Influences on Clinton's Welfare Reform Proposal

When President Clinton assembled his cabinet for his first term, he brought a group of well-known researchers and academics into prominent positions within the U.S. Department of Health and Human Services (HHS). David Ellwood, a professor at Harvard's Kennedy School of Government, assumed leadership within the office of Assistant Secretary of Planning and Evaluation in HHS. Ellwood's book, *Poor Support,* promulgated the notion of a work-based welfare system, including a time limit on benefit receipt.

Republican Welfare Reform Plan

The Republican coalition of state's rights advocates, budget cutters, and those who wanted to impose tough requirements on welfare recipients produced a welfare reform proposal in 1995 far bolder than anything the GOP had proposed during the first two years of the Clinton administration (1993–1994). Earlier GOP proposals preserved the federal entitlement to welfare benefits while providing states more money to move welfare recipients into jobs. The new Republican plan sought to eliminate the federal entitlement altogether and convert federal welfare spending to block grants. The plan offered no promise of guaranteed federal jobs for those who sought work and could not find it. Where the previous Republican plan would have saved taxpayers $19.5 billion over five years, the new plan would have reduced federal spending by $102 billion over seven years.

Source: Excerpted from: Christopher Conte, "Welfare, Work and the States," *CQ Researcher,* December 6, 1996, 1071.

Ellwood argued that the welfare system did not address the problems of the poor, because it only attempted to redress the symptoms (lack of money) rather than the causes (joblessness, low wages, single parenthood, illness) of poverty.[14] Instead, he argued that the country should adopt a system of "transitional support." This was a system that offered a variety of services, including cash assistance, job training, and help with finding a job, to families who experienced temporary financial difficulties. Ellwood never specified how "temporary" transitional support should be, and he advocated community service jobs for those unable to find regular employment when their time limit for benefits expired. However, as he noted, "ultimately, there ought to be some expectation that people provide for themselves through work."[15] The notion of a work-based, transitional form of assistance became the basis for the Clinton welfare reform plan, unveiled on June 14, 1994.

Pressure from the Republicans and the States

As more states sought waivers and as welfare caseloads reached historic highs in the early 1990s (more than 5 million families received assistance in 1994),[16] governors, particularly Republican ones, began exerting pressure on the federal government to reform the system. Tired of "supplicating themselves to HHS" for approval for waivers, governors demanded maximum discretion at the state level. Their success in implementing new reforms argued for a system in which welfare policy decisions would be made at the state level, since this arrangement could take into account the different situations faced by program administrators in different areas of the country.

This federal-state arrangement, known as devolution, received further political backing when Republicans gained control of Congress in 1995. During the previous fall's election campaign, almost all Republican House candidates had signed on to the "Contract with America," a ten-point agenda of conservative legislation that Newt Gingrich, the new House Majority Leader, promised to bring to the floor in the first hundred days of the new Congress. The contract's welfare reform provision committed the new majority to legislation that would "discourage illegitimacy and teen pregnancy by prohibiting welfare to minor mothers and denying increased AFDC for additional children while on welfare, cut spending for welfare programs, and enact a tough two-years-and-out provision with work requirements to promote individual responsibility."

Cutting federal welfare spending was a key element of the contract because Republicans were also looking for ways to fund a large tax cut. Many prominent Republican governors recognized this budget necessity and were willing to accept fewer federal funds if they had more discretion with those funds.[17] These governors favored a "block grant" structure, whereby states would receive a set amount of federal money for their welfare programs but would gain the power to determine how to fund particular aspects. In the existing system, certain funds could only be used for certain purposes, for example, to provide child care, and funding regulations prohibited states from shifting funds to other programs.

Some Republicans did not favor turning over a great deal of authority for welfare reform to the states. Their views were particularly influenced by the Heritage Foundation, a conservative think tank. In addition to promoting work, Heritage Foundation staff viewed welfare reform as the opportunity to promote values such as marriage and the reduction or elimination of out-of-wedlock childbearing. However, many governors, including influential Republicans Tommy Thompson of Wisconsin and John Engler of Michigan, objected to any "unfunded mandate"[18]—that is, states being told the circumstances under which families could receive federally funded benefits. These governors felt that those people denied benefits would ultimately be the responsibility of states, potentially straining their state budgets further. In the end, Gingrich was able to bring conservatives in Congress and Republican governors into agreement on a welfare reform plan of their own.

Passage of the Personal Responsibility and Work Opportunity Reconciliation Act

Faced with a reelection race and a Republican majority in both the House and Senate, President Clinton was under increasing pressure to sign a welfare reform bill in 1996. Clinton's welfare reform proposal had gone nowhere in 1994, and he had vetoed in December 1995 and January 1996 two different versions of the Republican plan. It was imperative for Clinton to make good on his pledge to "end welfare as we know it." In his 1996 State of the Union speech, he issued a further challenge to Congress. If given a bipartisan welfare reform bill, he would "sign it immediately."[19]

Senate Majority Leader Bob Dole, who wrapped up the Republican nomination for president in spring 1996, also faced obstacles in passing a reform bill. Dole's challenge was appeasing the more conservative members of his party, several of whom had been his rivals in the primaries, while passing a law palatable to a broad range of the electorate.[20] By 1996 Dole had assumed the mantle of leadership of the Republican Party—especially after firebrand Gingrich had lost some public support for conservative welfare reform by touting orphanages for children born to teen mothers or to parents who were unable to support them.[21]

The National Governors Association (NGA) played a key role in the debate by proposing a bipartisan welfare reform plan of its own. Most of what the NGA proposed were modifications to provisions that were being debated in Congress, such as making the family cap optional, increasing from 15 to 20 percent the proportion of cases that could be exempt from the time limit, and increasing funding for child care. The political pressure on both parties helped bring the House and Senate together on a bill, entitled the Personal Responsibility and Work Opportunity Reconciliation Act (PRWORA) of 1996. Congress passed the measure at the end of July 1996, and President Clinton signed it into law on August 22, 1996.

PRWORA created the Temporary Assistance for Needy Families (TANF) program, which replaced AFDC. TANF was authorized and funded through September 30, 2002, and included the following features:

Governors and Welfare Reform

State governors, acting in part through the National Governors Association (NGA), played a critical role in shaping Republican welfare reform plans, including the welfare reform act of 1996. Perhaps the two most influential Republican governors during this time were John Engler of Michigan and Tommy Thompson of Wisconsin.

Engler, a former state legislator, was elected governor of Michigan in 1990 and quickly began restructuring the state's welfare system. In 1991 he eliminated Michigan's General Assistance program that provided benefits to single adults and other low-income families ineligible for Aid to Families with Dependent Children (AFDC). The next year his administration unveiled a blueprint for further reforms. Known as To Strengthen Michigan Families (TSMF), the plan proposed reforms to a variety of social programs including AFDC, JOBS, child welfare, and child support. Under TSMF the state attempted to increase the obligation of welfare recipients to participate in work and training activities by requiring them to enter into "social contracts" with the state. Many of the welfare changes outlined in TSMF required Michigan to seek waivers from the federal government, which the state was mostly able to attain.

Similar to Engler, Tommy Thompson was a state legislator before being elected governor of Wisconsin in 1986. During his first two terms in office, his administration undertook many welfare experiments, culminating in Wisconsin Works, or W-2, a proposal to replace AFDC with a completely work-based welfare system. W-2 was pending waiver approval within the U.S. Department of Health and Human Services while Congress wrestled with welfare reform in 1996.

Both governors were strong proponents of devolution—bringing welfare control to the states. Believing that the waiver process was too cumbersome, Engler and Thompson joined the national debate over welfare reform, traveling to Washington to testify and otherwise promote their visions of what a new welfare system should look like. Some critics speculated that Engler and Thompson's involvement was spurred by a desire to focus national attention on their welfare reform efforts—as well as aspirations of national office. Regardless of motives, Engler and Thompson, along with Governor William Weld of Massachusetts, began working on their reform proposals. When Thompson assumed leadership of the NGA in 1995, he and his Republican colleagues were able to take advantage of mounting political pressures to pass welfare reform to promote NGA proposals in Congress.

After passage of PRWORA, Engler and Thompson retained prominence in the welfare arena. Engler became vice-chair of the NGA for the 2000–2001 term and was expected to be a leading voice for governors during welfare reauthorization debates in 2002. Thompson left the governor's office in early 2001 to become secretary of Health and Human Services under President George W. Bush.

Sources: Kristin S. Seefeldt, Laura Kaye, Christopher Botsko, Pamela Holcomb, Kimura Flores, Carla Herbig, and Karen C. Tumlin, *Income Support and Social Services for Low Income People in Wisconsin*, (Washington, D.C.: Urban Institute, 1998); Carol S. Weissert, "Learning from Leaders," in *Learning from Leaders: Welfare Reform Politics and Policy in Five Midwestern States*, ed. Carol S. Weissert (Albany, N.Y.: Rockefeller Institute Press, 2000), 9.

- An end to federal entitlement to cash assistance
- Funding to states for welfare (cash assistance) in the form of a capped block grant
- Work requirements
- A five-year lifetime limit on benefit receipt
- Increased amounts of discretion for states and localities in defining and operating cash assistance programs.

In addition, PRWORA made major changes to the food stamp program, the federal program that provides food assistance to low-income families and individuals in the form of vouchers. Although food stamps were not included in the TANF block grant, PRWORA imposed restrictions on food stamp receipt for childless adults between the ages of eighteen and fifty. Unless these recipients were working at least part-time, they would only be eligible to receive food stamps for three months during a three-year period. Most legal immigrants were completely barred from receiving benefits through food stamps, Medicaid (government funded-health insurance), and the Supplemental Security Income (SSI) program, a program to assist low-income individuals who are disabled, blind, or elderly.

Although Clinton objected to several aspects of the bill, he faced tremendous pressure to sign welfare reform before the 1996 election. Public opinion polls conducted shortly before the bill passed Congress showed that nearly half of respondents thought the president had not made a real effort to reform welfare.[22] Dole, meanwhile, in his campaign for the White House was criticizing Clinton for his inaction, while leading Democrats such as Senator Daniel Patrick Moynihan of New York were equally strident in protesting against the bill.[23]

Liberal Reaction to Welfare Reform Act

President Bill Clinton signed the Personal Responsibility and Work Opportunity Reconciliation Act (PRWORA) on August 22, 1996, despite staunch opposition from liberals, including officials within his own administration and Marian Wright Edelman, president of the Children's Defense Fund and a long-standing friend of the president. Edelman said the welfare reform act "makes a mockery of [Clinton's] pledge not to hurt children . . . . It will leave a moral blot on his presidency and on our nation that will never be forgotten."

Several prominent high-ranking officials at the Department of Health and Human Services, including Edelman's husband Peter, decided to leave the administration in protest of Clinton signing the bill. The first to leave was David Ellwood, assistant secretary for planning and evaluation. Ellwood complained that Republicans had seized on the president's rhetoric—in particular, his pledge to "end welfare as we know it"—while ignoring the president's other pledge to provide jobs to those who cannot find them. Acknowledging that the White House had lost control of the issue after Republicans took control of Congress in 1995, Ellwood said glumly, "We got hit by a freight train, in part, of course, because our own train moved too sluggishly."

Source: Excerpted from: Christopher Conte, "Welfare, Work and the States," *CQ Researcher*, December 6, 1996, 1072.

State Implementation of the Welfare Reform

Once PRWORA became law, states began implementing the provisions of the TANF program. Some states, including Michigan, Wisconsin, and Florida, had already been experimenting with welfare reform through the waiver process and had previously passed legislation that outlined their plans for further reform. These states were ready to start their new welfare programs as soon as the federal law was passed. Other states needed to pass enabling legislation to come into compliance with the new federal law. In some states, such as California and New Mexico, this process was somewhat contentious, with Democratic legislators often battling Republican governors over specifics of welfare reform, including time limits and work requirements. However, in many states, lawmakers passed legislation quickly or simply followed the federal law. In these states, the details of states' welfare reform plans were left up to the state agency designated in charge of TANF funds, with policies hammered out by state bureaucrats.

Even so, devolution of responsibility for welfare to states has not completely resulted in "fifty different programs." The work participation requirements in TANF has resulted in the implementation of "work first" programs in most states. These programs focus on quickly placing recipients into employment, as opposed to a "human capital" approach, which emphasizes participation in education and training programs.

Beyond this distinction, though, describing a state's TANF program is a complex task. First, some states such as California, New York, and Ohio give fairly wide latitude to counties in shaping their welfare reform programs. Even when states have a coordinated plan, PRWORA allows states to make a number of choices about certain policy options (for example, adhering to the federal sixty-month time limit on cash assistance or adopting a shorter limit). PRWORA is silent on other issues, such as how much of their wages recipients can keep without losing their benefits. Time limits, work sanctions, diversion policies, family caps, earned income disregards, and benefit levels are a few of the more important policies about which states have made very different choices. Each is discussed in turn below.

Time Limits

One of the most radical aspects of PWRORA is the curtailment of the federal guarantee of welfare benefits. Although states have always had very different welfare benefit levels, the federal guarantee meant that recipients could receive cash welfare as long as they met the state's eligibility requirements. Time limits, which restrict the number of months for which an eligible recipient can receive benefits, change this system dramatically. The federal lifetime limit of sixty months (five years) on receiving federal welfare payments is meant to ensure that assistance will only be temporary.

In operation, time limits are a relatively new policy tool designed to influence the behavior of welfare recipients. In most states, time limits are *lifetime* limits: that is, individuals are eligible for some number of months of welfare but can never become eligible for welfare again if they use all the months that they are allowed. Advocates of time limits argue that they provide an incentive for recipients to find employment quickly, so as not to use up their lifetime limit. This practice is often referred to as "banking" months of assistance for future use.[24] Another possibility is that some families will avoid "starting their clock" by not applying for welfare until absolutely necessary, while others will go to work because they have used up all their months.[25] Opponents of time limits fear, however, that some families will find themselves without jobs and other resources when they reach the end of their time on assistance. Without guaranteed jobs, such as the community service ones proposed at one time by Ellwood, entire families could find themselves with no income at all.

Generally, states have taken four different approaches in setting time limit policies:

- Following the federal limit (sixty months over a lifetime)
- Setting a lifetime time limit shorter than the federal limit
- Instituting "fixed period" time limits (allowing receipt of benefits for a certain number of months, followed by a period of ineligibility)
- Applying a time limit only to adults.

As of early 2001, more than half (twenty-eight) of states follow the federal, sixty-month cumulative time limit. (See Table 2-1.) Five states have chosen to impose shorter time limits, ranging from twenty-one months in Connecticut to forty-eight months in Georgia. Prior to PRWORA, a number of these states experimented with shorter time limit policies, which they chose to continue. For example, Florida was one of the first states to operate a time-limited welfare system via waivers, albeit on a small scale (two counties). Then-governor Lawton Chiles (D), with bipartisan support from legislators, established a program with time limits ranging between twenty-four to thirty-six months intended to ensure that welfare recipients "assume some responsibility for their future."[26]

Another thirteen states use "fixed period" time limits. In all but one of these states, the cumulative time on assistance is sixty months. That is, a recipient may receive welfare benefits for a certain amount of time, for example, twenty-four months. Then an individual cannot receive TANF again for a period of time. Nevada's policy sets this at twelve months. After this time passes, individuals may go back on assistance, but their benefits would be terminated once they accrued a total of sixty months.

Finally, five states specify that the time limit only applies to adults on assistance; children continue to receive assistance, either up to sixty months or indefinitely. In California, which allows children to continue receiving grants after sixty months, the process of determining a time limit policy was contentious.[27] Originally,

Table 2-1 State Time Limit Policies on Receiving Welfare Benefits

States that Follow the Federal Sixty-Month Time Limit	States that Use "Fixed Period" Time Limits	States with Shorter Time Limits	States with Shorter Time Limits on Adults Only
Alabama	Delaware	Arkansas	Arizona
Alaska	Florida	Connecticut	California
Colorado	Louisiana	Georgia	Indiana
District of Columbia	Massachusetts	Idaho	Maryland
Hawaii	Nebraska	Utah	Rhode Island
Illinois	Nevada		
Iowa	North Carolina		
Kansas	Ohio		
Kentucky	Oregon		
Maine	South Carolina		
Michigan	Tennessee		
Minnesota	Texas		
Mississippi	Virginia		
Missouri			
Montana			
New Hampshire			
New Jersey			
New Mexico			
New York			
North Dakota			
Oklahoma			
Pennsylvania			
South Dakota			
Vermont			
Washington			
West Virginia			
Wisconsin			
Wyoming			

Sources: National Governors Association Center for Best Practices, "Round Two Summary of Selected Elements of State Programs for Temporary Assistance for Needy Families," March 14, 1999; State Policy Documentation Project, a joint project of the Center for Law and Social Policy and the Center on Budget and Policy Priorities. Accessed at http://www.spdp.org; L. Jerome Gallagher, Megan Gallagher, Kevin Perese, Susan Schreiber, and Keith Watson, *One Year After Federal Welfare Reform: A Description of State Temporary Assistance for Needy Families (TANF) Decisions, as of October 1997* (Washington, D.C.: Urban Institute, 1998); State Plan Database, Welfare Information Network. Accessed at http://www.welfareinfo.org/SPD_reports.htm.

then-governor Pete Wilson recommended that new recipients be limited to twelve months of aid in any twenty-four-month period, while other recipients would be limited to twenty-four cumulative months of aid. Democrats, who controlled the legislature, were divided among themselves as to how long a time limit the state should have. After months of stalemate, a compromise was reached on the current sixty-month limit with extensions available for children. However, part of that compromise may lead to early termination of benefits: if applicants and recipients are not working or performing community service, and the welfare office determines that jobs are available, assistance may be limited to eighteen months for new recipients and twenty-four months for all others.

The resulting differences in time limits from state to state can be considerable. Take, for example, the case of a single mother with two children who has been receiving TANF for twenty-four months. If she lives in Iowa, she still has thirty-six more months of TANF eligibility on her "clock." If she lives in Louisiana, which has a "fixed period" time limit of twenty-four months within any sixty-month period, she would not be eligible for TANF again until another thirty-six months had passed. If she lives in Arizona, she would receive nothing more except a smaller grant for her two children for another thirty-six months. If she lives in Michigan or Vermont and is abiding by all program rules, she would receive assistance for another thirty-six months and perhaps even beyond that. However, states are barred from using federal funds to provide more than sixty months of assistance; they have chosen to use state funds instead. Finally, if she moves to Connecticut, she would not be ineligible to receive TANF, since Connecticut has a twenty-one-month lifetime time limit.

By contrast, several factors may enable this family to continue receiving assistance, no matter what state they live in and regardless of the time limit policy in that state. First, PRWORA allows states to exempt up to 20 percent of the caseload from the time limit, because of hardship. Nearly all states have policies to determine to which families the exemption might apply or to extend the time limits under certain circumstances, primarily circumstances that would make it difficult for the adult recipient to work. Common instances under which a family might be granted an extension include:

- Experiences with domestic violence
- Inability to find employment despite good faith efforts
- Disability of the adult and/or other member of the household.

All but eighteen states exempt certain categories of families, such as families with a disabled family member.[28] In some states, caring for a very young child can also temporarily exempt a family from time limits. These circumstances from state to state are typically defined strictly. For instance, in Massachusetts, several recipients brought suit against the Massachusetts Department of Transitional Assistance (MDTA) for requiring that a child's disability must be expected to last at least a year to be considered disabled for the purposes of the welfare time limit. This set children's disabilities at a standard higher than that needed for adults (who may be certified "disabled" by a medical doctor). In 1999 a state judge ruled that the policy violated state law, granting a preliminary injunction.[29]

Of families who have left welfare because of time limits, relatively little is known. In part, this is because only a small number of recipients have left because their "clock has expired." According to calculations by the Center on Budget and Policy Priorities, an estimated 60,000 families had left the welfare rolls because of time limits as of mid-2000.[30] However, more than 2.2 million families have left welfare in total since PRWORA was signed. The first families to reach the federal five-year lifetime limit did not do so until October 2001.

In states that have shorter time limits, or that have implemented time limits under waivers before 1996, few families have accumulated the total number of months. Of those families who have, few have lost benefits. For example, in Virginia recipients receiving welfare in June 1996 could have reached that state's twenty-four-month fixed period time limit in June 1998. However, in June 1998 just 15 percent of those recipients had accumulated twenty-four months. Many recipients left welfare because of employment. Others left welfare for a period and then returned, but they had not accumulated twenty-four straight months of benefits.[31] In Connecticut, which has a time limit of twenty-one months—one of the shortest in the country—less than half of families who reached that point as of mid-1998 had their benefits terminated. According to early evaluation results, families who lost benefits were working and had earnings over the poverty line, while the majority of families with very low or no earnings were granted extensions to the time limit.[32]

Massachusetts, which in December 1996 enacted a time limit of twenty-four months in any sixty-month period, commissioned a study to determine the well-being of families who had left welfare.[33] Compared to a group of recipients who left for reasons other than the time limit, families who reached the time limit were employed at similar levels (around 70 percent of the cases in both groups) and received other forms of public assistance (for example, food stamps and medical coverage) at similar rates. High proportions (about 80 percent) were facing debt (overdue utility and credit card bills). Studies in other states have found that those who left welfare because of time limits, and were employed, had higher incomes than families who left welfare for other reasons. However, these families reported more difficulty paying for food (North Carolina and Virginia) and were less likely to have health insurance (Florida).[34]

As more recipients begin to reach time limits, issues such as these may appear in other states. However, no national database or tracking system currently exists for TANF recipients. If a recipient moves from one state to another, workers in the new state of residence have no quick and reliable way of determining whether and for how long that family received welfare elsewhere. Theoretically, a family could use up its sixty months in one state and then move and continue to receive benefits in some other part of the country. However, there is no evidence yet that this is happening.

Sanctions

Sanctioning, or penalizing recipients by reducing their benefit amount, is a practice that predates the 1996 welfare reform. These reductions take place when a welfare worker determines that a recipient is "noncompliant": not following certain rules and expectations, particularly expectations to participate in work or work-related activities. Each state (and sometimes locality) determines noncompliance differently. In general, though, not attending required activities (such as work first programs), not making a "good faith" effort in finding employment, or quitting or being fired from a job may result in a sanction. However, welfare workers have varying levels of discretion when deciding whether or not to sanction a family. For example, all states include "good cause" provisions in their sanction policies. That is, if a recipient can show a valid reason for not complying with requirements, such as a lack of child care or transportation, he or she may not be sanctioned.

In theory, sanctioning may accomplish several ends. Some believe that sanctions motivate recipients to comply with program requirements. Without sanctions, this theory holds, recipients have no reason to leave welfare for work.[35] A corollary of this theory is that sanctions mirror the work world—employees who miss work are not paid, so recipients should be held to similar standards.[36]

All of these theories assume that welfare recipients are rational actors who will choose to comply or not comply with requirements based on their economic situation. A client whose benefits are reduced should come back into compliance, with the end goal of avoiding further financial punishment.[37] Similarly, recipients who are *not* motivated by sanctions may have other sources of income. As such, sanctions may "smoke out" those who do not need cash assistance (for example, individuals committing welfare fraud).

Whether or not sanctions change client behavior and result in "rational" decisions is a point of debate.[38] A major criticism of the sanction policy under JOBS, which reduced but never eliminated benefits over a long period of time, was that it was never strong enough to be an incentive for compliance or to make recipients feel any financial "pain."

Under PRWORA, states must sanction recipients who do not comply with work requirements, but states are free to set their own policies. With the exception of Wisconsin, the types of sanctions states use fall into three broad categories (see Table 2-2):

- Partial reduction, but never termination of benefits (fourteen states)
- Partial reduction of benefits followed by termination of benefits for repeated noncompliance (twenty-two states)
- Termination of benefits at the first (and subsequent) instance of noncompliance (fourteen states).

Arkansas, for example, uses a partial reduction sanction policy. If a single mother on TANF does not attend a mandatory job search class, her welfare worker could sanction her by reducing the family's grant by 25 percent until she attended. If, later on, she is noncompliant again, the same 25 percent reduction would be put in place. However, if this scenario played out in another state, the family could lose its benefits entirely. In Illinois, for instance, repeated noncompliance may result in loss of all benefits for a minimum of three months. In states such as Maryland, Nebraska, and Ohio, the family could lose all benefits the first time the mother did not attend job search class. Finally, if this family lives in Delaware, Georgia, Idaho, Mississippi, Nevada, Pennsylvania, or Wisconsin, they could potentially be ineligible for assistance forever. These states have policies allowing for a lifetime bar on assistance if a family is repeatedly out of compliance. In states with lifetime bans, a sanction functions like a time limit.

Table 2-2 State Sanction Policies

States that Have Partial Reduction of Benefits	States that Have Partial Reduction/ Eventual Termination of Benefits	States that Have Termination at First Instance of Noncompliance	Other Policies
Alaska	Alabama	Florida	Wisconsin[1]
Arkansas	Arizona	Hawaii	
California	Colorado	Idaho	
District of Columbia	Connecticut	Iowa	
Indiana	Delaware	Kansas	
Maine	Georgia	Maryland	
Minnesota	Illinois	Mississippi	
Missouri	Kentucky	Nebraska	
Montana	Louisiana	Ohio	
New Hampshire	Massachusetts	Oklahoma	
New York	Michigan	South Carolina	
Rhode Island	Nevada	Tennessee	
Texas	New Jersey	Virginia	
Washington	New Mexico	Wyoming	
	North Carolina		
	North Dakota		
	Oregon		
	Pennsylvania		
	South Dakota		
	Utah		
	Vermont		
	West Virginia		

1. In Wisconsin, TANF recipients who receive a cash grant may be sanctioned in two ways. First, for every hour they are not compliant, their grant is reduced by the minimum wage. Second, in severe or repeated instances of noncompliance, "strikes" may be issued against recipients. Recipients who accumulate three strikes are barred for life from receiving TANF. Jennifer Ehrle, Kristin S. Seefeldt, Patricia McMahon, and Kathleen Snyder, *Changes to Wisconsin's Welfare and Work, Child Care, and Child Welfare Systems Since 1997* (Washington, D.C.: Urban Institute, 2001).

Sources: National Governors Association Center for Best Practices, "Round Two Summary of Selected Elements of State Programs for Temporary Assistance for Needy Families," March 14, 1999; State Policy Documentation Project, a joint project of the Center for Law and Social Policy and the Center on Budget and Policy Priorities. Accessed at http://www.spdp.org; L. Jerome Gallagher, Megan Gallagher, Kevin Perese, Susan Schreiber, and Keith Watson, *One Year After Federal Welfare Reform: A Description of State Temporary Assistance for Needy Families (TANF) Decisions, as of October 1997* (Washington, D.C.: Urban Institute, 1998); U.S. General Accounting Office, *State Sanction Policies and Number of Families Affected* (Washington, D.C.: Government Printing Office, 2000); State Plan Database, Welfare Information Network. Accessed at http://www.welfareinfo.org/SPD_reports.htm.

As is the case with time limits, information is limited regarding the extent of sanctioning and the circumstances of families who have been sanctioned. According to the most recently available data, in 1998 about five percent of families receiving TANF across the nation were in sanction status during a given month. The range was zero to 29 percent of families, depending on the state.[39] The proportion of welfare cases closed because of sanctions is not large—in fiscal year 1998 it amounted to about six percent of cases, compared to 22 percent that were closed because of employment.[40] However, many in the advocacy community view these numbers as underestimates, because for the majority of welfare cases closures, no reason is recorded.[41]

To date, several studies have analyzed the circumstances of sanctioned families. While the methodologies and data sources of the studies vary tremendously, a few common themes have emerged:

- Sanctioned families have lower employment rates compared to families who left welfare for other reasons
- Sanctioned families may have more barriers to employment, including lower education levels, mental health problems, and child care and transportation difficulties
- Sanctioned families have fewer earnings and less income compared to families who left welfare for other reasons.[42]

Earned Income Disregards

On the other end of the spectrum from sanctions are policies designed to encourage work through rewards or incentives, such as earned income disregards, which is the practice of exempting part of a client's earnings when computing the amount of welfare benefits. If sanctions are a "stick," earned income disregards are a "carrot." A "dollar-for-dollar" policy would reduce recipients' welfare grants one dollar for every dollar they earned while working. This type of policy gives recipients no incentive to combine work and welfare. Disregard policies, however, allow recipients to mix welfare and work. For instance, under AFDC policies, recipients could keep the first $120 of their paycheck, plus 33 percent of the remaining amount. Any additional earnings were deducted from their cash grant. However, this disregard policy was limited to the first four months of employment; after that, recipients were faced with a near dollar-for-dollar reduction in welfare benefits. If earnings were high enough to render the family ineligible for AFDC, families also faced the loss of subsidized health care (Medicaid). These factors, welfare critics argued, kept many recipients from seeking work.

In an effort to remove this disincentive to work, many states sought waivers to change the benefit calculation and allow recipients to keep more of their earnings. Along with increasing the incentive to work, more generous earned income disregards are also thought to ease the transition from welfare to work by phasing out benefits over time, rather than canceling them abruptly once a recipient goes to work.

PRWORA allows states to set their own policies in this area, and only three states have maintained the old AFDC policy. The rest have implemented more generous earned income disregards. As of mid-2000, eighteen states allow recipients to keep a set amount of their earnings and a proportion of the balance. For example, Kansas's disregard policy is "$90 per month and 40 percent of the remainder." If a single mother earned $200 one month, the first $90 would not be counted against her welfare grant, and she would be able to keep another $44 (40 percent of the balance of $200 - $90). Another seventeen states use a proportion when calculating a disregard, ranging from 20 percent of earnings for clients in Nebraska to 100 percent of earnings in Connecticut, Indiana, and Virginia (as long as total earnings are below the federal poverty level, which was roughly $14,600 for a family of three in 2001). Louisiana, Tennessee, and Wyoming disregard a flat dollar amount. Eight states use a combination of these approaches, for example, disregarding a set amount and a proportion of the remainder for the first few months of employment, then switching to a flat dollar amount. Only Wisconsin, because of the structure of its TANF program, does not have an earnings disregard policy. In this state, recipients who are considered work ready do not receive a cash grant.

Family Caps

While earned income disregard policies allow working recipients to keep more of their cash welfare benefits, family cap policies limit benefits. During the early 1990s, the notion that welfare promoted out-of-wedlock childbearing gained credence. Proponents of this theory argued that because AFDC benefits increased with each additional child born, single mothers had an incentive to have more children. Prior to passage of PRWORA, a few states applied for waivers to test this theory. New Jersey had the most well-known policy: once families were receiving welfare, they were not eligible for any increases in their grants if they had more children. This type of policy is commonly called a "family cap." PRWORA gives states the option to institute family caps, and nineteen states (including New Jersey) have chosen to do so.

Whether or not family caps are an effective policy tool in reducing out-of-wedlock births is a source of much debate. The evidence linking higher AFDC benefits to out-of-wedlock births is itself a source of great controversy. Perhaps the two most vocal proponents of this theory are social critics Charles Murray and Robert Rector. Both claim that welfare is linked to out-of-wedlock childbearing, because it gives single mothers a financial alternative to marriage. Rector attributes the availability of welfare payments to the rise in out-of-wedlock childbearing because, as he writes, "For over three decades, the U.S. welfare system has massively subsidized and promoted illegitimacy and single parenthood." [43] A few social scientists have also found an association. [44] However, other researchers found very weak links or no links at all. [45] In addition, advocates against family caps argue that reducing out-of-wedlock births should not be done at the expense of the children who are born to unwed mothers.

The evaluation of New Jersey's family cap waiver policy produced controversial results. While recipients in the "experimental" group (those subject to the family cap policy) had lower birth rates and increased use of family planning services compared to the "control" group (a group of recipients not subject to the policy), abortion rates among the experimental group increased. [46] After this controversial finding, New Jersey legislators introduced legislation in 1998 that would repeal the state's family cap, and Kansas decided not to implement a family cap policy. As Kansas policymakers noted, "Since the purpose of the family cap is to assure adults do not continue having children in order to receive increased public assistance, the five-year time limit does an effective job of curtailing such practice." [47]

TANF Cash Benefits

Sanctions, earned income disregards, family caps, and ultimately time limit policies all interact with the amount of cash benefits a state provides through TANF. For example, a sanction policy that reduces a family's benefits by 25 percent could have more or less of a financial impact depending on the base amount of its check.

Even before PRWORA, states had the ability to set their own cash grant amounts, and great variation existed between the states. In 1996, before PRWORA was implemented, the amounts (for a family of three with no income) ranged from $120 a month in Mississippi to $923 a month in Alaska. (See Table 2-3.) In part, these differences reflect different costs of living in various states (Alaska and Hawaii, the two states with the highest cost of living, also have the highest benefit levels). To some degree, cash welfare benefit differences are also offset by the amount of food stamps available to families in different states. In lower benefit states, families are eligible for more from the food stamp program than are families living in higher cash benefit states.

Differences in welfare benefits also reflect varying degrees to which states have made increases to those benefits over time. However, even those states that periodically increased the maximum benefit level have not routinely adjusted benefits to keep pace with inflation. Between 1970 and 1996, the purchasing power of AFDC benefits declined by half nationwide.[48] This trend has continued in the years after passage of PRWORA. Between 1996 and 2000, if states had made adjustments to keep pace with inflation, benefit levels should have increased by about 10 percent. As shown in Table 2-3, however, the majority of states (thirty) did not adjust cash grant amounts at all. Six states (Colorado, the District of Columbia, Hawaii, Idaho, Oklahoma, and Wyoming) even reduced the amount of assistance recipients receive under TANF. Of the fifteen states that increased benefit levels during this time period, eight did so at a level that kept pace with inflation. The median increase was $29, representing a 7.7 percent increase in the amount of assistance received.

In general, there has been very little political support for increasing welfare benefit amounts. This was true even before welfare reform passed. In the late 1980s and early 1990s, a number of higher benefit states feared that they were becoming "welfare magnets": attracting low-income families from other, less generous states. Similar to the debate about the impact of benefits on out-of-wedlock childbearing, the welfare magnet theory has received much attention from policymakers and academics. Recent research, however, has found no support for it. Yet news reports of busloads of Chicago housing project residents arriving across the border in Wisconsin to apply for welfare benefits were used to show the necessity of that state's "two-tiered" benefit demonstration, implemented in several counties through waiver in 1992. Instead of getting AFDC payments at the level set by Wisconsin, new arrivals to the state received the benefit amount of their former state of residence. California enacted a similar provision, but other states were denied waivers for this type of policy because of a constitutional challenge to residency requirements.

Table 2–3 Change in State Welfare Benefits, 1996–2000

State	January 1996 Maximum Benefit (Family of Three, No Income)	January 2000 Maximum Benefit (Family of Three, No Income)	Change in Benefit Levels 1996–2000	
			Dollars	% Change
Alabama	$164	$164	$0	0%
Alaska	$923	$923	$0	0%
Arizona	$347	$347	$0	0%
Arkansas	$204	$204	$0	0%
California	$607	$626	$19	3.0%
Colorado	$421	$357	−$64	−15.0%
Connecticut	$636	$636	$0	0%
Delaware	$338	$338	$0	0%
District of Columbia	$420	$379	−$41	−9.8%
Florida	$303	$303	$0	0%
Georgia	$280	$280	$0	0%
Hawaii	$712	$570[1]	−$142	−20.0%
Idaho	$317	$293	−$24	−7.6%
Illinois	$377	$377	$0	0%
Indiana	$288	$288	$0	0%
Iowa	$426	$426	$0	0%
Kansas	$429	$429	$0	0%
Kentucky	$262	$262	$0	0%
Louisiana	$190	$190	$0	0%
Maine	$418	$461	$43	10.3%
Maryland	$373	$417	$44	11.8%
Massachusetts	$565	$565[1]	$0	0%
Michigan	$459	$459	$0	0%

Table 2–3 *continued*

State	January 1996 Maximum Benefit (Family of Three, No Income)	January 2000 Maximum Benefit (Family of Three, No Income)	Change in Benefit Levels 1996–2000	
			Dollars	% Change
Minnesota	$532	$532	$0	0%
Mississippi	$120	$170	$50	41.7%
Missouri	$292	$292	$0	0%
Montana	$425	$469	$44	10.4%
Nebraska	$364	$364	$0	0%
Nevada	$348	$348	$0	0%
New Hampshire	$550	$575	$25	4.5%
New Jersey	$424	$424	$0	0%
New Mexico	$389	$439	$50	12.9%
New York	$577	$577	$0	0%
North Carolina	$272	$272	$0	0%
North Dakota	$431	$457	$26	6.0%
Ohio	$341	$373	$32	9.4%
Oklahoma	$307	$292	−$15	−4.9%
Oregon	$460	$460	$0	0%
Pennsylvania	$421	$421	$0	0%
Rhode Island	$554	$554	$0	0%
South Carolina	$200	$204	$4	2.0%
South Dakota	$430	$430	$0	0%
Tennessee	$185	$185	$0	0%
Texas	$188	$201	$13	7.0%
Utah	$426	$451	$25	5.9%
Vermont	$696	$708	$12	1.7%

Table 2–3 *continued*

State	January 1996 Maximum Benefit (Family of Three, No Income)	January 2000 Maximum Benefit (Family of Three, No Income)	Change in Benefit Levels 1996–2000	
			Dollars	% Change
Virginia	$354	$354	$0	0%
Washington	$546	$546	$0	0%
West Virginia	$253	$328	$75	29.6%
Wisconsin	$517	$673	2	
Wyoming	$360	$340	–$20	–5.6%

1. Benefit levels for Hawaii and Massachusetts are those for families not exempt from the work requirement.

2. Only certain types of families in Wisconsin's TANF program receive a cash grant, so the 1996 (AFDC) and 2000 (TANF) benefits are not comparable.

Source: Computations based on data reported to the U.S. Department of Health and Human Services. 1996 data reported in U.S. Department of Health and Human Services, Office of the Assistant Secretary for Planning and Evaluation, "Aid to Families with Dependent Children: The Baseline," June, 1998, Table 5.5. 2000 data reported in U.S. House of Representatives, Committee on Ways and Means, *The 2000 Green Book, Background Material and Data on Programs within the Jurisdiction of the Committee on Ways and Means* (Washington, D.C.: Government Printing Office), Table 7–7.

PRWORA initially gave states authority to enact residency requirements, and some states took this option. Court action often ensued. Ultimately, California's policy (new residents were eligible to receive only the amount of the cash benefit in their state of prior residence, unless California's benefits were lower) was contested all the way to the U.S. Supreme Court. In *Saenz v. Roe et al* (1999) the Court ruled that such a requirement unconstitutionally infringed on the right to travel. All states with residency requirements were forced to repeal them.

How Welfare Policies Work Together in Three States

All of the welfare policies described above function together to determine the amount of assistance a family may receive and the length of time for which assistance is available. But once again, the effect of policies on welfare benefits can vary greatly from state to state. This section looks at how a single mother with two children applying for TANF would fare in three states: Connecticut, Illinois, and Mississippi. (See Table 2-4.)

Under certain circumstances, if this mother applied for assistance in Connecticut, she would have the option of taking a cash payment instead of TANF benefits. In 1998 Connecticut governor John Rowland announced a new policy whereby working families (or families in which the adult has a recent history of employment) could receive cash payments worth up to three months of the state's TANF benefit to use for short-term needs, such as assistance with utility bills, child care, or car repairs. The governor noted, "This program offers an important alternative to welfare for those who just need temporary help."[49]

One-time cash payments, such as those offered by Connecticut, are part of a broader set of policies referred to as "diversion" programs, because a potential recipient is diverted from applying for monthly TANF benefits. Other types of diversion program include requiring applicants to search for work as a condition of eligibility (with applicants potentially diverted into employment) or referring applicants to other social services agencies to see if their needs can be met through other services.

If instead the mother decided to apply for TANF in Connecticut, was eligible, and had no earnings or other income, she would receive a TANF benefit of $636 each month plus food stamps and Medicaid. If the mother went to work, she could make up to $1,157 a month (the federal poverty level for a family of that size) and still receive her grant, because Connecticut does not count any earnings under the poverty level when computing the grant. In other words, she could take a forty-hour a week job paying $6.70 and hour and receive income of $1,994 a month (earnings plus TANF benefit). However, at this level of work, she would lose eligibility for food stamps. In addition, if the mother has another child while on welfare, her TANF benefits would not increase, because the state has a family cap policy. Assuming she works continuously, the family would lose its TANF benefits twenty-one months later, when Connecticut's time limit goes into effect.

On the other hand, if this family lived in Illinois, the mother could not have worked as much as in Connecticut and remained on assistance. In Illinois, the earning disregard is lower. If the mother took a part-time (twenty hours a week) job at minimum wage ($5.15 an hour), the family would receive her earnings ($443) as well as $229 in TANF benefits (the result of "disregarding" 67 percent of earn-

Table 2-4 Comparisons of State Welfare Policies

State	Diversion Program	TANF Benefit Level	Family Cap?	Earnings Disregard	Sanction Policy (First sanction and most severe)	Time Limit
Connecticut	Cash payment	$636	Yes	100% as long as earnings below poverty level	20% reduction for at least three months; eventual termination for three months	Twenty-one months
Illinois	None	$377	Yes	67% of earnings not counted against grant	50% reduction until compliance; eventual termination for at least three months	Sixty months
Mississippi	None	$170	Yes	$90 unless full-time work obtained within thirty days of initial benefit receipt or placement into work search—then disregard 100% for first six months of employment, then $90	Termination for at least two months; eventual termination for lifetime	Sixty months

ings). Like Connecticut, Illinois would not increase the grant amount if the mother had additional children while receiving assistance. As long as she worked, however, she would not be using up her future eligibility for welfare: in Illinois, any month that the mother has earnings does not count toward the time limit.

In Mississippi, if the mother took even a part-time, minimum-wage job, the family would receive only $9 in TANF benefits. This is because Mississippi has one of the lowest benefit payments in the United States ($170 for a family of three), and the earned income disregard for part time work is a flat $90. In addition, the state also has a family cap policy, so the family would receive no additional assistance if another child was born. However, if the mother took a full-time job within the first month of the family being on assistance, she could keep all earnings for six months as well as the entire TANF grant. After that, the disregard reverts to $90, and most likely the family would lose benefits if the mother worked full time. Given the benefit levels and earning disregard policy in Mississippi, it is very difficult to combine work with welfare in that state. On the other hand, as in Illinois, this family would not be using up many months against its time limit in Mississippi.

So, while the mother may take a higher wage, full-time job and remain on assistance in Connecticut, her time on welfare there will be shorter than two years. In Illinois, a higher-paying job will render the family ineligible for full benefits, but the family may not lose benefits as quickly if the mother takes a lower-paying, part-time job. In Mississippi, low-wage, part-time work may render the family ineligible, while full-time work may keep the mother on the rolls for a few more months.

All three states operate programs in which recipients must participate unless they are already employed or exempt from the work requirement. Recipients who do not attend these programs or who are determined by welfare office staff to be "noncompliant" are sanctioned. In the example above, if the mother is not working and is not cooperating with the state's work requirements, the family's benefits would decrease from $636 to $509 in Connecticut and would stay at that level for at least three months, even if the mother quickly started meeting program expectations. In Illinois the family would also receive reduced benefits for at least three months. Because Illinois's grant is smaller and the sanction penalty is larger than Connecticut's (50 percent of benefits as opposed to 20 percent), the family would only receive $188.50. In Mississippi the family would lose all TANF benefits for a minimum of two months.

In Connecticut and Illinois the family could lose all benefits if the mother was noncompliant multiple times. This penalty would stay in effect for a minimum of three months. However, if the mother never complied, the family would simply lose benefits, and the sanction would function much like a time limit. In Mississippi the strictest sanction policy operates the same way as a lifetime time limit—the family loses all benefits and is barred for life from ever receiving them again in that state.

Delivery of Welfare Services Under TANF

Along with a lifetime limit on benefit receipt, PRWORA also requires that all nonexempt recipients be engaged in "work activities" once they have received assistance for twenty-four months. According to Bruce Reed, domestic policy advisor to President Clinton, the twenty-four month figure was derived directly from David Ellwood's book, *Poor Support,* in which Ellwood suggested that families might receive transitional assistance for eighteen to thirty-six months before being required to perform community service. Reed noted that twenty-four months was the midpoint of these two figures.[50]

In addition, PRWORA mandated states to meet "work participation rate" requirements each year. That is, a certain proportion of the state's caseload, regardless of the length of time a recipient has been on, must be working or participating in a work-related activity (for example, looking for a job, receiving short-term training in how to find a job, and, on a limited basis, participating in a short-term training program that will prepare the recipient for a specific job). Beginning in 1997, 25 percent of families had to be in a work activity, and the proportion increases to 50 percent in 2002. These work participation rate requirements, coupled with the twenty-four-month work time limit, have led most states to operate "work first" programs as a way to move welfare recipients into employment.

In addition to implementing work first programs, many states have put in place other changes designed to facilitate the movement of welfare recipients into work. Two of these, case management and privatized delivery of services, are also discussed in this section.

Work First

The phrase "work first" can both refer to programs in which participants receive assistance in searching for jobs as well as a philosophical belief about how to move welfare recipients into employment. This philosophy assumes that finding a job and developing work skills through direct experience—rather than participating in education and training—will be more effective in moving recipients off the welfare rolls. As mentioned earlier, the work first philosophy gained increasing acceptance during the mid-1990s. Many policymakers found fault with the poor results from the JOBS program, which emphasized participation in basic education, postsecondary education, or other education and training programs.

Although the details of each state's program vary (and may vary greatly within each state), the primary focus of work first programs under PRWORA is to assist clients in finding employment quickly, as opposed to placing them in education and training programs first. Typical activities in a work first program may include workshops on a variety of "job readiness" skills, ranging from resume writing and interviewing to activities that are designed to help recipients manage daily life. For example, participants might attend budgeting and money management classes; they might be required to go to seminars on being better parents; or they could receive instruction in time management. However, the key activity in work first programs is job search. Recipients must go out in the community and apply for jobs. Depending on the program, they receive varying degrees of assistance in this task. Some programs may require recipients to search for work on their own, reflecting beliefs that (1) people will stay longer in jobs they find on their own, and (2) learning how to find work is just as important as working. Other programs offer more hands-on assistance to clients, such as calling employers on clients' behalf or bringing employers to the program or to the welfare office to conduct interviews on-site.

With PRWORA entering its sixth year, a number of states, however, have started to combine a work first approach to welfare reform along with more education and training services. With the dramatic decline in welfare caseloads, many policymakers believe that those left on the rolls are "harder to serve" and need more training in order to enter the workforce. However, most states that allow some education and training place limits on the amount of time and type of program in which recipients may participate. Following are some examples of state and local programs for moving welfare recipients into work.

Case Management

As states began instituting a work first approach, the catch phrase "changing the culture of the welfare office" took hold. This phrase is frequently used to illustrate how the welfare system's previous focus on providing cash assistance has changed to one on moving recipients into jobs. An integral piece of that change requires welfare offices to reorient what they do—"changing the culture" within the welfare office from its focus on determining eligibility and providing cash benefits to the provision of employment and social services with staff acting as "case managers."

The case management model, along with the expectation that welfare office staff will work intensively with clients to help them move off welfare, marks a significant contrast from the traditional staffing model within welfare offices. Prior to welfare reform, eligibility workers performed the main duties of welfare offices—eligibility determination and benefit provision. These positions were considered more clerical in nature. Under JOBS, if the welfare office provided employment-related services inhouse (instead of awarding contracts to other entities), a comparatively small number of staff who were not eligibility workers were assigned to carry out these tasks.

By contrast, many states have now moved to a case management system within their welfare offices, either by retraining existing staff, hiring new staff, or a combination of both. "Case manager" is frequently used as a generic description for welfare service workers who are responsible for addressing a variety of their clients' needs. But the specific functions of the position and the qualifications needed to perform them vary widely. As case managers, staff responsibilities may include determining eligibility for TANF, providing services needed to assist clients getting to work, helping clients devise a plan to move into employment, determining other social services the client may need, and, in some cases, providing counseling. States have developed different approaches to case management. (See box on page 88.)

The Private Sector and Welfare Reform

Before 1996, it was public welfare agencies that administered AFDC at the state and/or local levels. PRWORA, however, gives states the option to use private agencies to determine eligibility and administer benefits for TANF.

Historically, private agencies, particularly nonprofit organizations, have been involved in the public welfare system for many years. Under JOBS, for example, state or local public welfare agencies frequently contracted with nonprofit human service agencies, adult education providers, and community colleges to provide education and training or job search services. With welfare reform, many states

Three Approaches to Case Management

The following are different approaches to case management that three states have developed in their current welfare programs.

MICHIGAN: INTEGRATED CASE MANAGEMENT ROLE

In mid-1997 Michigan transformed its welfare office staff, most of whom previously determined and monitored financial eligibility for welfare, into case managers. These staff members—renamed "family independence specialists"—were given the responsibility to, "identify and develop plans for self-sufficiency, . . . provide direct services when needed and necessary, such as counseling in instances of noncompliance, initiate referrals for community services, and [build] a trusting relationship with families."

Michigan's integrated approach, however, initially resulted in challenges for state welfare directors and staff. The added role of case manager took up more of the staff members' time, while the paperwork associated with the job did not decrease. The amount of time staff members had to devote to case management activities, such as going to recipients' homes and talking with them about barriers to employment, was limited. To address this time obstacle, the state has recently simplified some of the eligibility policies and paperwork.

UTAH: SOCIAL WORKERS AS CASE MANAGERS

In Utah, rather than retrain existing welfare office staff to become case managers, the state hired counselors, most of whom were social workers, to work specifically with welfare recipients identified as having the greatest challenges in finding employment, particularly those with mental health and substance abuse problems.

Referral of a welfare recipient to a counselor, though, depends on the ability of existing welfare staff to identify individuals who might need additional help. Counselors in Utah have trained welfare office staff in how to identify signs of mental health problems or substance abuse.

DELAWARE: USE OF TWO CASE MANAGERS

The welfare arrangement in Delaware involves two sets of case managers. One set carries out the typical functions of welfare office staff (determining eligibility for governmental programs) as well as a new function of preparing a "contract of mutual responsibility," which outlines what activities the recipient must do to move off welfare. Once this contract is prepared, the recipient is referred to an employment case manager in an outside contracted agency who is responsible for helping the recipient find and keep a job.

A major challenge of this type of case management setup is that it requires frequent communication between workers in two separate organizations. To facilitate communication, the state has developed a computer system that both sets of case managers can use to obtain updated information on recipients.

Sources: Kristin S. Seefeldt, Sandra K. Danziger, and Nathaniel Anderson, *What FIA Directors Have to Say About Welfare Reform,* (Ann Arbor: University of Michigan, 1999), 5; Julie Strawn, "Substance Abuse and Welfare Reform Policy," Welfare Information Network Issue Note, January 1997, 1 (no. 1). Accessed at http://www.welfareinfo.org/hardtoplace.htm; Nanette Relave, "Using Case Management to Change the Front Lines of Welfare Service Delivery," Welfare Information Network Issue Note, February 2001, 5 (no. 4). Accessed at http://www.welfareinfo.org/casemanagementissuenote. htm.

and localities have greatly increased the involvement of the private sector in the welfare system, particularly in running work first programs.[51] Large-scale privatization, though, has not taken place, in part because the food stamp and Medicaid programs are not included in the TANF block grant structure. Public workers must still handle these programs. However, Texas and Wisconsin have contracted out all other services, minimizing the role of public workers in many areas of the state to just eligibility determination for food stamps and Medicaid.

Most private agencies involved in the welfare system tend to be nonprofit organizations, but with welfare reform there has been an increase in the number of for-profit corporations entering the arena. Some of these for-profit organizations, for example, America Works, were formed with the purpose of helping welfare recipients gain employment. Others, such as Curtis and Associates, moved into the welfare system as a way to expand their businesses. Previously, Curtis provided job search services to other groups of workers such as farmers. Some companies, in particular Maximus and Lockheed Martin, moved into the business of providing welfare to work services by first providing information and technology services to state governments, including state human service agencies. Maximus is a key player in the welfare programs of Los Angeles, Milwaukee, and Phoenix, while Lockheed is notable in Florida and Texas.

The decision to privatize certain aspects of the welfare system may have come about because of a number of factors.[52] First, PRWORA, with its emphasis on work, changes the role of the welfare system from one of income support to one of work support. Traditional public welfare bureaucracies, while experienced in providing benefits, have not been as involved in helping recipients find employment. Second, the notion of "reinventing government" has gained popularity over the last decade. This phrase, made popular by former Vice President Al Gore, brings to mind a leaner and more cost-effective public sector that not only ensures services are delivered, but often relies on the private sector to deliver them. The assumption is that the private sector is concerned with the bottom line and can deliver services more cost-effectively than government. In addition, supporters of privatization believe that if contracts to run welfare services are put out for bid, competition should increase not only the cost-efficiency of operation but also bring innovation. Private agencies, when competing against each other to secure a contract, will strive to offer services that give them an edge over their competitors.

Privatization, however, may not have these desired effects, particularly if contracts encourage cost savings over all other outcomes. One of the major arguments against privatization stems from this concern: in order to save money, private agencies may turn away clients who need more services, especially if the agencies receive a fixed amount of funds per client.[53] There is also the issue of accountability. Public agencies, by nature, are accountable to taxpayers for expenditures of public money. When private agencies run welfare programs, the direct link of accountability to taxpayers is gone. Private agencies may be more accountable to their board of directors.

However, not enough evidence is available to make a definitive assessment of the benefits and costs of privatization. A review of past studies finds some support for the notion that private agencies may provide higher quality services than public agencies, but little support for the notion of increased cost-effectiveness.[54] Allegations of misuse of public welfare funds and of poor treatment of clients by private agencies have also come to light. In Milwaukee, an audit revealed that two private providers were improperly using funds from their welfare contract for activities ranging from paying large bonuses to employees to trying to secure contracts in other states.[55] When public agencies run welfare programs, however, similar problems can arise.

Looking Toward the Future: Possible Emerging Policy Issues

Welfare reform was implemented in 1996 during a period of unprecedented economic growth. In the mid-1990s, unemployment dropped dramatically and jobs became plentiful, making it easier for recipients to meet work requirements and cushioning the impact of the cuts in immigrant benefits. The rate of economic growth slowed after mid-2000, but its effect on the welfare system and recipients is not yet known. The first families to hit the federal sixty-month time limit started to do so in October 2001. Evidence is mixed about the readiness of this group to enter the workforce. With PRWORA coming up for reauthorization in 2002, all of these are important issues that could shape the direction of welfare policy in coming years.

Welfare Reform and Immigrants

PRWORA greatly restricted the eligibility of legal immigrants for public assistance. Specifically, newly arrived legal immigrants are barred from receiving TANF for the first five years after their arrival (exceptions are made for certain refugees and immigrants with asylum status). States, however, have the option of providing TANF, as well as Medicaid, to eligible immigrants already in the United States. Nearly all states have taken this option.

Other provisions in PRWORA would have had a greater impact on legal immigrants, had the law not been amended. Originally, PRWORA barred immigrants from receiving food stamps and SSI. In the year after passage, an estimated 940,000 immigrants, one-fifth of them children, lost food stamp benefits and the Social Security Administration was prepared to drop 580,000 immigrants from the SSI rolls.[56] In the 1997 budget, Congress and the president restored these benefits to many immigrants, primarily children, the elderly, and the disabled. Pressure to do so came primarily from immigrant advocacy groups, but governors and mayors of cities with large immigrant populations were also concerned about shouldering the bill for services to immigrants.

Despite the changes in the law, large numbers of immigrants, particularly the newly arrived, remain ineligible for federal benefits. This has left states to decide how and to what extent to provide services to noncitizens not covered by federal programs. Some states have filled gaps in coverage by creating, for example, state-funded food assistance programs. California, New York, and Texas, three states with a large share of the immigrant population, all have such programs.[57] However, tension remains about the degree to which states should or can provide these types of services. If state budget surpluses shrink, fewer funds may be available to run these programs. In such a climate, resistance may grow to providing state-funded services to immigrants, whose entry into the country is controlled by federal policy.

Caseload Declines, Welfare "Leavers," and Welfare "Stayers"

A primary goal of PRWORA was to move welfare recipients off the rolls and into work. Slightly less than four years after passage of the law, TANF caseloads nationwide have been cut in half, from 4.4 million families (August 1996) to 2.2 million (June 2000), although that decline started in 1995 after welfare caseloads peaked at more than 5 million families in 1994.[58] According to state reports to HHS, at least 20 percent of recipients that leave welfare do so because of increased earnings.[59]

The extent to which the large decline in caseloads is a result of welfare reform, a good economy, or some combination of both is a source of much debate. While PRWORA puts increased pressure on both states and recipients to leave welfare for work, PRWORA was implemented during a period of unprecedented growth in the availability of jobs. During 1997–2000, unemployment in the United States dropped from 4.7 to 4.0 percent, as opposed to the early 1990s, when caseloads were rising and unemployment was between 6 and 7 percent. Given this economy, some welfare recipients may have entered the labor force even in the absence of welfare reform.

In 1999 the Council of Economic Advisors, a group of presidential appointees, attempted to sort out the effect of welfare reform on employment versus the effect of the economy. By their estimates, welfare reform policies accounted for approximately one-third of the caseload declines between 1996 and 1998, whereas the good economy and increases in the federal minimum wage contributed much less (about 8 to 10 percent each).[60] An earlier report released by the council attributed 26 to 36 percent of caseload declines in the prewelfare reform 1990s (1993–1996) to economic conditions, with welfare reform policies under waivers playing a "smaller yet important role."[61]

Other analysts disagreed with the council's assessment: some attribute more of the decline to welfare reform policies, others less. The conservative Heritage Foundation used sanction policies (described above) and work requirements to determine whether states pursued aggressive reforms (for example, immediate entry into a work first program and case closure for failure to do so) or "weak" ones (delayed work first requirement and partial benefit reduction sanction). These analyses found that, independent of their unemployment rates, states with more aggressive policies had larger caseload declines.[62] This led the authors to conclude that:

The huge state variations in the rate of caseload decline cannot be attributed to differences in state economic factors. But they can be explained convincingly by differences in the rigor of the state's work-related welfare reforms. Policy reform—not economics—is the principal engine driving the decline in [welfare] dependence.[63]

Others, though, question the importance of welfare policies on caseload declines, noting that other, nonwelfare policies, primarily the expansion of the earned-income tax credit (EITC), made it much more attractive for welfare recipients to go to work.[64] The EITC provides tax relief to families with low and moderate incomes in the form of a refund, even if the family's earnings were so low that they did not owe taxes. Finally, as one review of studies on this topic notes, all analyses to date find a substantial proportion of caseload decline attributable to *neither* the economy or welfare policies.[65]

Regardless of the cause of the large declines in welfare caseloads, those who study welfare have raised questions about how families who left welfare are faring. Across the nation, a number of states, as well some research institutes, have undertaken studies to attempt to answer this question. These studies are often referred to as "leavers" studies, since the group of interest are families who have left welfare.

State leaver studies vary a great deal in terms of the methodology they use and who they consider a "leaver." For example, some states conducted telephone surveys with former welfare recipients while others relied solely on state administrative data, such as welfare and employment records, to obtain information. "Leavers" might be defined as families who left welfare during a certain time period, regardless of whether or not they returned to welfare. Other states considered "leavers" to be only those families who left welfare and did not return. Keeping these differences in mind, findings from various state leaver studies have produced some similar results. According to a review of several state studies, more than 50 percent of welfare "leavers" were employed, and more than half of that group was employed nearly full-time. Most, however, were not earning enough to raise their family income above the poverty line.[66] Another review of state leaver studies found that between 23 and 35 percent of leavers returned to welfare for at least a month at some point during the year following their exit.[67]

Two national studies, "The National Survey of America's Families," conducted by the nonpartisan Urban Institute, a think tank in Washington, D.C., and "Welfare, Children, and Families," run by Johns Hopkins University, found similar patterns in employment and earnings. The Urban Institute study also reported that former welfare recipients are much more likely than other low-income families to struggle with paying bills and keeping adequate food in the household.[68] In addition, the Johns Hopkins study cautions that not all leavers are alike; women who relied on welfare for longer periods of time prior to leaving were found to earn less and have lower household incomes than those who had spent less time on welfare.[69]

With welfare caseloads declining so sharply, many speculate that those left on the rolls are increasingly "hard-to-serve," with many impediments to employment, ranging from low education levels to health and substance abuse problems. The status of welfare "stayers" is very important to the reauthorization debate, since states may have to make a case for funding TANF at similar levels to 1996. If "stayers" are harder to serve, states may need to spend the same amount of money to provide services to fewer clients.

As is the case on many issues related to welfare reform, evidence on this particular question is mixed. The Urban Institute's study, "Assessing the New Federalism," finds no statistical difference in terms of disadvantage (such as physical and mental health problems) between adults on welfare in 1997 and adults receiving welfare in 1999.[70] On the other hand, studies that examine a range of employment barriers, including specific mental health disorders and a variety of skill deficiencies, find that many of those who continue to receive welfare postreform exhibit characteristics that could make them harder to serve. A University of Michigan study of current and former welfare recipients, for example, finds that women who relied primarily on welfare for support were much more likely to have five or more barriers to employment than were women who primarily worked.[71]

In the future, the experience of welfare stayers and leavers will likely continue to be shaped by economic conditions and welfare policies. How the latter affects families remains to be seen, with the effect of five-year time limit unknown and with TANF up for reauthorization in Congress in 2002.

Family Formation

In PRWORA's legislative language, the goals of the TANF program are to:

- Provide assistance to needy families so that children may be cared for in their own homes or in the homes of relatives

- End the dependence of needy parents on government benefits by promoting job preparation, work, and marriage
- Prevent and reduce the incidence of out-of-wedlock pregnancies and establish annual numerical goals for preventing and reducing the incidence of these pregnancies
- Encourage the formation and maintenance of two-parent families.[72]

However, the details of the law primarily focus on work and work-related requirements and not on efforts to end out-of-wedlock pregnancies and encourage marriage. States were allowed to spend TANF funds on efforts to promote abstinence education, and five states with the largest reductions in out-of-wedlock births received financial bonuses from HHS. However, states were not mandated to implement programs targeted on this outcome. In other words, the reduction in these states could have been because of demographic or economic factors rather than policy changes.

For some welfare critics, the lack of attention to out-of-wedlock childbearing and to marriage is a severe shortcoming of current state welfare programs. Conservative organizations such as the Heritage Foundation encouraged the administration of George W. Bush in 2001 to hold states more accountable for results in these areas. New policies, for instance, might set marriage and out-of-wedlock reduction goals and require states to spend TANF funds on implementing and evaluating programs to meet these goals.[73]

Aside from media and public education campaigns, there are few tested models for programs that would increase family formation. Programs that encourage the involvement of fathers in the lives of their children are becoming more widespread. Many of these have as an underlying objective an increase in the likelihood of the father paying child support, thus reducing the mother's need for government assistance. An example of such a program is the Fragile Families initiative, run in several large U.S. cities, that seeks to promote paternal involvement as soon as a child of an unwed couple is born.

In the coming years, these types of programs may gain greater prominence, and their focus may shift to promoting marriage. One of the major advocates of fatherhood involvement programs, Wade Horn, was nominated by the Bush administration to fill a prominent position within HHS. Shortly before his appointment, he wrote that Congress, in reauthorizing TANF in 2002, should require states to provide job training programs to low-income fathers, earmark TANF funds for programs that work on marital and parenting skills, and allow TANF funds to go to nonprofit and religious organizations to run programs promoting marriage and reducing out-of-wedlock births.[74]

Faith-Based Involvement

Including religious organizations as welfare service providers is allowed under PRWORA in a provision, known as "charitable choice," which allows faith-based organizations to compete for contracts for state and federal welfare funds on the same basis as other organizations. While faith-based entities receiving TANF funds cannot require client participation in religious activities or refuse to take clients not of their organizations' faith, they do not have to create a secular environment for activities.

Shortly after entering the White House in 2001, Bush announced his intention to open up the contracting process to faith-based groups. While much debate surrounds this proposal, including potential constitutional problems (separation of church and state) and civil rights questions (can faith-based organizations discriminate in their hiring practices if they receive government funds?), little is known to date about the use of the current charitable choice option in welfare programs today or about its impact.

When TANF comes up for reauthorization in 2002, Congress and the president could simply reauthorize TANF in its current form, extending funding beyond its September 30, 2002 end date. However, it is probable that issues such as caseload declines will figure into discussions about appropriate funding levels for state block grants. In addition, the new administration's attention to issues such as family formation and delivery of programs promoting those and other goals by faith-based providers seem likely to enter reauthorization hearings. Even without another round of major welfare reform, the policies and goals of PRWORA could shift in coming years.

Notes

1. Anne Marie Cammisa, *From Rhetoric to Reform?* (Boulder, Colo.: Westview Press, 1998), 47.

2. U.S. House of Representatives, Committee on Ways and Means, *The 1996 Green Book, Background Material and Data on Programs within the Jurisdiction of the Committee on Ways and Means* (Washington, D.C.: Government Printing Office), 473.

3. Mary Jo Bane and David T. Ellwood, *Welfare Realities* (Cambridge, Mass.: Harvard University Press, 1994), 61.

4. U.S. House of Representatives, Committee on Ways and Means, *The 1996 Green Book, Background Material and Data on Programs within the Jurisdiction of the Committee on Ways and Means* (Washington, D.C.: Government Printing Office), 443–445.

5. R. Kent Weaver, *Ending Welfare as We Know It* (Washington, D.C.: Brookings Institution Press, 2000), 230–231.

6. Data reported by the Administration for Children and Families, U.S. Department of Health and Human Services. Accessed at http://www.acf.dhhs.gov/news/stats/3697.htm.

7. See, for example, Robin Toner, "New Politics of Welfare Focuses on Its Flaws," *New York Times*, July 4, 1992, A1.

8. Weaver, *Ending Welfare as We Know It*, 128.

9. Lawrence M. Mead, *The New Politics of Poverty* (New York: Basic Books, 1992), 24.

10. Mark Greenberg and Steve Savner, *The CLASP Guide to Welfare Waivers: 1992–1995* (Washington, D.C.: Center for Law and Social Policy, 1995), 2.

11. Ibid.

12. Gil Crouse, "State Implementation of Major Changes to Welfare Policies, 1992–1998," Prepared for the Office of Human Services Policy, Assistant Secretary for Planning and Evaluation, U.S. Department of Health and Human Services, 1999, Table W-1. Accessed at http://aspe.hhs.gov/hsp/Waiver-Policies99/W1tim_limt.htm.

13. Weaver, *Ending Welfare as We Know It*, 132.

14. David Ellwood, *Poor Support* (New York: Basic Books, 1988), 6.

15. Ibid., 13.

16. Data reported by the Administration for Children and Families, U.S. Department of Health and Human Services. Accessed at http://www.acf.dhhs.gov/news/stats/3697.htm.

17. Weaver, *Ending Welfare as We Know It*, 267.

18. Ibid., 267.

19. "Special Report/Social Policy—Issue: Welfare," *Congressional Quarterly Weekly Report*, August 31, 1996.

20. Weaver, *Ending Welfare as We Know It*, 298–299.

21. Ibid., 274–275.

22. Todd S. Putnam, "Clinton on Welfare: Fancy Footwork in a Box," *New York Times*, July 26, 1996, A1.

23. Ibid.

24. La Donna Pavetti and Dan Bloom, "Sanctions and Time Limits: State Policies, Their Implementation and Outcomes for Families" in *The New World of Welfare*, ed. Rebecca Blank and Ron Haskins (Washington, D.C.: Brookings Institution Press, 2001).

25. Pavetti and Bloom, "Sanctions and Time Limits," 16.

26. Robert E. Crew and Belinda Creel Davis, "Florida Welfare Reform: Cash Assistance as the Least Desirable Resource for Poor Families," in *Managing Welfare Reform in Five States: The Challenge of Devolution*, ed. Sarah L. Liebschutz (Albany, N.Y.: Rockefeller Institute Press, 2000), 27.

27. Rob Geen, Wendy Zimmermann, Toby Douglas, Sheila Zedlewski, and Shelley Waters, *Income Support and Social Services for Low-Income People in California*, (Washington, D.C.: Urban Institute, 1998), 39–40.

28. State Policy Documentation Project, "Time Limits: Findings in Brief," (Washington, D.C.: Center for Law and Social Policy/Center on Budget and Policy Priorities, 2000). Accessed at http://www.spdp.org.

29. *Minnefield, Taylor, and Miller v. McIntire, Massachusetts Law Reporter* 10 (no. 22), November 8, 1999, 517.

30. Liz Schott, "Ways that States Can Serve Families that Reach Welfare Time Limits" (Washington, D.C.: Center for Budget and Policy Priorities, 2000), 1. Accessed at http://www.cbpp.org/6-21-00wel.pdf.

31. Pavetti and Bloom, "Sanctions and Time Limits," 20–21.

32. Dan Bloom, Laura Melton, Charles Michalopoulos, Susan Scrivener, and Johanna Walter, "Jobs First: Implementation and Early Impacts of Connecticut's Welfare Reform Initiative" (New York: Manpower Demonstration Research Corporation, 2000), 56.

33. Massachusetts Department of Transitional Assistance, "After Time Limits: A Study of Households Leaving Welfare Between December 1998 and April 199," (Boston: Massachusetts Department of Transitional Assistance, 2000). Accessed at http://www.state.ma.us/dta/dtatoday/reform/CSR.pdf.

34. Pavetti and Bloom, "Sanctions and Time Limits," 25.

35. Mead, *New Politics of Poverty*, 173.

36. U.S. General Accounting Office, "Welfare Reform: State Sanction Policies and Number of Families Affected" (Washington, D.C.: Government Printing Office, 2000), 7.

37. David Fein and Wang S. Lee, "Carrying and Using the Stick: Financial Sanctions in Delaware's A Better Chance Program," (Cambridge, Mass.: Abt Associates, 1999), 1.

38. Fein and Lee, "Carrying and Using the Stick," 2; Joel F. Handler, *The Poverty of Welfare Reform* (New Haven: Yale University Press, 1995), 86–87.

39. U.S. General Accounting Office, "Welfare Reform," 30.

40. U.S. Department of Health and Human Services, *Temporary Assistance for Needy Families (TANF) Program: Second Annual Report to Congress*, (Washington, D.C.: Department of Health and Human Services, 1999), 108.

41. Heidi Goldberg and Liz Schott, "A Compliance-Oriented Approach to Sanctions in State and County TANF Programs," (Washington, D.C.: Center for Budget and Policy Priorities, 2000), 5.

42. Ibid., 7–12.

43. Robert Rector, "Illegitimacy a Major Cause of Poverty and Dependency," *Intellectual Ammunition*, February/March 1997. Accessed at http://www.heartland.org/ia/febmar97/ contents.htm.

44. These studies include Robert Plotnick, "Welfare and Out-of-Wedlock Childbearing: Evidence from the 1980s," *Journal of Marriage and the Family* 52 (August 1990); and Shelly Lundberg and Robert Plotnick, "Adolescent Premarital Childbearing: Do Economic Incentives Matter?" *Journal of Labor Economics* 13 (April 1995).

45. See, for example, Gregory Acs, *The Impact of AFDC on Young Women's Childbearing Decisions* (Washington, D.C.: Urban Institute, 1993); Chong-Bum An, Robert Haveman, and Barbara Wolfe, "Teen Out-of-Wedlock Births and Welfare Receipt: The Role of Childhood Events and Economic Circumstances," *The Review of Economics and Statistics*, 75, (May 1993); Greg Duncan and Saul Hoffman, "Welfare Benefits, Economic Opportunities, and Out-of-Wedlock Births Among Black Teens," *Demography*, 27 (November 1990).

46. Michael J. Camasso, Carol Harvey, Radha Jagannathan, and Mark Killingsworth, "Final Report on the Impact of New Jersey's Family Development Program: Results from a Pre-Post Analysis of AFDC Case Heads from 1990–1996 (Trenton: New Jersey Department of Family Services, 1998). Accessed at http://www.state.nj.us/humanservices/rutfdp.html.

47. Center for Law and Social Policy, "Caps on Kids: Family Cap in the New Welfare Era, A Fact Sheet," (Washington, D.C.: Center for Law and Social Policy, 1999). Accessed at http://www.clasp.org/pubs/caps_on_kids.htm#top.

48. U.S. House of Representatives, Committee on Ways and Means, *The 1996 Green Book*, 443–445.

49. State of Connecticut, Executive Chambers, "Governor Rowland Announces Program to Help Keep People Off of Welfare." Press release September 28, 1998. Accessed at http://www.dss.state.ct.us/pressrel/980930.htm.

50. Matthew Cooper, "Where Do I Sign?" *The New Republic*, August 12, 1996, 12.

51. Richard Nathan, "The Newest New Federalism for Welfare: Where Are We Now and Where Are We Headed?" *Rockefeller Reports*, October 30, 1997, 6.

52. Demetra Smith Nightingale and Nancy Pindus, "Privatization of Public Social Services: A Background Paper," (Washington, D.C.: Urban Institute, 1997), 9.

53. Ibid., 11.

54. Ibid., 15.

55. Steve Schultze, "W-2 Agency Misspent $370,000: Welfare Money Used for Parties, Soliciting Business, Audit Finds," *Milwaukee Journal Sentinel*, February 17, 2001, 1A.

56. U.S. General Accounting Office, "Welfare Reform: Many States Continue Some Federal or State Benefits for Immigrants," HEHS-98-132 (Washington, D.C.: Government Printing Office, 1998), 3, 10.

57. Karen C. Tumlin, Wendy Zimmermann, Jason Ost, "State Snapshots of Public Benefits for Immigrants: A Supplemental Report to 'Patchwork Policies,' " (Washington, D.C.: Urban Institute, 1999), 13, 41, 52.

58. U.S. Department of Health and Human Services, Administration for Children and Families, "Change in TANF Caseloads Since Enactment of New Welfare Law," accessed at http://www.acf.dhhs.gov/news/stats/aug-dec.htm; and "Temporary Assistance for Needy Families (TANF) 1996–1999," accessed at http://www.acf.dhhs.gov/news/stats/3697.htm.

59. U.S. Department of Health and Human Services, *Temporary Assistance for Needy Families (TANF) Program*, 108.

60. Council of Economic Advisers, "The Effects of Welfare Policy and the Economic Expansion on Welfare Caseloads: An Update," August 3, 1999. Accessed at http://clinton3.nara.gov/WH/EOP/CEA/html/welfare.

61. Ibid.

62. Robert Rector and Sarah Youssef, *The Determinants of Welfare Caseload Decline* (Washington, D.C.: Heritage Foundation, 1999), 7

63. Ibid., 10.

64. See, for example, Liz Schott, Robert Greenstein, and Wendell Primus, "The Determinants of Welfare Caseload Decline: A Brief Rejoinder," (Washington, D.C.: Center for Budget and Policy Priorities, 1999). Accessed at http://www.cbpp.org/6-22-99wel.htm.

65. Stephen Bell, "Why Are Welfare Caseloads Falling?" Assessing the New Federalism Discussion Paper 01-02 (Washington, D.C.: Urban Institute, 2001), 59.

66. Sarah Brauner and Pamela Loprest, "Where Are They Now? What States' Studies of People Who Left Welfare Tell Us," (Washington, D.C.: Urban Institute, 1999), 4–6.

67. Julia Issacs and Matthew R. Lyon, "A Cross State Examination of Families Leaving Welfare: Findings from ASPE Funded Leaver Studies," paper delivered at the National Association for Welfare Research and Statistics 40th Annual Conference, Scottsdale, Arizona, August 1, 2000, 8.

68. Pamela Loprest, "How Families That Left Welfare Are Doing: A National Picture," (Washington, D.C.: Urban Institute, 1999), 5.

69. Robert Moffitt and Jennifer Roff, "The Diversity of Welfare Leavers," (Baltimore: Johns Hopkins University, 2000), 6.

70. Sheila R. Zedlewski and Donald W. Alderson, "Before and After Reform: How Have Families on Welfare Changed?" (Washington, D.C.: Urban Institute, 2001), 1.

71. Sheldon Danziger, "Comment on TANF and the Most Disadvantaged Families' Well-Being," in *The New World of Welfare*, ed. Rebecca Blank and Ron Haskins (Washington, D.C.: Brookings Institution Press, 2001).

72. H.R.3734, "Personal Responsibility and Work Opportunity Reconciliation Act of 1996," Section 401, Public Law No: 104-193, August 22, 1996.

73. Patrick F. Fagan, "Encouraging Marriage and Discouraging Divorce," *Heritage Foundation Backgrounder*, March 26, 2001, 1–20.

74. Wade F. Horn and Isabel V. Sawhill, "Making Room for Daddy: Fathers, Marriage and Welfare Reform," in *The New World of Welfare*, ed. Rebecca Blank and Ron Haskins (Washington, D.C.: Brookings, Institution Press, 2001).

3 Businesses and Nonprofit Organizations

The underlying goal of welfare reform to "change the culture of the welfare office" has shifted the focus of those offices from writing checks to moving recipients into work. The old stereotypical images of welfare offices as drab public buildings in which long lines of people waited to be served by uncaring bureaucrats is no longer true in many states. With public welfare offices no longer mandated to be the sole providers of welfare services, businesses and nonprofit organizations have taken on an increased role in providing those services.

The role of many businesses in welfare reform is, of course, simply in employing welfare recipients. However, the Personal Responsibility and Work Opportunity Reconciliation Act (PRWORA) also opened the door to businesses and nonprofit social service agencies to bid for contracts to provide work first and other welfare services. Another role of nonprofit organizations in welfare reform is monitoring the types of services provided and making recommendations for their improvement. These nonprofit organizations, including professional associations of state officials and policy-makers, think tanks, and advocacy groups, have exercised varying degrees of influence in shaping the most recent welfare reform and its implementation.

This chapter describes the roles of businesses and nonprofit advocacy and research organizations in the current welfare system. It discusses any influence businesses and nonprofit organizations had during the welfare reform debates in the mid-1990s and also describes what their roles might be in the coming years, either in providing services or in the reauthorization of welfare reform in 2002.

The Role of Businesses in Welfare Reform

Businesses primarily play two roles in the postwelfare reform system—as organizations that prepare recipients for entry into the labor market and as the employers who hire those recipients into jobs. Since passage of welfare reform in 1996, there has been a marked increase in the number of corporations, or "for-profits," involved in job search and placement efforts. The major firms profiled in this chapter operate welfare-to-work or work first programs in multiple locations throughout the country. Although firms that hire welfare recipients are too numerous to cover individually, this chapter also describes several large corporations and partnerships that have made concerted efforts to employ welfare recipients.

Businesses as Job Search and Placement Providers

Providing welfare services may not seem to be very lucrative for businesses, yet an increasing number of for-profits have been entering the arena. Businesses would be unlikely to bid for welfare contracts if there were no hope for financial gain. In fact, conventional wisdom about the profitability of welfare services as a business may be wrong: analysts from Lehman Brothers, a major Wall Street investment company, estimated the welfare "market" in 1998 at $20 billion a year.[1]

For-profits involved in providing welfare services usually are under contract with public welfare agencies to help clients find and attain jobs. Four national for-profits are generally recognized as the major leaders in placing welfare recipients into jobs:

- America Works
- Curtis and Associates
- Lockheed Martin/IMS
- Maximus[2]

These four companies have programs in a number of states and localities to move welfare recipients into work. (For mission statement and contact information, see Table 3-1 on page 108.) Two other notable national companies, Electronic Data Systems (founded by H. Ross Perot) and Anderson Consulting, are management and information companies that are mostly involved in designing computer and other automated systems for welfare offices. Thus, while their contracts with state welfare systems are increasing, they do not provide services directly to clients.

AMERICA WORKS.   America Works was one of the first for-profits to provide welfare services, helping state and local welfare offices move recipients into jobs. Founded in 1984 by entrepreneur and self-described "social activist" Peter Cove, the company places welfare recipients into jobs that are found by America Works staff.

The America Works program, however, goes beyond just locating available jobs. When recipients are hired, they remain employees of America Works—which in turn bills the employer for their wages. Recipients only move onto the employer's payroll after successfully staying on the job for several months.[3] During this probationary period, America Works staff may visit recipients periodically to deal with issues such as child care and transportation in an effort to keep recipients employed.

America Works also sets itself apart from other private employment firms by operating completely on performance-based criteria. In contracting with public welfare agencies, the company stipulates it will only receive payment for each recipient placed into a job, as opposed to other contractual arrangements in which the contractor may receive all or part of its funding up-front.

CURTIS AND ASSOCIATES.   Dean Curtis, a communications professor, founded Curtis and Associates in 1985 to run programs for unemployed Nebraska farm workers. The company eventually shifted its focus to welfare recipients. It has more than 500 employees located in more than ninety offices across the country.[4] In July 2000 Curtis and Associates was acquired by Benova, Inc., a firm that provides program management assistance to state and local health and human services agencies (for example, designing systems to help determine Medicaid eligibility).

Curtis and Associates operates work first type programs in a number of states, including Arizona, California, Nebraska, New York, Wisconsin, and the District of Columbia. It has distinguished itself from other private providers by developing its own set of instructional materials, which the company markets to organizations and businesses in the job placement field, including those that serve welfare recipients. For example, Curtis sells a two-week curriculum entitled, "Steps to Self-Sufficiency," which is designed to teach the "elements of job search" and "polishing the [job] interview," among other skills.[5]

LOCKHEED MARTIN/IMS.   Defense contractor Lockheed Martin is a surprising example of a corporation that provides welfare services. A subsidiary of the company, Information Management Systems (IMS), works with public-sector agencies to, as the division's Web site notes, "address some of the nation's most pressing public policy issues and improve the delivery of public services that enhance the quality of life in our cities, counties and states."[6]

In 1996 the IMS hired Gerry Miller, who was then director of Michigan's welfare agency and a key state bureaucrat involved in the welfare reform debates, to oversee its efforts to secure welfare-related contracts. The company operates work first programs in Florida and Texas—two states with large welfare caseloads. IMS also holds contracts to automate welfare and other social service assistance programs.

MAXIMUS. Of the major for-profits operating welfare-to-work programs, Maximus is the largest in terms of its share of the market. In 1999 the company held 30 percent of the private social services market (including, but not limited to welfare-related contracts). It is estimated that if Maximus were a state providing social services, it would have the twenty-ninth largest caseload.[7]

Maximus CEO David Mastran founded the Reston, Virginia, company in 1975 to provide consulting services to government agencies, such as assistance in program management and identification of additional sources of federal funding for various government projects. Over time, Maximus moved into development of computer systems for public programs and actual operation of social service programs, including welfare-to-work programs.

Maximus holds contracts to provide work first and other welfare-related services in five states, including numerous contracts within California. Its contract in Milwaukee, Wisconsin, to operate the Wisconsin Works (W-2) program, is particularly notable: in addition to overseeing job search and placement activities for clients, Maximus also determines eligibility for Temporary Assistance for Needy Families (TANF) cash benefits. In most states, this function is still usually handled by public welfare agencies.

The Ups and Downs of For-Profits in Welfare Reform

The movement of profit-seeking firms into welfare services has generated much controversy. Defenders of for-profits contend that they will provide services more efficiently than other types of service providers, mostly notably public bureaucracies, because these companies must make a profit to stay in business. Many also believe that for-profits will be more innovative in providing welfare services and more capable of making quick and needed organizational changes than the public sector.

On the other hand, critics contend that a focus on the bottom line could be detrimental to welfare recipients, some of whom may need costly services (for example, mental health treatment or remedial education) before moving into the labor market. Since the entry of for-profits into the welfare services arena, no formal studies have been conducted to determine whether or not for-profits (1) place more clients into jobs (compared to nonprofits and public agencies), or (2) provide fewer services to clients in efforts to increase profits. Both scenarios have been reported in the media.

One potential measure of the "success" of for-profits is the sheer number of state contracts they procure. Curtis and Associates attributes its ability to secure additional welfare-to-work contracts in Indiana to the high number of welfare recipients who found employment through its first two offices in the state.[8] The company found jobs for 61 percent of the welfare recipients who went through its Indiana program. However, according to state data, this rate is no better or worse than the job placement rate for Indiana as a whole.[9]

In Nebraska, Curtis and Associates has been criticized for cutting costs at the expense of clients' needs. The Nebraska Appleseed Center for Law in the Public Interest, an advocacy group, contends that Curtis's state programs have been understaffed and filled with employees who are not qualified to be caseworkers. More problematic, the group believes, is that recipients are required to fill out complicated paperwork on their own. If done incorrectly, the paperwork can then be used as a reason for the company to deny recipients benefits.[10]

Similarly, Maximus's track record is mixed. The company received kudos in 1997 from then-Virginia governor George Allen for its Fairfax County program that moved 84 percent of clients into jobs.[11] However, the company has also made headlines in Wisconsin over allegations of improper use of welfare funds. In 2000 a state audit revealed that the firm had used funds from its Wisconsin's TANF contract for activities not strictly related to state welfare services. For example, according to the audit Maximus spent $23,000 for a motivational speech and concert for clients performed by a popular singer, $22,000 for social events for employees, and more than $50,000 for expenses related to obtaining a contract in New York City.[12] Wisconsin, however, later determined that these expenditures were because of "sloppy bookkeeping." Maximus agreed to pay back the costs as well as to spend $500,000 on extra services such as child care, transportation, and emergency food.[13]

Similar to Maximus, Lockheed Martin/IMS can also boast of high rates of job placement. In its Dallas program it helped move 76 percent of its welfare-to-work clients into employment.[14] However, in the late 1990s a Texas district attorney's of-fice launched an investigation to determine whether or not IMS engaged in illegal lobbying (hiring current and former state officials) in its failed attempt to secure a contract to operate Texas's entire welfare system.[15]

Finally, America Works has been criticized for charging high service fees. In the 1980s Ohio cancelled its contract with America Works, when some state officials alleged that it was costing the state approximately $24,000 for every client that America Works placed in employment.[16] America Works, though, estimated that the average charge to the state was $5,000 per client (in 1996). America Works jus-tifies its fees by contending that its track record of job placement and retention saves states money by keeping clients from returning to welfare.[17]

America Works has also come under fire for its employment practices. During the probationary period in which welfare clients work at a company but remain employees of America Works, America Works pays a wage lower than what clients would receive if they were regular employees. America Works, though, bills the company for the regular, higher wage and keeps the difference as payment for its services. In addition, America Works receives some government tax credits desig-nated for businesses that hire welfare clients. Although America Works does pro-vide services to both recipients and employers during this probationary time, some critics argue that the company is boosting its profits at the expense of its low-paid clients.[18]

This drive for profitability is the most troublesome aspect of for-profits for some critics who see these companies as "making a buck" off of a steady stream of welfare recipients who, under current welfare policies, must participate in welfare-to-work programs. Yet while for-profits have been criticized for problems in their delivery of welfare services, programs run by public agencies and by nonprofit or-ganizations are not trouble-free. In fact, while Maximus was able to rectify the problems it faced in Wisconsin, the state did not renew a similar contract it had with Employment Solutions, a nonprofit subsidiary of Goodwill Industries of Southeastern Wisconsin and Metropolitan Chicago. An audit found that the non-profit agency had spent $1.7 million of its TANF funds on staff bonuses as well as improperly billing the state for travel and other expenses related to other con-tracts.[19] If states and localities are unsatisfied with the performance of any type of contractor, for-profit or otherwise, they do have the option of canceling or not re-newing the contract.

Table 3-1 Major Businesses Involved in Providing Welfare Services

Company	Mission Statement	Importance to Welfare Reform	Contact Information
America Works	"We change peoples lives by lifting them from welfare dependency into the productive world of employment."	One of first for-profit firms to become involved in delivering job search and placement services to welfare recipients. Operates programs in New York, Baltimore, Boston, Indianapolis, and Miami.	America Works 575 8th Avenue, 14th Floor New York, NY 10018 Phone: (212) 244-5627 Fax: (212) 244-5628 Web: http://www.americaworks.com
Curtis & Associates, Inc.	"Curtis and Associates, Inc., will have an international impact on reducing poverty and unemployment. Through our efforts millions of people will have higher self-esteem, higher hopes for the future, and jobs that will enhance their self-sufficiency. Governments and businesses will save millions of dollars through the efforts of our company."	Has contracts in fourteen states either to operate work first programs directly or develop training materials for existing welfare office staff. Produces material widely used by welfare-to-work providers throughout the country.	Curtis & Associates, Inc. 315 West 60th Street Kearney, NE 68845 Phone: (308) 234-2676 Fax: (308) 237-7981/ 338-8024 Web: http://selfsufficiency.com
Lockheed Martin (Information Management Systems)	None	Has work first and other employment contracts in numerous locations, including many in Texas and Florida.	Information Management Systems 3000 Frank W. Burr Blvd. Teaneck, NJ 07666 Phone: (201) 996-7000 Web: http://www.lmims.com/about/index.html

Organization	Slogan	Description	Contact Information
Maximus	"Helping Government Serve the People."	Largest for-profit welfare to work contractor in terms of amount of funds from these types of contracts. Has contracts to provide welfare-related services in numerous states.	Maximus 11419 Sunset Hills Road Reston, VA 20190 Phone: (703) 251-8500 Fax: (703) 251-8240 Web: http://www.maxinc.com/
Marriott (Pathways to Independence)	None	One of several major corporations that has hired many welfare recipients and provides specialized training services to help recipients keep their jobs.	Fred Kramer, Project Director Pathways to Independence Marriott Drive, Department 935.47 Washington, DC 20058 Phone: (301) 380-8583 Fax: (301) 380-4710 E-mail: fred.kramer@marriott.com
United Parcel Service (Welfare to Work Program)	"Through more than forty Welfare to Work programs across the country, UPS collaborates with government agencies, faith-based groups, and non-profit organizations to develop, train, and mentor qualified candidates for positions at UPS and other area businesses."	One of several major corporations that has hired many welfare recipients and provides specialized training services to help recipients keep their jobs.	United Parcel Service 55 Glenlake Parkway, NE Atlanta, GA 30328 Phone: (404) 828-7123 Web: http://www.ups.com/ (main site) or http://www.community.ups.com/community/resources/helping/welfare_to_work.html (site describing welfare-to-work initiatives)
The Welfare to Work Partnership	"A nonpartisan, nonprofit organization created by the American business community to provide innovative workforce solutions for companies through hiring, retaining and promoting welfare recipients and other unemployed and low-income workers."	Has recruited thousands of businesses to hire welfare recipients and serves as a clearinghouse of information for businesses wanting to get involved in efforts to hire recipients.	The Welfare to Work Partnership 1250 Connecticut Avenue, Suite 610 Washington, DC 20036 Phone: (202) 955-3005 Fax: (202) 955-1087 E-mail: info@welfaretowork.org Web: http://www.welfaretowork.org

Business Involvement as Employers

The most common way in which businesses are involved in welfare reform is as employers of recipients. Employers do not always know, however, that the person they hire is or had been receiving welfare. Some welfare-to-work programs send staff members along with welfare recipients to job interviews or bring employers to their offices to conduct interviews there. On the other hand, other work first programs encourage recipients to search for work on their own, in part because of concerns about avoiding stigmatizing the recipient in the eyes of the employer.[20]

The extent to which employers do or do not discriminate against welfare recipients in hiring is unknown. Certainly, since the passage of welfare reform large numbers of former recipients have moved into the workforce. However, two major concerns of those who opposed welfare reform were (1) whether there would be enough jobs for everyone on welfare, and (2) whether employers would be willing to hire welfare recipients. Surveys of employers indicated that PRWORA's goal of total employment for welfare recipients may be difficult to achieve. For example, a survey of employers in Michigan found that while employers endorsed a general willingness to hire welfare recipients, employers also noted that many job openings required a certain skill level (high school diploma and skills such as reading, writing, and the ability to work with computers).[21] Other studies indicated that a significant number of welfare recipients lacked the education and skills necessary to obtain these jobs permanently.[22] Another obstacle to full employment was that many of the available jobs were at companies located far from the central cities in which many welfare recipients live.[23]

To address these concerns, a number of state and local welfare programs have embarked on efforts to involve employers directly in hiring welfare recipients. These efforts include customized training for employers who hire recipients, as well as the use of TANF money to support mentorship activities for recipients once they are employed.[24] The Welfare to Work Partnership is a nonprofit organization that has been attempting to accomplish this goal on the national level. The Partnership's mission is to recruit businesses to hire welfare recipients and other low-income individuals. Founded in 1997 by Eli Segal, former National Service advisor to President Bill Clinton, the Partnership initially brought together the CEOs of United Airlines, Burger King, Sprint, Monsanto, and United Parcel Services (UPS) to set up programs to hire and retain welfare recipients in their, and other, companies. By 2000, the Partnership included more than 20,000 businesses of varying sizes, with 1.1 million recipients hired by these companies. (For mission statement and contact information, see Table 3-1 on page 108.)

Recruiting employers into the Partnership often is done through visits to particular communities. In 1997, for example, the Partnership targeted thirteen major cities with high poverty rates. According to Partnership literature:

> In each of these cities, partnerships with local and state government leaders, businesses, service providers, and welfare recipients are the key to success. The Partnership works to develop and implement creative strategies, such as training and mentoring programs, for successful welfare-to-work initiatives. The goal is to determine and assess the local need, package and supply the appropriate technical tools, identify an infrastructure within targeted communities, facilitate local relationships and exchange information, increase the number of Business Partners through local community efforts, and increase the local welfare-to-work placements.[25]

After a business becomes involved in the program, the Partnership continues to help by providing information and assistance. This assistance may be in the form of conferences, publications, and directories of service providers that provide training and other services needed by recipients moving into the workforce.

United Parcel Services (UPS), a major shipping company, is one of the founding businesses within the Partnership. According to company literature, UPS has been working to hire welfare recipients for more than twenty-five years. It currently operates more than forty specific welfare-hiring efforts across the country. In the Chicago program, for example, newly hired welfare recipients are assigned mentors who help the recipient learn skills needed for the job. In particular recipients learn "soft skills," such as time management and appropriate customer relations. A number of UPS sites offer transportation assistance, which is important because many of UPS's distribution sites are located at airports far from city centers. For example, welfare recipients working for UPS at Philadelphia International Airport are driven to and from work if they lack transportation. Other entry-level workers who are not on welfare may be eligible to receive some of the extra services provided to welfare recipients, including transportation and tuition assistance. The company has placed some 35,000 welfare recipients in jobs with benefits.[26] (For mission statement and contact information, see Table 3-1 on page 108.)

The Marriott hotel chain was one of the first corporations to launch a large-scale effort to hire and train welfare recipients for work in the hotel industry. Its

"Pathways to Independence" program begun in 1991 has been showcased on national television and by politicians, including President Clinton, as an example of the potential for private businesses working with welfare recipients. The program consists of a six-week training program, which includes onsite training at one of the chain's hotels. Costs for operating the program are shared between Marriott and public and private agencies involved in welfare reform. (For mission statement and contact information, see Table 3-1 on page 108.)

By 1998, about 850 people had graduated from the program, about a 90 to 95 percent success rate. One year later, about 60 percent of graduates were still employed by Marriott. One criticism of Marriott, however, is that the company has the option of screening out individuals it believes might fail its program. For example, in North Carolina, only five of twenty-two referrals from the local welfare office were accepted into Marriott's Pathways program, with the others dropped because of bad personal references or evidence of drug use.[27]

Given the expense associated with offering training, mentoring, and transportation services, such as those provided by UPS and Marriott, why have private companies taken on these costly efforts? In part, the strong economy in the mid- to late 1990s left many companies with unfilled positions, either because the businesses were expanding or because employees left to take better jobs elsewhere. When the Welfare-to-Work Partnership surveyed business members in 1998, it found that 71 percent reported employee shortages.[28] In addition, the entry-level labor market traditionally experiences high turnover, which increases the expense associated with training new workers. Many of the programs run by Partnership businesses report that welfare recipients are more likely to stay in an entry-level job than other employees.

Some welfare watchers are wondering if the strong economy and the selection criteria used by businesses when hiring welfare recipients are the reasons why many work first programs have been so successful. Because of good economic conditions, many recipients who have gone off of welfare may have done so in the absence of welfare reform. And businesses that have the ability to pick and choose among recipients (as Marriott does) may have already hired the best workers. If welfare recipients who have not yet found employment are "harder to serve," companies in the future may not be able or willing to invest what is needed to make them employable. After Marriott's Pathways to Independence program began recruiting clients with many more problems, such as substance use and domestic violence, Janet Tully, the head of the program predicted, "There's no way we're going to go any deeper into the well [caseload]. You're not going to find any company going that far down."[29]

Nonprofit Organizations

Many nonprofit organizations, or "nonprofits," across the country are also providing welfare-to-work services in the wake of welfare reform. However, there are no major national nonprofits providing welfare programs. Nonprofits that provide services to welfare recipients tend mostly to be locally based organizations. In a number of localities across the country, national organizations such as Goodwill and Jewish Vocational Services operate some programs, but their local independent affiliates are the ones making the decisions. Instead, national nonprofits have taken a more prominent role in the welfare reform effort by analyzing policy and/or performing advocacy activities. This section highlights some of the major associations, policy research nonprofits, advocacy groups, and religious organizations that are most relevant to welfare and welfare reform.

Associations

A number of associations, or member groups, have played a role in shaping the welfare reform debate as well as in implementing the new law. For the most part, these nonprofit groups represent the interests of various levels of state and local government. The National Conference of State Legislatures (NCSL), the National Association of Counties (NACo), and the U.S. Conference of Mayors (association group for mayors of large cities), for example, all have provided analysis of welfare-related issues and taken positions on behalf of their members around proposed welfare legislation and regulations. Two of the more prominent groups in this area, though, are the National Governors' Association, representing governors and their staff, and the American Public Human Services Association, the member group for state human services administrators. (For mission statement and contact information, see Table 3-2 on page 122.)

NATIONAL GOVERNORS ASSOCIATION. The National Governors Association (NGA) was founded in the early 1900s to provide a forum for governors to discuss interstate issues and to provide a unified voice from the states to Congress on national policy. In other words, the NGA serves as a lobbying force for governors. The primary way in which the NGA undertakes this activity is by taking formal positions on various policy issues and by serving as a conduit of information between the governors and Congress.[30] The NGA maintains a professional staff based in Washington, D.C. All governors (including those of the five U.S. territories) are automatically members of NGA, and the organization strives to be bipartisan. Each year a new chair and vice-chair are elected, with a stipulation that these positions be filled by members of different parties. These positions are rotated between Democrats and Republicans. In 2000 Democrat Parris Glendening of Maryland was chair, while Republican John Engler of Michigan was vice-chair; in 2001, Engler was chair and Democrat Paul Patton of Kentucky was vice-chair.

Although Republicans held the majority of governorships in the states and territories from the mid-1990s through 2002 (in January 2002 there were twenty-eight Republicans, twenty-five Democrats, and two independents), Republicans did not necessarily control the agenda of the NGA. In order to maintain the association's bipartisan stance, the NGA requires that two-thirds of governors support positions before they are adopted by the group as a whole. These national positions also expire after two years.[31] During the mid-1990s, the two-thirds majority provision curbed the influence the NGA as a whole was able to have on Congress during the course of the welfare reform debates.

In 1994, for example, many Republican governors supported House Republicans' desire to cut welfare spending and other "Contract with America" provisions if states were given increased flexibility in designing and running their welfare programs. However, Republicans, while in power in a majority of state capitals, were still shy of the two-thirds needed for NGA endorsement of Republican welfare proposals put forward at that time. The NGA's role in the early debates, then, was minimal. By 1996, though, political winds had shifted: both Congress and the president were under pressure to pass some form of welfare legislation. At the same time, the NGA was able to reach consensus on what it wanted out of welfare reform and put forth its own plan. Under the NGA's proposal, more conservative policies, such as family caps, were made optional. With welfare caseloads declining, liberal opposition to block grant funding waned. By putting forth what was viewed as a bipartisan alternative to Republican and Democratic proposals, the NGA was able to help shape the final legislation.[32]

Since passage of PRWORA, the NGA, through its professional staff, has been active in providing technical assistance to states as they implement the law. An arm of the NGA, the "Center for Best Practices," is charged with helping "[g]overnors and their key policy staff develop and implement innovative solutions to governance and policy challenges facing them in their states."[33] Welfare reform is one of the topic areas on which the Center concentrates. Since enactment of the law, Center staff have organized conferences for state officials and produced numerous reports on successful strategies states are using or could use in their welfare programs. These reports have covered topics such as serving welfare recipients with learning disabilities, helping children and youth with TANF dollars, and working with employers in the context of welfare reform.

In anticipation of the reauthorization of TANF in 2002, governors, through NGA, have adopted several policy positions. Areas of agreement reflected in the NGA policy document are around funding for the program—maintaining current levels of funding and the block grant structure, increasing flexibility of states, and simplifying or creating ways to align the rules of related programs (for example, Medicaid and food stamps) with TANF rules.[34] The NGA does not formally support more controversial issues, such as including provisions to promote family formation, because of the lack of a two-thirds consensus.

AMERICAN PUBLIC HUMAN SERVICES ASSOCIATION. The American Public Human Services Association (APHSA) is similar to NGA in a number of ways. APHSA is a professional organization for state government officials—those working in each state's human services agency. Affiliate membership is open to others in the human services field, such as nonprofit social service agencies. Also like NGA, APHSA lobbies the federal government on behalf of its members, and "educates members of Congress, the media, and the broader public on what is happening in the states around welfare, child welfare, health care reform, and other issues involving families and the elderly."[35] Founded in 1930, the organization was known as the American Public Welfare Association (APWA) until 1998, with the name change recognizing that the association addresses human service policy issues broader than what is conveyed by the phrase "public welfare."[36]

In the original debate over welfare reform, APHSA did not have as much involvement or influence as did the NGA. Because directors of state human service agencies are appointed by governors, APHSA's positions on major legislation tend to be in line with those of the NGA. However, during the welfare reform debates in the mid-1990s, the president of the APHSA, Gerry Miller, then-director of Michigan's Family Independence Agency, was closely involved in welfare reform with Michigan governor John Engler.

APHSA also provides technical assistance to members through conferences, professional development training, and policy documents. The latter include information sharing reports on state and local practices in TANF and other human services programs. This is an important function, since through these outlets APHSA may be able to influence the direction of welfare policy implementation and the day-to-day operations of welfare programs.

With reauthorization of TANF slated for 2002, APHSA has adopted positions similar to NGA on a number of issues, including maintaining the current level of block grant funding. However, APHSA has also been advocating several specific policies. One is the addition of funding bonuses for states that reduce the number of teen out-of-wedlock births. This is similar to a current TANF provision that awards states funds for reductions in all out-of-wedlock births. Another policy position is the requirement that all TANF recipients be engaged in work or work preparation activities. The latter could include counseling, adult literacy classes, and other types of activities to remove barriers to employment.[37]

Policy Research Organizations

In very broad terms, policy research organizations share a common trait with associations in conducting research and analysis on issues pertinent to policy makers within government. Organizations that conduct policy research generally are composed of individuals with backgrounds in economics, political science, or sociology who use nonpartisan research methodologies to prevent the introduction of any bias. However, as political scientists Andrew Rich and Kent Weaver note, some policy research organizations tend also to advocate policy. This, along with the growth in the number of policy research organizations, may have diluted the impact of social science research in shaping welfare policy. Because so many organizations that label their activities as "policy research" have, in fact, other agendas, policy research organizations in general have faced more and more skepticism over their objectivity.[38]

This section examines three of the more prominent policy research organizations—the Manpower Demonstration Research Corporation, the Urban Institute, and the Heritage Foundation—in the context of their background, the types of "research" they produce, and their influence on welfare policy. (For mission statement and contact information, see Table 3-2 on page 122.)

MANPOWER DEMONSTRATION RESEARCH CORPORATION. Of the three nonprofit research organizations discussed here, the Manpower Demonstration Research Corporation (MDRC) is the only one created in part by the federal government. Founded in 1974 by several federal agencies and the Ford Foundation, MDRC was to establish "a new kind of organization that would build a body of unassailable evidence about whether social programs do or do not work."[39] Although the term "social policy" encompasses a broad range of issues, a primary focus of MDRC's work relates to welfare, with much of their research focusing on programs designed to move recipients off the welfare rolls and into jobs.

As its name implies, MDRC largely engages in "demonstration" research projects. These projects are evaluations of the effectiveness of new initiatives, often done on a pilot (or demonstration) basis using a social science technique called "random assignment." MDRC is considered one of the pioneers in using this research technique to evaluate welfare programs. In random assignment evaluations, participants (in this case welfare recipients) are randomly assigned to a "treatment" or "control" group. In welfare experiments, treatment group members are subject to the new policy being tested, while the control group faces the existing or old policy. MDRC or other researchers using this technique then collect a variety of data from administrative sources, such as state welfare and employment records, to determine if those in the treatment group exhibit the desired behavior more often than those in the control group.

For example, a treatment group faced with stricter sanctions for nonwork might be expected to find work earlier than a control group that did not face the same sanctions. If more people in the treatment group than in the control group find employment, then sanctions would be evaluated as "successful." If the people in the treatment group were not employed at higher rates, however, the sanctions policy would be evaluated as having "no effect" or as "unsuccessful."

Random assignment is generally considered superior to other evaluation techniques, because it accounts for possible differences between people receiving and not receiving the "treatment." Take the example of welfare recipients in an evening training program for restaurant work (the "treatment group") as compared to recipients who do not receive the training (the "control group"). If recipients were allowed to decide whether to participate in the treatment group, those who chose to participate might also be the ones who were most motivated to go to work or the ones who were most successful in finding evening child care. If recipients in the treatment group have a higher employment rate than those in the control group, it would be unclear whether their success was because of their training, motivation, or ability to arrange child care. Thus, any evaluation results showing differences in employment between the two groups would be difficult to interpret.

Random assignment (if conducted correctly) greatly alleviates this problem. In the example above, if recipients were assigned randomly to either the restaurant training group or the control group, there should be some motivated recipients in each group. Therefore, any difference between the two groups should not be because of the possibility that one group was more motivated than the other. Similarly, if recipients are assigned randomly to each group, there should be some who have access to child care and some who do not. Again, any differences between the two groups would not be influenced by access to child care. Random assignment thus increases the probability that any differences between the two groups would be because of the training, and the training alone.

During the 1980s and early 1990s, MDRC was the primary evaluator of the major welfare waiver demonstration programs, including the national evaluation of the 1986 JOBS program, California's welfare-to-work program (Greater Avenues to Independence or GAIN), and Florida's experiment with time limits. MDRC studies of these waiver programs helped shape the welfare reform debate in a couple of ways. First, in large part because of their rigorous methods, MDRC studies have been free from being labeled as conservative or liberal, giving MDRC credibility with both political parties.[40] MDRC President Judith M. Gueron was invited multiple times to testify before Congress at welfare hearings. The success of the MDRC-evaluated welfare waiver program in Riverside, California, and MDRC evaluations from the 1980s showing that participation in work-oriented programs increased employment and decreased welfare use, were used by many policy makers in the 1994–1996 period to promote work first programs over education and training.

On the other hand, more current and larger MDRC evaluation results—for example, evaluations of the JOBS program and of training and education as a way to move welfare recipients into work—were not completed in time to inform the reform debates. This is often a problem with social policy research in general. Careful evaluation and study take time, and often relevant outcomes (for example, whether or not welfare recipients keep their jobs) cannot be determined for several years after a project is implemented. As economist and welfare expert Sheldon Danziger notes, the consequence is that "social science research on welfare tended to be one cycle behind the welfare reform policy debate and to have had little impact on policy outcomes."[41]

With passage of welfare reform, states have gained much freer rein to experiment with their welfare programs along with no federal mandate to conduct evaluation research. Even so, MDRC continues to be involved with states in conducting research. The organization has done evaluations for several states that chose to continue their waiver programs, and it has conducted studies of postwelfare reform policies in other states. It is also undertaking a large-scale study of the effects of welfare reform in four urban areas. Finally, MDRC has produced a series of technical assistance reports for states and localities, which, similar to those reports produced by association groups, may influence welfare policy development at the state and local level.

URBAN INSTITUTE. The Urban Institute is a Washington, D.C., think tank that started operations in 1968. Researchers at this policy research organization study a slightly broader array of social policies than MDRC, including health policy, particularly Medicaid and Medicare, tax policy, and other public finance issues. Welfare, however, continues to be a major issue tackled by the organization. The Urban Institute was the evaluator for Washington state's waiver project and is involved with another research firm in evaluating Indiana's welfare waivers. However, it has not generally engaged in running large-scale demonstration projects like MDRC.

The Urban Institute is nonpartisan, "leaving politics to others" as its Web site says, but it is frequently labeled by the media and others as liberal or left-leaning. For example, the *Washington Post,* in 1996 referred to the organization as "the liberal think tank" when citing an institute study on the underrepresentation of minority firms in the government contracting process.[42] The *Wall Street Journal* used a similar label in 2000 when reporting on the institute's research on public housing.[43]

This perception of a liberal bias may have affected the influence the Urban Institute had during the welfare reform debates. The institute produced many reports on welfare-related issues in the period leading up to PRWORA, and a number of its researchers were actively involved in shaping the original welfare plan of the Clinton administration. However, the Urban Institute received the most attention from a highly controversial study released shortly before PRWORA was signed. In July 1996 its researchers reported that, based on their analyses, the proposed House welfare bill

would increase poverty and reduce incomes of families in the lowest income group. With the legislation fully phased in, spending on the current social safety net would be reduced by about $16 billion per year compared to current law. We estimate that 2.6 million more persons would fall below the poverty line as a result, including 1.1 million children.[44]

In 1995 the Urban Institute had conducted similar analyses on a different Senate welfare bill, estimating in that an additional 1.5 million children would be thrown in poverty if that bill became law. The Senate study was commissioned by the U.S. Department of Health and Human Services and personally given to President Clinton by HHS Secretary Donna Shalala.[45] But the institute undertook the 1996 study of the House bill on its own. As researcher Isabel Sawhill noted, "As a country, we should not be adopting such dramatic changes in our social welfare law without first knowing what the likely consequences will be."[46] White House officials chose to ignore the findings, echoing Republican sentiments that the analysis did not take into account the benefits of welfare reform, such as the benefit to children of growing up in a household with working parents.[47]

Since the enactment of welfare reform, however, the Urban Institute has emerged as one of the leading sources of information for what has happened to families in the postreform period. Their study, "Assessing the New Federalism," is one of the largest ongoing research projects in the country focusing on the circumstances of families leaving and staying on welfare, and on how different states and localities have implemented welfare reform.

HERITAGE FOUNDATION. The Heritage Foundation may be the most ideological of the policy research groups and also the most influential in the current political climate. The Heritage Foundation was established in 1973 as a "research and educational" institution, but it makes no secret of its ideological bent. Its mission statement acknowledges that it seeks to "formulate and promote conservative public policies." Unlike other research organizations, it receives more than half of its funding from individuals—a very high proportion.[48] Contributors who give more than $1,000 a year are invited to policy seminars featuring conservative and controversial speakers such as Rush Limbaugh and Kenneth Starr. Furthermore, Heritage has been accused of overstepping the boundary between analyzing policies and lobbying for specific policies. The *Wall Street Journal* reported "unlike most other think tanks, Heritage not only suggests ideas but actively pushes them in Congress. And in some cases, its legislative efforts would benefit the goals of major donors."[49]

Unlike MDRC, the Urban Institute, and other (but not all) research firms study-ing welfare reform, the Heritage Foundation does not engage in large evaluations of programs or surveys of recipients. Instead, it conducts some data analyses, such as its recent analysis of trends in child poverty, but it also produces many issue pa-pers. These papers summarize trends and existing research about a particular topic and then present specific recommendations based on the review.

Robert Rector, a Senior Research Fellow, is the foundation's leading voice on is-sues related to welfare and poverty. Along with others at the Heritage Foundation, he has been closely involved with politicians and their staff on Capitol Hill. R. Kent Weaver, who has written an extensive volume on the passage of PRWORA, notes that during the debates, Rector was an extremely influential figure, "providing a steady stream of critiques of the current welfare system, building coalitions among groups, drafting legislation, and working with individual legislators and commit-tee staffs."[50] Despite these efforts, Rector and the foundation's vision for welfare reform—which would have included mandatory family caps and stricter work re-quirements—were not fully embraced in 1996.

However, the influence of Rector and the foundation on policy makers may per-haps be even stronger as reauthorization draws near in 2002. By March 2001 Rec-tor had testified twice before the U.S. House of Representatives on TANF reautho-rization. His proposals to revise TANF, which include promoting marriage and discouraging divorce, are also in line with the beliefs of many key officials in the administration of George W. Bush.

Policy Advocacy Organizations

The third type of nonprofit organizations considered in this section are those groups that advocate on behalf of low-income families, including welfare recipi-ents. However, this definition does not clearly distinguish these organizations from the research organizations highlighted above. To varying degrees, advocacy groups involved in welfare reform also conduct some of their own research. How-ever, like the Heritage Foundation, these organizations also advocate for very spe-cific policies based on their research or reviews of others' research, indicating again that the line between research and advocacy may often be blurry.

The organizations described in this section, the Center on Budget and Policy Priorities, the Center for Law and Social Policy, and the Children's Defense Fund, are three of the largest and best known advocacy/research groups that work on

Table 3-2 Major Nonprofit Organizations Involved in Providing Welfare Services

Organization	Mission Statement	Importance to Welfare Reform	Contact Information
American Public Human Services Association	"The association's mission is to develop, promote, and implement public human service policies that improve the health and well-being of families, children, and adults."	Membership agency of all state human services agencies, whose oversight includes welfare. Did not have a large role in welfare reform debates but has influenced implementation.	American Public Human Services Association 810 First Street N.E., Suite 500 Washington, DC 20002-4267 Phone: (202) 682-0100 Fax: (202) 289-6555 Web: http://www.aphsa.org
Catholic Charities USA	"Catholic Charities USA's mission is to provide service for people in need, to advocate for justice in social structures, and to call the entire Church and other people of good will to do the same."	Religious membership organization for local Catholic Charities agencies. Was critical of the welfare reform legislation but limited in its influence.	Catholic Charities USA 1731 King Street, Suite 200 Alexandria, VA 22314 Phone: (703) 549-1390 Fax: (703) 549-1656 Web: http://www. catholiccharitiesusa.org
Center for Law and Social Policy (CLASP)	"A national nonprofit organization with expertise in both law and policy affecting the poor. Through education, policy research, and advocacy, CLASP seeks to improve the economic security of low-income families with children and secure access for low-income persons to our civil justice system."	Advocacy/research organization. Had a large role in the welfare debates in critiquing the proposed legislation but did not have a large influence in the final law because of its perceived "liberal" bias. Instructs states on maximizing flexibility given the language of the reform law.	Center for Law and Social Policy 1616 P Street N.W., Suite 150 Washington, DC 20036 Phone: (202) 328-5140 Fax: (202) 328-5195 Web: http://www.clasp.org

Organization	Description	Contact
Center on Budget and Policy Priorities	"The Center on Budget and Policy Priorities is a nonpartisan research organization and policy institute that conducts research and analysis on a range of government policies and programs, with an emphasis on those affecting low- and moderate-income people." Advocacy/research organization. Had a large role in the welfare debates in critiquing the proposed legislation but did not have a large influence in the final law because of its perceived "liberal" bias.	Center on Budget and Policy Priorities 820 First Street S.E., Suite 510 Washington, DC 20002 Phone: (202) 408-1080 Fax: (202) 408-1056 Web: http://www.cbpp.org
Children's Defense Fund	"The mission of the Children's Defense Fund is to Leave No Child Behind and to ensure every child a Healthy Start, a Head Start, a Fair Start, a Safe Start, and a Moral Start in life and successful passage to adulthood with the help of caring families and communities." Preeminent advocacy organization focused on children's issues. Highly critical of welfare reform and of President Clinton for signing it.	Children's Defense Fund 25 E Street N.W. Washington, DC 20001 Phone: (202) 628-8787 Web: http://www.childrensdefense.org
Christian Coalition	"Represent the profamily point of view before local councils, school boards, state legislatures and Congress; speak out in the public arena and in the media; train leaders for effective social and political action; inform profamily voters about timely issues and legislation; protest anti-Christianity bigotry and defend the rights of people of faith." Faith-based organization closely aligned with the Heritage Foundation and other socially conservative groups. Advocates policies to discourage out-of-wedlock pregnancies and encourage family formation.	Christian Coalition of America 499 South Capitol Street S.W., Suite 615 Washington, DC 20003 Phone: (202) 479-6900 Fax: (202) 479-4260 Web: http://www.cc.org/

Table 3-2 *continued*

Organization	Mission Statement	Importance to Welfare Reform	Contact Information
Heritage Foundation	"The Heritage Foundation is a research and educational institute—a think tank—whose mission is to formulate and promote conservative public policies based on the principles of free enterprise, limited government, individual freedom, traditional American values, and a strong national defense."	Conservative research organization with advocacy tendencies. Had much influence in Congress during the welfare debates and in early reauthorization discussions. Concerned with promoting marriage and family stability within the welfare system.	Heritage Foundation 214 Massachusetts Ave N.E. Washington DC 20002-4999 Phone: (202) 546-4400 Fax: (202) 546-8328 Web: http://www.heritage.org
Manpower Demonstration Research Corporation (MDRC)	"MDRC is dedicated to learning what works to improve the well-being of low-income people. Through our research and the active communication of our findings, we seek to enhance the effectiveness of social policies and programs."	Nonpartisan research organization. Research results for its large-scale demonstration projects that tested various types of welfare-to-work and welfare waiver programs helped to validate a "work first" approach to welfare reform.	Manpower Demonstration Research Corporation 16 East 34 Street, 19th Floor New York, NY 10016-4326 Phone: (212) 532-3200 Fax: (212) 684-0832 Web: http://www.mdrc.org

National Governors' Association (NGA)	"The association's ongoing mission is to support the work of the governors by providing a bipartisan forum to help shape and implement national policy and to solve state problems."	Bipartisan membership association for governors. Influential in final stages of welfare reform debates as its nonpartisan proposal helped Congress reach consensus on final welfare bill.	National Governors Association Hall of States 444 North Capitol Street Washington, DC 20001-1512 Phone: (202) 624-5300 Web: http://www.nga.org
Urban Institute	"The Urban Institute is a nonprofit policy research organization established in Washington, D.C., in 1968. The Institute's goals are to sharpen thinking about society's problems and efforts to solve them, improve government decisions and their implementation, and increase citizens' awareness about important public choices."	Nonpartisan research organization, although sometimes labeled as "liberal." Produced controversial analyses during the welfare reform debates predicting that 1.1 million children would be in poverty as the result of reform legislation.	Urban Institute 2100 M Street, N.W. Washington, DC 20037 Phone: (202) 933-7200 Web: http://www.urban.org

issues related to welfare reform. All are located in Washington, D.C.; none accept money from the federal government to fund their activities; and all label themselves as nonpartisan but are considered "liberal" in their policy orientation. In large part because of this, their role in the welfare reform debates was limited to critiquing the various bills and proposals that came out of Congress and the White House. (For mission statement and contact information, see Table 3-2 on page 122.)

CENTER ON BUDGET AND POLICY PRIORITIES. After serving in the Carter administration as director of the food stamp program, Robert Greenstein founded the Center on Budget and Policy Priorities (CBPP), and in 2001 he remained as its executive director. The Center on Budget and Policy Priorities (CBPP) describes itself as:

> one of the leading organizations in the country working on fiscal policy issues and issues affecting low- and moderate-income families and individuals . . . [specializing] in research and analysis oriented toward policy decisions that policymakers face at both federal and state levels.[51]

Although the CBPP works on a variety of policy issues, including taxes, housing, health, and overall federal budget priorities, welfare is a major focus of its activities. Some of its analysis resembles that produced by other research organizations. CBPP conducts its own data analysis, but it also synthesizes research of others and draws policy conclusions. While CBPP is often labeled a think tank (although a liberal one), it does engage in advocacy activities. For example, according to the Center for Responsive Politics, a nonprofit that tracks political contributions, in 1998 CBPP spent $40,000 on lobbying.[52]

During the debate over welfare reform in the mid-1990s, Greenstein was a strong critic of proposed welfare changes. He led CBPP's attempts to modify what the organization perceived to be the harsher parts of the proposed law, such as time limits, family caps, and cuts in food stamps to immigrants.[53] News organizations interviewed Greenstein on a regular basis. But with its "liberal" label and viewpoints far removed from those of Republicans who controlled Congress, the only avenue for CBPP to pursue its agenda was through the White House. However, as noted in Chapter 2, President Clinton's strategy on welfare reform was to move away from a traditional liberal stance. With many of the White House's reform ideas being, in fact, conservative in origins, CBPP, as well as the Center for Law and Social Policy and the Children's Defense Fund, had little say in the outcome of the final legislation. Given that the administration of George W. Bush is a conservative Republican one, and with Democrats only holding tenuous control of the Senate, CBPP's ability to influence the reauthorization of TANF in 2002 may again be limited.

CENTER FOR LAW AND SOCIAL POLICY. The Center for Law and Social Policy (CLASP) is frequently considered the partner to the Center on Budget and Policy Priorities.[54] A group of lawyers, including Charles Halpern, who later went on to be the first Dean of the Law School at the City University of New York, founded CLASP as a public interest law organization in 1968. Currently CLASP does not provide direct legal help, but it lends legal and other consultation to programs funded by the Legal Services Corporation, the nonprofit established by Congress in the 1970s to provide civil legal assistance to low-income individuals. However, the bulk of its work today is performing policy analysis and advocacy around welfare issues affecting low-income people.

Like CBPP, CLASP is known for its timely analysis of federal legislation, regulations, and policy issues around welfare and other "family policy" issues, such as child support and employment and training. Its most prominent advocate is Mark Greenberg, an attorney who frequently puts his legal background to use by analyzing the ramifications of various proposed changes in welfare regulations or law—including PRWORA. For example, during the debates, he wrote a discussion piece examining what the end to the entitlement to benefits would mean in practical terms to poor families.[55] However, because of the political climate at the time, CLASP's influence on modifying provisions of the new welfare law were limited in the same ways as CBPP's.

In the years after passage of PRWORA, CLASP has extended its focus to working directly with states. In 1997 the *Wall Street Journal* profiled Greenberg as he traveled to various states to, as the article characterized it, "cut the heart out of the new federal welfare law."[56] By analyzing the language of PRWORA, Greenberg has been able to determine ways in which states can exempt more families from the time limit or work requirements while staying within the letter of the law. As with many other laws, PRWORA has unintentional loopholes, and Greenberg has encouraged states to take advantage of these clauses to keep fewer families from losing benefits.[57]

CHILDREN'S DEFENSE FUND. Of the nonprofit organizations profiled here, the Children's Defense Fund (CDF) comes closest to being a pure advocacy organization.

Although it conducts some of its own research, particularly on child care and early childhood education issues, CDF does not bill itself as a research organization. Marian Wright Edelman formed CDF in 1973, and in 2001 she remained as president. CDF and Edelman are probably two of the best known names in advocating on behalf of children. Long before President George W. Bush pledged during his campaign to "leave no child behind," CDF coined and trademarked the phrase.

As with CBPP and CLASP, during the welfare reform debates CDF was unable to push its agenda—which included, among other policies, maintaining the entitlement to assistance and providing more funds for child care. However, disagreements between the CDF and the Clinton administration over welfare reform became very personal. Both President Clinton and First Lady Hillary Rodham Clinton were close friends of Marian Wright Edelman and her husband, Peter Edelman. Up until September 1996, Peter Edelman served in the Clinton administration as assistant secretary for planning and evaluation in the Department of Health and Human Services. When Clinton signed PRWORA, Edelman resigned in protest, writing that, "I have devoted the last thirty-plus years to doing whatever I could to help in reducing poverty in America. I believe the recently enacted welfare bill goes in the opposite direction."[58]

Hillary Clinton had even closer ties to CDF, serving on its board of directors from 1986 to 1992. When President Clinton indicated he would sign PRWORA, Marian Wright Edelman issued a statement saying the law would

> hurt and impoverish millions of children and abolish the 61-year-old national safety net for children . . . [making] a mockery of [Clinton's] pledge not to hurt children. It will leave a moral blot on his Presidency and on our nation that will never be forgotten.[59]

The passage of PRWORA was said to have caused a large rift in their friendship.[60]

After welfare reform passed, CDF decided to take efforts "to minimize the harms of the new welfare bill, and to shape programs that genuinely help parents work and lift families out of poverty."[61] As they do in many of their advocacy efforts, CDF has called upon its wide network of state and local child advocates (including those in CDF's regional offices in Minnesota, New York, and Ohio). These advocates monitor welfare reform implementation in their states and press state legislatures and welfare agencies to take action to minimize some of what it views as the more harsh provisions of the law.

Religious Organizations

Religious or faith-based organizations involved in welfare reform vary a great deal in terms of size and purpose. PRWORA included a provision, known as "charitable choice," that required states to allow faith-based organizations to compete for grants to administer programs related to TANF. PRWORA also included provisions to protect the religious identity and character of faith-based contractors, including giving these organizations the right to give preference to members of their own congregation in hiring and to explain the religious motivations behind their service to clients.

The effects of charitable choice, however, are unclear. Some religious organizations have provided social services, funded by government grants, for a long time. The Salvation Army, for instance, has been receiving government funds since the 1890s and currently depends on federal money for 18 percent of its budget.[62] Umbrella religious social service groups, such as the Lutheran Services of America and Catholic Charities USA, also use TANF money, as well as other government grants, to provide and expand their services.

The charitable choice provision has not resulted in an explosion of new programs from religious organizations that did not provide services in the past. Individual congregations and churches were expected to be most affected by the new provision, because charitable choice allows these groups to receive TANF funds. However, according to the Center for Public Justice, only eighty-four groups in nine states have received funding under the charitable choice provision, and fewer than fifteen states have made progress towards encouraging religious organizations or issuing regulations for their participation.[63]

This delay on the part of state welfare agencies to fund this provision is often matched by reluctance on the part of religious groups who have not sought government contracts in the past. Pastors and leaders of religious social service organizations in southern California, for instance, expressed reservations about welfare reform in general and the charitable choice provision in particular. James Lawson, pastor of Holman United Methodist Church in Los Angeles, argued, "Welfare reform hurts African Americans. It's one more form of involuntary servitude. Churches shouldn't be in that kind of a system."[64]

Religious organizations, however, have also been active in advocating welfare reform policy. This is especially true of large parent organizations, whose functions include not only lobbying on behalf of their member groups but also bringing their

distinctive theological viewpoints into the public debate. Serving in this role for local Catholic charitable agencies, Catholic Charities USA provide various social
services throughout the country. (For mission statement and contact information,
see Table 3-2 on page 122.) During the welfare reform debates, Catholic Charities
was frequently aligned with organizations such as the CBPP, CLASP, and CDF in its
criticism of Republican welfare proposals. Catholic Charities was most often concerned about the fate of poor children under welfare proposals that sought to end
the federal entitlement to assistance. When PRWORA passed, Catholic Charities
USA came out strongly against the bill, with spokesperson Sharon Daly saying,
"This bill will create a social catastrophe by cutting off critically needed assistance
to millions of our poorest children without assuring their parents jobs to support
them."[65]

Other faith-based organizations were much more supportive of PRWORA and
lobbied for its passage. These groups, which include the Christian Coalition (for
mission statement and contact information, see Table 3-2 on page 122) and the Eagle Forum, do not necessarily align themselves with a particular religion or even
consider themselves to be "religious" entities. Their leadership, however, is composed of conservative Christians. The Christian Coalition was founded by televan-
gelist Pat Robertson, and the Eagle Forum is led by Phyllis Schlafly, an activist
whose support of "profamily" causes has included opposition to the Equal Rights
Amendment, government-funded day care, and abortion. Another common unify-
ing theme is their concern with out-of-wedlock pregnancy and the demise of the
"traditional" two-parent family—a shared concern of the Heritage Foundation.
During the welfare reform debates, Heritage analyst Robert Rector worked closely
with these groups, providing them with information and strategies for their lobbying and helping to increase their visibility and influence with Congress.[66]

What Next for Businesses and Nonprofits in Welfare Reform?

Businesses, whether they are for-profit service providers or employers hiring welfare recipients, were not instrumental in shaping PRWORA. However, they have
played a large role in the postwelfare reform era. For-profit firms, such as Maximus and Curtis, have been instrumental in moving welfare recipients into employment.

How involved businesses continue to be in welfare reform may depend on a couple of factors. First, if the reauthorization of welfare reform provides for greater in-

volvement of faith-based organizations that place an emphasis on services to promote family formation, for-profits may see their contracts for employment-based services shrink. Second, an economic downturn may mean that employers become less willing to hire welfare recipients, making the job of finding employment more difficult for for-profit organizations. While many companies can boast of success in placing welfare recipients into work since PRWORA passed in 1996, it is unclear if the success will remain if the recession that begun in March 2001 continues for an extended period. Welfare recipients hired through these programs could be particularly vulnerable to lay-offs if companies follow the "last hired, first fired" philosophy.

Evidence from the employer surveys highlighted earlier indicates that this scenario may come to pass. Economist Harry Holzer found that employers' willingness during this period to hire welfare recipients and to provide "workplace supports" (for example, assistance with transportation or child care) was greatly affected by the tight labor market.[67] In other words, low unemployment rates and difficulties filling vacant jobs made welfare recipients more attractive to employers. If the nation's economy changes adversely, this willingness to hire welfare recipients may no longer be the case.

Nonprofit organizations exerted varying degrees of influence during the original debate over welfare reform, with NGA, MDRC, and the Heritage Foundation having perhaps the most sway. As PRWORA nears reauthorization in 2002, the Heritage Foundation seems to be emerging as the think tank to which the Bush administration and Republicans in Congress look for advice. Conservative Christian groups seem to have a great deal of sway within the administration as well. The role the NGA will play in the future reauthorization debate is unclear. How much influence more "liberal" groups will have with Congress (especially the Democrat-controlled Senate) in the reauthorization discussions is also unclear.

Welfare recipients themselves, or organizations attempting to speak directly on their behalf, were markedly absent from the welfare reform debates in the 1990s. Only during the late 1960s did a national organization for welfare recipients exist. This group, the National Welfare Rights Organization (NWRO), died out as did many protest groups of that time. Currently, grassroots organizations of current and former welfare recipients exist at local levels and with varying degrees of membership, but there is no large national coordinating body. Groups such as the National Organization for Women (NOW) have advocated their positions on welfare reform: in 1995 NOW president Patricia Ireland was arrested while protesting the welfare bills being debated in Congress.[68] However, NOW's agenda is much broader than issues affecting welfare recipients or low-income women, and it remains to be seen how much energy and political capital it can devote to welfare reform in the future. The Children's Defense Fund organized a rally, called "Stand for Children," in June 1996 to call attention to the needs of children. However, welfare reform and its impact on children was only one of many themes raised during that rally.

In the postwelfare reform era, there has been some activity on the welfare rights front. In early 2001, a group of about fifty welfare rights advocates disrupted the proceedings at an academic conference in Washington, D.C., on the next stages of welfare reform.[69] In addition, welfare activists are part of the "Women's Committee of 100," a group composed primarily of university professors, who have developed a platform around the issue of welfare reform. Specifically, they call for:

> ending women's poverty by rewarding women's work on the job and at home. We recommend replacing TANF with a set of policies that address the economic plight faced by those doing the work of caregiving—most of whom are women. Such a caregiving allowance would allow women (or other caregivers) to choose among caring for dependents themselves, purchasing high quality services, or some combination of both.[70]

Francis Fox Piven, a member of the committee and a well-known sociologist and activist on behalf of the poor, reports that incidences of grassroots activity are springing up throughout the United States. These grassroots activities range from local protests against specific policies to lobbying efforts for policies that, for example, allow welfare recipients to attend college.[71] If welfare activists continue to engage in these activities, welfare recipients and groups representing them may at least have a voice in reauthorization decisions, in contrast to their absence from the initial debates over PWRORA.

Notes

1. Adam Cohen, "When Wall Street Runs Welfare," *Time*, March 23, 1998, 64–65.

2. Nina Bernstein, "Giant Companies Entering Race to Run State Welfare Programs," *New York Times*, September 15, 1996, 1.

3. Summary of services based on Peter Cove, "Prepared Testimony," testimony before the U.S. House of Representatives, Committee on Small Business, Subcommittee on Empowerment, "Welfare to Work: What Is Working, What Is Next?" May 25, 1999.

4. Bill Berkowitz, *Prospecting Among the Poor: Welfare Privatization,* (Oakland, Calif.: Applied Research Center, 2001), 14.

5. Curtis and Associates, Overview of "Steps to Self-Sufficiency." Accessed at http://selfsufficiency.com/p_employ.htm.

6. Lockheed Martin, "About IMS." Accessed at http://www.lmims.com/about/index.html.

7. Lorraine Woellert, "Maxiums Inc.: Welfare Privatizer," *Businessweek Online,* May 31, 1999. Accessed at http://www.businessweek.com.

8. Profile on Indiana programs from Curtis and Associates' Web site. Accessed at http://selfsufficiency.com.

9. U.S. Department of Health and Human Services, Administration for Children and Families, "High Performance Bonus Awards, FY 1999 State Performance and Percentage Change (Increase or Decrease) over FY 1998, by Work-Related Measures." Accessed at http://www.acf.dhhs.gov/programs/opre/hpb/table5.htm.

10. Bill Berkowitz, *Prospecting Among the Poor: Welfare Privatization* (Oakland, Calif.: Applied Research Center, 2001), 14.

11. John Rubino, "Privatization's Profit Potential," *Virginia Business Magazine,* August 1997. Accessed at www.virginiabusiness.com.

12. Christopher Drew, "Audit Faults Firm Seeking City Contracts," *New York Times,* July 29, 2000, B1.

13. Steve Schultze, "Maximus to Pay Back $500,000: Firm Also Plans Extra Spending for Poor After Audit," *Milwaukee Journal Sentinel,* October 14, 2000, 1B.

14. Cohen, "When Wall Street Runs Welfare," 64–65.

15. William D. Hartung and Jennifer Washburn, "Lockheed Martin: From Warfare to Welfare," *The Nation,* March 2, 1998, 11–12.

16. Esther B. Fein, "For Job-Finding Concern, a Troubled Past," *New York Times,* March 24, 1994, A1.

17. Pete Cove and Lee Bowes, "How to Make Sure the New Welfare-to-Work Really Works," (New York: Manhattan Institute, 1996). Accessed at http://www.manhattan-institute.org/html/cb_6.htm.

18. Mark Dunlea, "The Poverty Profiteers Privatize Welfare," *Covert Action Quarterly* Winter 1996–97. Accessed at http://www-pluto.informatik.uni-oldenburg.de/~also/welar008.htm.

19. Steven Schultze, "Agency Getting Out of W-2: Employment Solutions Was Dogged by Criticism," *Milwaukee Journal Sentinel,* June 8, 2001, 1A.

20. Kristin S. Seefeldt, Jodi Sandfort, and Sandra K. Danziger, "Moving Toward a Vision of Family Independence: Local Managers' Views of Michigan's Welfare Reforms," (Ann Arbor: University of Michigan, 1998), 34.

21. Harry Holzer, "Will Employers Hire Welfare Recipients? Recent Survey Evidence from Michigan," (Madison, Wisc.: Institute for Research on Poverty, 1998), 35–36.

22. See, for example, Gary Burtless, "Welfare Recipients Job Skills and Employment Prospects," *The Future of Children* 7 (Spring 1997): 41–51; LaDonna Pavetti, "How Much More Can They Work? Setting Realistic Expectations for Welfare Mothers," (Washington, D.C.: Urban Institute, 1997).

23. Harry Holzer, "Will Employers Hire Welfare Recipients? Recent Survey Evidence from Michigan," (Madison, Wis.: Institute for Research on Poverty, 1998), 35–36.

24. For more examples, see Amy Brown, Maria L. Buck, and Erik Skinner, "Business Partnerships: How to Involve Employers in Welfare Reform," (New York: Manpower Demonstration Research Corporation, 1998).

25. Welfare-to-Work Partnership, "City Link: Partnerships Across the Nation." Accessed at http://www.welfaretowork.org/wtwpapps/wtwphome.nsf/home?openframeset.

26. Information in this paragraph comes from the following sources: United Parcel Services, "Helping People to Succeed." Accessed at http://www.community.ups.com/community/resources/helping/welfare_to_work.html; Richard Wolf, " 'Welfare-to-Work' Provides Benefits Beyond Reducing Rolls; Companies Learning That It Pays to Give Other Workers Same Help," *USA Today,* August 27, 1999, 6A.

27. Information about Marriott's Pathways program comes from the following sources: Amy Brown, Maria L. Buck, and Erik Skinner, "Business Partnerships: How to Involve Employers in Welfare Reform," (New York: Manpower Demonstration Research Corporation, 1998); Michael Grunwald, "Welfare-to-Work: The Challenge Grows Harder," *Boston Globe,* April 20, 1998, A1; Dana Milbank, "Under the Underclass," *The New Republic,* August 4, 1997.

28. Welfare-to-Work Partnership, "Member Survey, Executives Speak Out Partnership and Promise: Business Leaders Support Welfare to Work," 1998. Accessed at http://www.welfaretowork.org.

29. Dana Milbank, "Under the Underclass," *The New Republic,* August 4, 1997, 20–24.

30. Weaver, *Ending Welfare as We Know It,* 208.

31. Ibid, 209.

32. This paragraph draws heavily from Cammisa, *From Rhetoric to Reform,* 74, 78; and Weaver, *Ending Welfare as We Know It,* 266–267, 321–322.

33. NGA Center for Best Practices, "Mission Statement." Accessed at http://www.nga.org/center/1,1188,00.html.

34. National Governors' Association, Human Resources Policy Committee, "Welfare Reform Policy," revised 2001. Accessed at http://www.nga.org/nga/legislativeUpdate/1,1169,C_POLICY_POSITION,00.html.

35. APHSA, "About APHSA." Accessed at http://www.aphsa.org/about/about.asp.

36. APHSA, "What's in a Name?" Accessed at http://www.aphsa.org/name.htm.

37. American Public Human Services Association, "Crossroads: New Directions in Social Policy" (Washington, D.C.: APHSA, 2001), 25–37.

38. Weaver, *Ending Welfare as We Know It*, 136, 143.

39. Manpower Demonstration Research Corporation, "Why was MDRC Created?" Accessed at http://www.mdrc.org/WhatIsMDRC/WhatIsMDRC1.htm.

40. Weaver, *Ending Welfare as We Know It*, 144; Michael Wiseman, "Welfare Reform in the United States: Historical Background," in *Informing the Welfare Debate: Perspectives on the Transformation of Social Policy*, Institute for Research on Poverty Special Report no. 70, (Madison, Wisc.: Institute for Research on Poverty, 1997), 97.

41. Sheldon Danziger, "Welfare Policy from Nixon to Clinton: What Role for Social Science?" (Paper prepared for the conference "The Social Sciences and Policy Making," Institute for Research on Poverty, Madison, Wis., March 13–14, 1998), 25.

42. Michael A. Fletcher, "Study Says Minority Firms Underrepresented in U.S. Contracts," *Washington Post*, October 31, 1996, A3.

43. Jonathan Eig, "Hanging on: A Housing Project Falls, but the Poor Resist Orders to Move Out," *Wall Street Journal*, December 19, 2000, A1.

44. Sheila Zedlewski, Sandra Clark, Eric Meier, and Keith Watson, "Potential Effects of Congressional Welfare Reform Legislation on Family Incomes," (Washington, D.C.: Urban Institute, 1996), 1.

45. Peter Edelman, "The Worst Thing Bill Clinton Has Done," *Atlantic Monthly*, March 1997, 43–46.

46. Elizabeth Shogren, "Study Warns of Welfare Reform Impact," *Los Angeles Times*, July 26, 1996, 16.

47. Ibid.

48. Heritage Foundation, "2000 Annual Report." Accessed at www.heritage.org.

49. Christopher Georges, "Conservative Heritage Foundation Finds Recipe for Influence: Ideas Plus Marketing Equal Clout," *Wall Street Journal*, August 10, 1995, A10.

50. Weaver, *Ending Welfare as We Know It*, 213.

51. Center on Budget and Policy Priorities, "What Is the Center on Budget and Policy Priorities." Accessed at http://www.cbpp.org/info.html.

52. Center for Responsive Politics. Accessed at http://www.opensecrets.org/lobbyists/98profiles/4250.htm.

53. Weaver, *Ending Welfare As We Know It*, 203–204.

54. Weaver, *Ending Welfare As We Know It*, 203.

55. Mark Greenberg, "No Duty, No Floor: The Real Meaning of 'Ending Entitlements,' " (Washington, D.C.: Center for Law and Social Policy, 1996).

56. Dana Milbank, "Lawyer Helps States See the Loopholes in Welfare Law," *Wall Street Journal*, March 14, 1997, A18.

57. Ibid.

58. Barbara Vobejda and Judith Havemann, "2 HHS Officials Quit Over Welfare Changes; Protest by Clinton Friend, Influential Academic Shows Split in Administration," September 12, 1996, A1.

59. Jerry Gray, "The Welfare Bill: The Liberals; Amid Praise, a Peppering of Criticism and Dismay," *New York Times*, August 1, 1996, A23.

60. Neil Lewis, "A Friendship in Tatters Over Policy," *New York Times*, September 13, 1996, A23.

61. Nancy Ebb and Deborah Weinstein, "Implementing the New Welfare Law," (Washington, D.C.: Children's Defense Fund, 1996), 1.

62. Mark Silk, "Old Alliance, New Ground Rules," *Washington Post*, February 18, 2001, B3.

63. Sarah Glazer, "Faith Based Initiatives: Current Situation," *CQ Researcher*, May 4, 2001.

64. John Orr with Carolyn Mounts and Peter Spoto, "Religion and Welfare Reform in Southern California: Is Charitable Choice Succeeding?" Center for Religion and Civic Culture in Southern California, University of Southern California, April 2001, 7–8.

65. Catholic Charities USA, "Catholic Charities USA Calls Welfare Bill Reckless and Wrong." Press release dated August 1, 1996.

66. This paragraph draws heavily on Weaver, *Ending Welfare as We Know It,* 211–216.

67. Harry Holzer, "Employer Demand for Welfare Recipients and the Business Cycle: Evidence from Recent Employer Surveys," (Madison, Wis.: Institute for Research on Poverty, 1998).

68. "The First 100 Days; NOW Chief Handcuffed, Arrested in Capitol Protest; Demonstrations Are Staged in the House Gallery and Newt Gingrich's Office," *Atlanta Journal and Constitution,* March 24, 1995, 10A.

69. Karen MacPhearson, "Experts Laud Welfare Reform, but Say More Is Needed," *Pittsburgh Post-Gazette,* February 2, 2001, A7.

70. Women's Committee of 100, "An Immodest Proposal: Rewarding Women's Work to End Poverty," 2000. Accessed at http://www.welfare2002.org.

71. Francis Fox Piven, "Welfare Movement Rises," *The Nation,* May 8, 2000, 4–5.

4 International Implications

The capability of any country to provide income assistance for its poor presupposes particular economic structures and a level of economic development. The United Nations notes that:

> In developing country contexts, the great majority of the population stands outside formal systems of social protection, being engaged in rural or urban self-employment. Extending social protection meaningfully to these groups is a huge challenge. It also raises real questions concerning what we mean by social protection, as it can be difficult to separate promotional activities that seek to strengthen people's capacity to sustain their own independent livelihoods from forms of protection that guarantee a collective public response for those deprived or seriously at risk.[1]

When poverty is a way of life for most citizens in a country, its government often does not have the resources to provide economic assistance in the form of "welfare" payments. Nor do work requirements or the substitution of work for welfare make much sense in a country without the economic development to sustain formal paid employment. Thus, how U.S. welfare policy is viewed internationally requires comparisons with countries that resemble it in terms of economic performance and government: in particular, the developed economies of western Europe.

The U.S. welfare system is distinctive and not as broad-based as the welfare systems of industrialized European countries. Even if other U.S. social programs, such as Social Security, disability insurance, and unemployment insurance, are considered with Temporary Assistance for Needy Families (TANF), food stamps, and Medicaid, the United States has more eligibility requirements for its welfare recipients than western European nations do for theirs. The United States provides a categorical, rather than a universal, safety net.[2] By contrast, most European nations offer a range of assistance to their citizens that is not contingent on financial resources and is designed to promote social well-being and help alleviate, or even prevent, poverty.

The degree to which low-income single mothers are treated differently for purposes of benefit provision is another area in which U.S. welfare policies are quite distinct when compared to those in most of Europe. With the possible exception of Great Britain, most western European countries provide financial support to single mothers to: (1) stay at home to raise children but not necessarily to work (Ireland); (2) enter the workforce (Sweden); or (3) either stay at home or enter the workforce (France and Germany—to a certain degree).[3] By contrast, single mothers who receive TANF in the United States are expected to work and tend to be concentrated in low-wage jobs with few benefits.

As these comparisons suggest, the United States and other Western industrialized nations differ not only in the level and range of benefits they provide, but also in the social purposes that benefits are meant to serve. The U.S safety net system is so different from those in Europe and elsewhere that even reforms with similar intentions—cutting costs or increasing responsibility—often take on very different forms. In recent years, however, a few countries, namely Great Britain and the Netherlands, have looked to the U.S. welfare system for guidance in reforming their systems. Changes in the global economy, the increased integration of the economies of these European nations into the European Union (EU), and increased immigration to Europe could, some hypothesize, lead other European nations to adopt U.S.-type welfare policies.

The first step in understanding why U.S. welfare reform policies are not currently widely copied abroad (and may never be) is to examine how the European and American welfare systems developed. This chapter opens with a description of the factors that have led U.S. welfare policy to diverge so widely from those in industrialized European countries. It then explores the ways in which welfare reform in the United States has influenced other countries in Europe and concludes with a discussion of the economic forces that might continue—or halt—this trend.

The Development of Social Welfare Systems

The modern welfare state grew out of industrialization and the movement of large segments of the population from farming and into wage-based employment. The new problems arising from urban living and the hazards of factory work (ranging from unemployment to industrial accidents) created a need for large-scale solutions. The need to deal with the problems of industrialization, however, cannot by itself explain U.S./European differences. Although industrialization occurred simultaneously in both places, the United States adopted social welfare policies much later than Europe.[4] Most scholars, therefore, have looked to political factors to explain the solutions that eventually developed.

One important factor in the development of welfare in industrialized nations is the strength of working-class pressure on the government and mobilization of labor unions. Scholars argue that the greater the solidarity and power of labor unions, the more comprehensive the resulting social welfare systems have become. Differences between United States and European social welfare systems, then, are partly the result of relatively weak U.S. labor unions in relation to powerful business interests. In contrast to those in the United States, unions in much of Europe are much stronger. For example, in Germany labor unions after World War II were deliberately reconstructed to give workers a say in managing the company that employs them.[5]

Yet another factor is the relative development of governmental bureaucracies and democratic government. Modern European welfare systems arose in the late 1800s and early 1900s as those nations moved away from monarchies and to democratic systems of governance. The new political parties needed to appeal to the working class, who were beginning to win the right to vote, and who exercised that power by organizing under the banners of labor unions and labor socialism. But access to one obvious reward for political support—jobs for votes—was foreclosed:

> In such instances, when political parties emerged and sought popular support, they could not simply offer the spoils of office as an inducement to voters and party activists, for access to jobs in civil administration was controlled by established bureaucratic elites.[6]

Although these bureaucracies blocked access to patronage jobs, they had the capacity to administer social welfare programs. So European political parties based their appeals to constituents on programs and services they could provide through government. In the late 1800s, for instance, Germany's Chancellor Otto von Bismarck faced challenges to his regime from a growing socialist movement. In response, his government created various social welfare programs, including public health insurance, old age pensions, and disability insurance. All of these programs were administered by an existing civil service.[7]

The United States, on the other hand, which began as a democracy in the late 1700s, did not develop a large government bureaucracy until more than a century later. U.S. political parties did not appeal to voters on ideas or policies but rather on promises of government jobs or other benefits available through highly organized political "machines."[8] The local nature of these "machines" also helped to cement an American tradition of local government, one that is wary of national programs and requirements, and jealous of local autonomy. As the discussion of devolution in Chapter 2 illustrates, this is still a feature of U.S. welfare reform. Finally, even the structure of the U.S. federal government, characterized by the "separation of powers" (executive, legislative, and judicial branches) makes development of national welfare policies more difficult.[9] Political opponents of a particular social welfare policy have many venues in which to block its operation. European government structures, by contrast, tend to be more centralized. When political parties in these countries that favor social welfare policies hold power, it is difficult for opposing parties to mount an effective challenge.

Models of Welfare States

Although the U.S. welfare system differs from the general European model, not all European systems are alike. In fact, there are numerous differences between European nations. Gosta Esping-Anderson, a Swedish political scientist, divides welfare systems into three types—social democratic, conservative-corporatist, and liberal.[10] Social democratic nations are typified by the Nordic states (Sweden, Finland, Norway, and Denmark), which provide the most comprehensive social welfare benefits as a matter of right to all citizens. The "conservative-corporatist" countries, by contrast, tie benefits to past employment and are concerned with preserving the status of employees who have contributed to a social insurance fund.[11] Many western European countries, including France, Germany, and the Netherlands, fit into this model. Finally, the United States, as well as Great Britain and Canada, are "liberal" nations. They provide only minimal benefits, based on recipients' need, as a last resort for those unable to support themselves through work.

Sweden: Social Democratic Welfare System

Of all the social democratic countries, Sweden has perhaps the most comprehensive welfare system, covering all citizens "from cradle to grave."[12] Governmental support is available in forms ranging from free health care (including prenatal visits and health care clinics at schools), universal day care, child allowances (cash benefits to help with the cost of raising children), and guaranteed benefits for the sick, the disabled, and the elderly. The origins of these policies can be traced back to the nation's temperance movement, which, along with other social change organizations, advocated for many of the benefits now in place in Sweden.[13] In addition, Sweden's ruling Social Democratic Party, which has held power in Sweden for nearly eight decades, has been unhindered in its pursuit of these universalistic policies.[14]

Sweden also has pursued "active labor market policies" (ALMP), instituted over the 1940s and 1950s. These policies include job training and retraining, subsidies to employers who hire the long-term unemployed, and the use of temporary, publicly funded jobs. The overall goal of these policies is to increase the labor supply in the country, promote full employment, and make taxpayers out of all citizens, thereby funding the comprehensive social safety net.[15]

Unlike in the United States, unmarried mothers in Sweden do not have a work program that especially targets them. Instead, the Swedish system attempts to equalize the status of all mothers and to promote work. Both married and single mothers are eligible for parental leave and cash assistance through the country's social insurance program, as long as they have been working or have been available for work.[16] Being "available for work" is defined as registering with the Swedish Employment Office and not declining job offers. Unwed mothers are not specifically singled out for any benefits or restrictions. However, they do receive priority in securing day care and receive financial support taken from the income of the absent parent (in effect, child support).[17] Single-parent families are viewed as another type of family. Policies in "social democratic" countries such as Sweden are designed to equalize the living conditions of all families, regardless of their structure.[18]

Germany: Conservative-Corporatist Welfare System

In contrast, conservative-corporatist welfare states

> typically are shaped by the church and are strongly committed to the preservation of the traditional family. Tax policies and family benefits encourage marriage and motherhood. . . . [W]omen and social services are the domain of the family. The state will interfere only when the family's capacity to serve its members is exhausted.[19]

As such, welfare policies in conservative-corporatist states, such as Germany, are designed to maintain the income of unemployed workers, not necessarily citizens as a whole. This is primarily done through a social insurance system that relies on employee/employer contributions—not unlike the U.S. Social Security system. However, in Germany, government policies have upheld a male breadwinner/female homemaker model.[20] To promote this traditional division of parental responsibilities, employed German mothers are allowed up to three years of partially paid maternity leave. The German tax system is also designed in such a way as to make it advantageous for the married couples to have unequal earnings.[21]

Germany does not explicitly exclude single mothers from these welfare policies. However, because the welfare system is primarily based on ties to the labor market through a male breadwinner, and the tax system favors two-parent families, the place of single mothers in society is somewhat tenuous.[22] German mothers, single or married, who want to work technically place their children in publicly funded child care, but most of this care is part-time and available for children over age three. Child-care benefits for mothers who want to work full time are limited, although German mothers have started to work full time in greater numbers in the 1990s.[23] Cash assistance is available to single mothers, although they are seen as "family dependents": parents and grandparents are the first source of support, with the state stepping in only when familial resources are not sufficient.[24] But this provision is not premised on a notion that single motherhood must be actively discouraged (as is the case with the U.S. Personal Responsibility and Work Opportunity Reconciliation Act (PRWORA). Rather, German single mothers are viewed as mothers of the future generation, and, as one writer notes, "The dominant popular discourse of single motherhood in Germany is that single mothers are poor, overworked, and to be pitied."[25]

The contrast between these views of the welfare state and the place of single mothers within it are striking when compared to those of the United States. The welfare reform debate in the United States was greatly influenced by conservative politicians and scholars who viewed the welfare system as an underlying cause of social problems ranging from out-of-wedlock childbearing to poor school performance to crime. Public opinion regarding the U.S. welfare system often mirrors these views. In a 1996 poll conducted by the Public Agenda Foundation, 65 percent of Americans surveyed agreed with the statement that the most troubling aspect of welfare is that it "encourages people to adopt the wrong lifestyles and values."[26] In addition, Americans are more likely to think of "welfare" as the cash assistance program for (primarily) single-parent families, rather than including in other so-cial support programs, such as Social Security and Medicare,[27] that not only bene-fit a very wide share of the population but also do not impose "income tests."

Great Britain: Liberal Welfare System

Given the differences in welfare systems and values about those systems, the extent to which nations with conservative-corporatist or social democratic welfare sys-tems will adopt U.S. welfare policies is probably rather limited. However, in coun-tries with somewhat similar "liberal" welfare systems and political philosophies about the welfare state, particularly Great Britain, the influence of U.S. policies can already be seen.

Although it has many of the features of other European nations (national health care, child allowances), Britain's welfare system more closely resembles that of the United States. Britain provides relatively low amounts of benefits to unemployed individuals, makes receipt of these benefits contingent on financial eligibility re-quirements, and, in general, focuses on alleviating the effects of poverty rather than on preventing it.[28] The broad similarities in government policy between the United States and Britain, coupled with increased British unemployment in the 1990s and a close relationship between British Labor Party officials and U.S. Presi-dent Bill Clinton when he was in office, all contributed to Britain in the late 1990s adapting some elements of the U.S. welfare reform.

During the course of the 1980s and 1990s, the British employment picture be-came bleak. Between 1979 and 1997, unemployment among families with two working-aged parents rose from 9 to 18 percent, while the unemployment rate for single mothers reached about 60 percent.[29] The number of single mothers in the nation also doubled between 1976 and 1996.

How to handle this increased unemployment became a cornerstone of the British Labor Party's bid to regain the majority in Parliament after its defeat in 1992. Traditionally, the Labor Party had advocated for universal and unconditional government benefits for all the unemployed. However, within the party there was a growing sense that change was needed in order to regain the political support of middle-class voters.[30] Many Labor Party leaders, in particular Tony Blair, closely monitored Bill Clinton's 1992 presidential campaign, which targeted middle-class voters with its pledge to "end welfare as we know it." Several top Labor strategists even worked with the Clinton campaign.[31]

Blair continued to forge a close alliance with President Clinton throughout the early days of his presidency. By 1994, Blair was voicing opinions on welfare reform that were strikingly similar to Clinton's. In a speech that year he said, "Work and welfare go together . . . welfare must enhance duties and responsibilities and not be a substitute for them."[32] As one British academic noted: "Blair's speeches, and the writings of his close colleagues, resonate with a potpourri of U.S. influences: Charles Murray, Lawrence Mead, . . . David Ellwood, [and] Clinton himself."[33]

When the Labor Party, under Blair's leadership, regained a majority in Parliament in Great Britain in 1997, welfare reform was one of the issues at the top of its political agenda. The party pledged to move 250,000 unemployed young adults (not including single mothers) off welfare and into employment. To accomplish this and other reforms, the party proposed the "New Deal," a program that has many similarities to current U.S. welfare policies. Officials in British government visited the United States, traveling to Wisconsin and Riverside, California, two places that started to experiment early with work-oriented welfare systems. The British adopted a "work first" strategy for the New Deal program, with program participants spending up to four months searching for work with the assistance of a "personal advisor," the British term for the U.S. "caseworker."[34] After this time, participants who have not found jobs are offered subsidized work in either the public or private sector, or they may enter an education or training program if they have few skills.

Beginning in 1998, participation in Britain's New Deal became mandatory for young adults (ages eighteen to twenty-four) who have been unemployed for at least six months, as well as for adults over age twenty-four who have been jobless for more than two years. Individuals who do not look for work, take a subsidized job, or participate in education and training can lose their benefits, just as is the case in the United States. As of mid-1999, partners of the unemployed are also mandated to take part in the New Deal.[35]

However, unlike in the United States, single mothers, called "lone parents" in Britain, are not required to participate in New Deal programs. Single mothers may volunteer for the program and receive help with finding a job and finding child care, but they are not compelled to look for work until their youngest child turns sixteen. In a British pilot program, called New Deal for Lone Parents, a quarter of participants found jobs. However, very few mothers, about five percent, volunteered for the program.[36] The low participation in the program has led to some efforts to increase British investments in child care (needed for single mothers to go to work), but it has also led others to speculate that the New Deal for Lone Parents program should become mandatory.[37]

Whether or not this will happen in Britain is the source of much debate. On the one hand, the country has increased its focus on moving single mothers into the labor force. Even before its New Deal programs of the early 1990s, the British government attempted to make work more attractive than receipt of public assistance by putting in place earnings disregards, similar to those in U.S. welfare policy (see discussion of disregards in Chapter 2). Britain provides this assistance to single mothers through the Family Tax Credit, a cash benefit for low-income working families.[38] In addition, the position of some U.S. social critics that single motherhood is a "threat to society," has gained some adherents in Britain. For example, the writings of U.S. social critic Charles Murray (see discussion of his writing in Chapter 2), who views single parenthood as the root of many societal ills, such as poverty and crime, have received attention in the British press.[39]

However, the British government's policies toward single mothers do not completely reflect American beliefs. For example, when Frank Field, the British minister for welfare reform, was quoted in late 1997 as saying, "it might be argued that sanctions might be required for some lone parents," he was also quick to note that a mandatory New Deal Program with sanctions might not increase participation "when it is all too often a lack of child care which prevents large numbers from working."[40] Also, when the Labor Party leadership proposed eliminating the "One Parent Benefit," the cash grant single mothers receive in addition to the universal "Child Benefit," it met with staunch opposition from members of its party. A contingent of women representatives called the proposed cuts "economically inept, morally repugnant and spiritually bereft."[41] In the end, the Labor Party backed off of this proposal. Unlike the United States, the British public lacks consensus on whether the primary role of single mothers should be as worker or caregiver.[42] In general, the British public has been more supportive of aid to the poor and more concerned about inequality than are Americans, and Tony Blair has even proposed raising benefit levels for those who truly cannot work.[43]

Privatization and the Delivery of Welfare Services in Europe

One aspect of the U.S. welfare system that Britain and other European countries have borrowed is an increased role for the private sector in providing services. Historically, Britain has maintained national control over the delivery welfare and assistance programs, and its public Employment Service (ES) has overall responsibility for operating New Deal programs. However, similar to welfare bureaucracies in the United States, the ability of the ES to move from an agency that establishes eligibility and provides benefits to one that is focused on employment has been questioned.[44] As a result, the British government opted to experiment with privatization in ten areas of the country, where private agencies are now under contract to deliver the program.[45] According to New Deal minister Andrew Smith:

> One of the key conditions for the success of the New Deal is the full involvement of the private sector. . . . Our decision to invite the private sector to lead the delivery of the New Deal in ten areas altogether will enable us to explore the private sector's capacity to head up local delivery arrangements. We want to raise the level of awareness of the New Deal in the commercial world and the opportunities for its involvement in local partnerships generally.[46]

In its efforts to serve older unemployed individuals as well as single mothers, Britain also sought to contract out the program in several parts of the country.

In the Netherlands, the Dutch, too, have started to involve private-sector organizations in running welfare programs while decreasing the role of government. Although this shift, unlike Britain's, was not linked to reforms in the United States, some of the ways in which the Dutch have opted to organize welfare services come from the United States. Again, Wisconsin's program (Wisconsin Works, or W-2) has been a model for the Netherlands.

As in Britain, the Dutch and U.S. welfare systems share some commonalities that make adaptation of U.S. welfare reform policies more likely there than in other European countries. First, the Netherlands has undergone significant economic restructuring since the 1980s. Throughout the 1970s and 1980s, the country's economy weakened, unemployment reached double-digit levels, and significant portions of the citizenry (nearly one of every seven adults in 1993) received disability insurance.[47] The cost of unemployment and welfare benefits rose significantly. In the Netherlands unemployed workers could receive up to 90 percent of their former annual wages, and welfare recipients could receive 70 percent of the nation's median income.[48] With such generous benefits, public expenditures on social programs were more than 50 percent of the country's GDP.[49]

In response to this, the conservative-led Dutch government cut taxes, sharply reduced spending on public welfare benefits, tightened eligibility for benefits, and introduced a new social welfare model, which the Dutch call the "poldermodel."

Roughly translated, "poldermodel" refers to the culture of cooperation in low-lying areas that is needed to keep water from spilling through the dykes ("polder" in Dutch).[50] In practical terms, the poldermodel represents the Dutch attempt to create a social welfare system in which receipt of benefits is linked to efforts to improve the employability of unemployed individuals and thus increase the labor supply of the nation.

Part of the poldermodel strategy is to promote work over benefit receipt. In 1997 Dutch delegations visited Wisconsin on several occasions to learn from that state's experience.[51] The Netherlands is in the process of creating 200 "Centers for Work," which are modeled after Wisconsin's Job Centers.[52] In both the Netherlands and in Wisconsin, instead of going to separate welfare offices, individuals go to these centers to apply for benefits as well as receive help with finding a job. In another idea, borrowed from Wisconsin, Dutch municipalities (which oversee the administration of welfare programs) are held accountable for their performance in moving welfare recipients into employment.[53] In part, these innovations may be more easily transferable from the United States to the Netherlands because of similarities in service delivery structures. Although the Netherlands is not as decentralized as the United States, more than 600 municipalities and their social service departments are charged with administering Dutch social assistance programs.[54]

While the Dutch have adopted certain aspects of Wisconsin's welfare program, most of what the Netherlands has borrowed have been changes in how welfare programs are administered, rather than changes in the philosophy of welfare. Even though the Dutch have a work-based welfare system, policies such as time limits, which are at the heart of W-2 and the current U.S. welfare system, have not been integrated into the Dutch model. As a Dutch social services administrator noted:

> The idea of leaving families without support because a certain time-frame has been exceeded is very controversial. It touches the heart of the Dutch (and European) welfare system and is unacceptable to many people.[55]

Economic Change and the European Welfare System

Despite large differences in existing welfare systems, economic factors could, theoretically, force more European nations to move toward policies that are more similar to those of the United States. First, European nations have begun to confront the costs of large-scale social welfare systems. Economic pressures from previous recessions have already forced many countries to cut benefits and otherwise re-think their social welfare systems. Second, membership in the European Union (EU) is likely to exert fiscal controls on government budgets. Membership in the EU requires that countries control debt, forcing some countries to scale back their welfare programs and other forms of social assistance. Finally, globalization, which can encourage both the out-migration of workers looking for lower taxes and healthier economies, as well as in-migration of workers whom natives may see as taking their jobs and threatening the social order, could decrease support for uni-versal welfare programs. Yet, for major change to occur, these pressures would have to alter long-held beliefs of the citizenry about the purpose of social welfare programs within European society.

Pressures from Domestic Budgets

European social welfare systems, particularly those in the Nordic countries, are quite expensive. While the United States spent just over 15 percent of its GDP on social programs in 1997, the average within the EU was 25 percent, with Sweden's expenditures topping all countries at about 33 percent of GDP.[56] Sweden experi-enced a much more rapid growth in social welfare spending during the 1970s and 1980s compared to the rest of Europe. By 1980, Sweden ranked at the top in every type of spending for welfare programs.[57] In the early 1990s all nations felt in-creased pressures on their social welfare systems from a worldwide recession, but the effect was particularly hard on Sweden. Swedish unemployment rose to double digits, with particularly large increases in the number of long-term unemployed and the number of people engaged in government-funded ALMP programs.[58] As a result, the Swedish government began to cut back these programs and the benefits levels for unemployment and sickness insurance,[59] and, to a lesser degree, for child allowances.[60] Finland, which saw unemployment rise to nearly 20 percent in the early 1990s, began to do the same.[61]

Added to these economic pressures are changes in European demographics, in particular the aging of the population. While this aging trend has occurred in most Western countries, the social welfare system for the aged is more generous in the Nordic countries. With more people living longer, the amount of government funds spent on pensions has increased. How to fund these and other services in the near future is a major issue for these countries.

Already the Nordic countries have very high tax rates to finance their social welfare systems. As noted in *The Economist*:

> Inevitably, the price of the Nordics' generous welfare system has been sky-high taxes. Income-tax rates in the four mainland countries are near the top of the world league, with the highest rate exceeding 60 percent, and kicking in at quite low income levels.[62]

Norway has felt less strain on its social welfare system because of outside economic conditions, at least in part because of its status as a major oil and natural gas exporter. Yet its tax rates are very high: in 1998, a family making $36,000 a year fell into the top income tax bracket of 49.5 percent.[63] Some speculate that the willingness of citizens to contribute more may have reached its upper limits.[64]

A comprehensive social welfare system is expensive to support, and, in good economic times, exerts a major pressure on national budgets. During recessionary periods, this budgetary pressure increases, because more people claim benefits. If Europe enters into another recession, governments may again feel the need to scale back social spending.

Pressures from the European Union

The formation of the European Union (EU) has compelled its member nations toward economic and political union, including use of a common currency and greater economic integration. In 1993 Belgium, Denmark, France, Germany, Great Britain, Greece, Ireland, Italy, Luxembourg, the Netherlands, Portugal, and Spain signed the Maastricht Treaty on European Union. The Maastricht Treaty sets out what are commonly described as the "three pillars" of the EU. These are:

- The institutional "pillar," which establishes guidelines for a single market, for entry into the union, and for formation of a single currency (the euro).
- The foreign policy "pillar," which sets policy in the area of foreign affairs and security, so that member nations can act as one body on these issues.
- The justice and home affairs "pillar," which facilitates closer cooperation and standardization on "domestic" issues such as asylum, immigration, and customs.[65]

In 1995 Austria, Finland, and Sweden joined the EU, accepting these provisions.

Membership in the EU puts pressure on European social welfare systems in several ways. First, in order to be a member of the EU, counties must meet certain economic conditions including low budget deficits and national debt. In order to attain this, many countries have had to reduce spending on social programs. For example, in the mid- to late 1990s Germany struggled with making cuts to social welfare spending to be compliant with EU standards. After many debates and protests, Germany cut government-funded sick pay and pensions, restricted eligibility for other benefits, but left unemployment benefits untouched.[66]

Sweden's welfare system has faced challenges in the past few years as well, as the county has run budget deficits and has a national debt much higher than those allowed by EU standards.[67] In order to bring its economy into line, more cutbacks in social welfare spending seem inevitable. In addition, as the EU evolves, individual countries will be competing with each other to keep and attract businesses. Nations such as Sweden, with high tax rates, may be at a disadvantage, because employers may not be willing to help pay for an expensive welfare system.[68]

What then, will be the outcome of these economic pressures? Some Swedish social scientists worry that their country is moving in the direction of more "liberal" countries, such as the United States, noting a retreat from a universal approach to social welfare to one that is starting to rely on more means-tested benefit programs.[69] Looking at EU countries more broadly, other commentators believe that the pressures of European integration and globalization *are* resulting in a scaling back or "retrenchment" of social welfare systems to be more similar to those of "liberal" countries.[70] As one notes:

> Financial globalization is the principal means by which the ultra-liberal model is disseminated throughout the world. Its power is such that even the best-organized economies . . . are unable to fight back effectively.[71]

Pressures from Migration

The increased integration of world economies is often seen as part of the larger "globalization" of national economies. But a somewhat different aspect of globalization is the increased porousness of national boundaries and the resulting mobility of workers. In an era of ease of travel, common languages, and transnational corporations, highly skilled workers can abandon their home countries for work environments that offer lower taxes and greater economic opportunity. Similarly, low-skilled workers who cannot find jobs in their home countries can also leave for wealthier countries. As these workers compete for jobs in their new environment, they put pressure on the job opportunities and wages of native-born workers at the low end of the income scale.

Changes in migration patterns such as these can put pressure on social welfare systems in many ways. If highly skilled workers leave a country that imposes high taxes to pay for a generous welfare system, that country will lose the very workers it depends upon to fund its programs. Such workers, by leaving, can also put pressure on countries to lower taxes and thus cut benefits. Similarly, competition from low-skilled immigrants can make it harder for native-born workers to get jobs, resulting in their greater dependence on the welfare system and thus its increased costs. Immigrants, who are particularly vulnerable to economic shifts, may also find themselves in need of social service programs during economic hard times.

This latter phenomenon could also change European social welfare systems by changing the ideological beliefs upon which they are based. Until relatively recently, the population of most European nations was homogenous, that is, made up of one race or ethnic group. Theoretically, at least, benefits for those of one's own ethnicity are easier to support: wealthier citizens find it easier to identify with those receiving benefits. But the increased immigration of non-Europeans to western Europe could change the willingness of Europeans to pay for benefits. The United States, which is characterized by its heterogeneity, or varied racial/ethnic makeup, provides an example. Although issues of race and ethnicity are not always openly raised in discussions of U.S. welfare policies, they frequently loom as a specter in any welfare reform debate. A common stereotype of a welfare recipient, for example, is an African American single mother with many children. In border states such as California, stories frequently circulate about Mexican women crossing into the United States to give birth, with public funds picking up the costs of the delivery. Stereotypes such as these make the welfare debate highly charged.

In Europe, the issue of race has only recently become entwined in debates over social welfare programs. Because citizens of European nations are, by and large, of one race, immigrants and asylum seekers, even though they tend not to be eligible for the full range of benefits offered to native-born citizens, have become targets of stigma. The ability of immigrants to obtain citizenship in European countries is also limited. This is particularly true in Germany, where citizenship hinges on birth and ethnic ties to Germany. Immigrants may face other hurdles when applying for benefits for which they are eligible. According to some reports, when applying for government assistance, asylum seekers from outside of Europe tend to be labeled more severely than, for example, refugees from the former Yugoslavia.[72] Increasingly, non-Nordic immigrants in Sweden live in highly segregated areas and are often stigmatized as "welfare cheats."[73] In the treatment of immigrants, therefore, Europe and the United States may increasingly resemble each other in the reluctance to extend full benefits to those who are not seen as full members of the polity.

Conclusion

Many of the historical factors that first caused the U.S. and European welfare systems to develop differently are no longer applicable. Recent trends in economic, political, and social pressures could have begun to bring about a convergence in governmental systems. But the differences between the social welfare systems of United States and its European counterparts, both in the reach of their policies and in the social bases of their support, in all likelihood will remain.

Despite some recent cutbacks in its benefits, Sweden still has one of the most generous and egalitarian social welfare systems in the world.[74] Great Britain, which more closely resembles the United States, has shaped its welfare reforms in the context of an integrated and comprehensive strategy to end poverty. The current British government's social policies include ambitious investments in education and early intervention programs, tax credits to raise the incomes of the working poor, and benefit increases for the most disadvantaged: policies that cost an additional 6.7 billion pounds, or about 1 percent of the nation's GDP.[75] To say that the European countries are on the verge of abandoning their more generous systems of social provision would, therefore, not be correct.

Prevailing societal norms about the role and purpose of the welfare system suggest that future changes in the European welfare systems will likely be limited. The most probable changes will be programmatic (that is, affecting benefit levels, eligibility, and service delivery) rather than systemic (that is, affecting the political environment within which the welfare system operates).[76] Many in European political and academic circles increasingly use the term "socially excluded" to describe the circumstances of those who need assistance, rather than "poor." The choice of terminology is important in that it extends concern about the disadvantaged beyond their lack of income (or poverty). Social exclusion implies that the government is concerned about increasing opportunities for all citizens to fully realize the social rights of citizenship, including a basic standard of living but also opportunities to participate in society and the economy.[77]

Public opinion in European nations also continues to reflect support for the basic elements of these nations' welfare systems.[78] Part of this may have to do with the broader coverage of the systems—unlike welfare in the United States, which is seen as benefiting the poor, social welfare programs in Europe benefit a larger segment of society. In Norway (which has not joined the EU), promoting equality and taking care of those not as well off are viewed as part of Norway's way of life. As the country's Minister for Social Affairs, Magnhild Meltveit Kleppa, said, "The philosophy is to keep the traditional equality we've had."[79] Even in Great Britain, a country that has taken on many U.S. policies and strategies for delivering welfare services, adoption of further reforms may be challenged by fundamental differences in philosophies between the two nations. British social scientist Robert Walker summarizes these differences by noting that:

> The British public does not seem to accept that it is lone [single] parenthood rather than poverty that disadvantages children, nor that welfare recipients are trapped by indolence rather than force of circumstance.[80]

In contrast, recent welfare reforms in the United States have been based on many of those very ideological assumptions regarding the causes and consequences of poverty and single parenthood. Although the differing perspectives of Europe and the United States on these issues are not immutable, the extent to which either might move closer to the other is debatable. The influence of a particular model of welfare (and the evidence that might support its viability) on another is likely to proceed much more slowly than advocates on either side might predict—or hope.

Notes

1. United Nations Social and Economic Council, Commission for Social Development. *Enhancing Social Protection and Reducing Vulnerability in a Globalizing World,* 11–12. Accessed at http://www.un.org/esa/socdev/csd/csd39docs/csd39e2.pdf.

2. James Midgley, *Social Welfare in Global Context* (Thousand Oaks, Calif.: Sage Publications, 1997), 81.

3. Simon Duncan and Rosalind Edwards, "Introduction: A Contextual Approach to Single Mothers and Paid Work," in *Single Mothers in an International Context: Mothers or Workers,* ed. Simon Duncan and Rosalind Edwards (London: UCL Press, 1997), v.

4. Margaret Weir, Ann Shola Orloff, and Theda Skocpol, "Understanding American Social Politics," in *The Politics of Social Policy in the United States*, ed. Margaret Weir, Ann Shola Orloff, and Theda Skocpol (Princeton: Princeton University Press, 1988), 10.

5. Christine Cousins, *Society, Work, and Welfare in Europe* (New York: St. Martin's Press, 1999), 14–17.

6. Ann Shola Orloff, "Origins of America's Welfare States," in *The Politics of Social Policy in the United States*, ed. Margaret Weir, Ann Shola Orloff, and Theda Skocpol (Princeton: Princeton University Press, 1988), 44.

7. Brigitte H. Schulz, "Globalisation, Unification, and the German Welfare State," *International Social Science Journal*, 52 (March, 2000), 41.

8. Ibid., 45.

9. Ibid., 80.

10. Summarized by Midgely, *Social Welfare in Global Context*, 94–95.

11. Jonah Levy, "Vice into Virtue? Progressive Politics and Welfare Reform in Continental Europe," *Politics and Society*, 27 (June 1999), 241.

12. Sven Hort, "From a Generous to a Stingy Welfare State? Sweden's Approach to Targeting," in *Targeting Social Benefits: International Perspectives and Trends*, ed. Neil Gilbert (New Brunswick, N.J.: Transaction Publications, 2001), 187.

13. Ibid., 190.

14. Ibid., 189.

15. Gregg M. Olsen, "Half Empty of Half Full? The Swedish Welfare State in Transition," *Canadian Review of Sociology and Anthropology* 36 (May 1999), 247. See also Hort, "From a Generous to a Stingy Welfare State?" 193.

16. Ulla Bjornberg, "Single Mothers in Sweden: Supported Workers Who Mother," in *Single Mothers in an International Context: Mothers or Workers*, ed. Simon Duncan and Rosalind Edwards (London: UCL Press, 1997), 250.

17. Ibid., 250, 251.

18. Ibid., 247.

19. Sonja Drobnic, Hans-Peter Blossfeld, and Gotz Rohwer, "Dynamics of Women's Employment Patterns over the Family Life Course: A Comparison of the United States and Germany," *Journal of Marriage and the Family* 61 (February 1999), 134.

20. Martina Klett-Davis, "Single Mothers in Germany: Supported Mothers Who Work," in *Single Mothers in an International Context: Mothers or Workers*, ed. Simon Duncan and Rosalind Edwards (London: UCL Press, 1997), 209.

21. Drobnic, Blossfeld, and Rohwer, "Dynamics of Women's Employment Patterns," 135.

22. Mary Daly, *The Gender Division of Welfare: The Impact of the British and German Welfare States* (Cambridge, UK: Cambridge University Press, 2000), 91.

23. Klett Davis, "Single Mothers in Germany,"193.

24. Ibid., 193.

25. Ibid., 187.

26. Gary Bryner, *Politics and Public Morality: The Great American Welfare Reform Debate* (New York: Norton, 1998), 33.

27. R. Kent Weaver, *Ending Welfare as We Know It* (Washington, D.C.: Brookings Institution Press, 2000), 172.

28. Robert Walker, "The Americanization of British Welfare: A Case Study of Policy Transfer," *Focus* 19 (Summer-Fall 1998), 32.

29. Ibid., 34.

30. Desmond King and Mark Wickham Jones, "From Clinton to Blair: The Democratic (Party) Origins of Welfare to Work," in *The Political Quarterly,* 70 (January/March, 1999), 63.

31. Ibid., 66.

32. Ibid., 68.

33. Walker, "The Americanization of British Welfare," 34.

34. Robert Walker and Michael Wiseman, "Britain's New Deal and the Next Round of U.S. Welfare Reform," (Madison, Wis.: Institute for Research on Poverty, 2001), 5.

35. Walker, "The Americanization of British Welfare," 36.

36. Simon Duncan and Rosalind Edwards, *Lone Mothers, Paid Work, and Gendered Moral Rationalities* (New York: St. Martin's Press, 1999), 288.

37. Ibid., 290.

38. Simon Duncan and Rosalind Edwards, "Single Mothers in Britain: Unsupported Mothers or Workers?" in *Single Mothers in an International Context: Mothers or Workers,* ed. Simon Duncan and Rosalind Edwards (London: UCL Press, 1997), 65.

39. Ibid., 56.

40. David Brindle, "Welfare to Work: Making It Work for Lone Parents," *Guardian,* December 31, 1997, 6.

41. Chris Deerin, "Labour Leaders Face Backlash at Conference," *Daily Mail,* February 21, 1998, 24.

42. Duncan and Edwards, *Lone Mothers, Paid Work, and Gendered Moral Rationalities,* 247; and Walker, "The Americanization of British Welfare," 38.

43. Jane Waldfogel, "Research on Poverty and Anti-Poverty Policies," in *Understanding Poverty*, ed. Sheldon Danziger and Robert Haveman (Cambridge: Harvard University Press, forthcoming).

44. Dan Finn, "A Comparison of Local Approaches to Welfare-to-Work in the United States, the United Kingdom and the Netherlands," in *The Local Dimension of Welfare-to-Work: An International Survey*, ed. Organization for Economic Cooperation and Development (Paris: OECD, 1999), 148.

45. Walker, "The Americanization of British Welfare," 35.

46. Press release, Department for Education and Employment (Britain), "Private Sector to Deliver New Deal in Five Areas," *M2 Presswire*, February 28, 1998.

47. Data from Organization for Economic Cooperation and Development, *Economic Surveys: Netherlands, 1997–1998* (Paris: OECD, 1998) cited in Finn, "A Comparison of Local Approaches," 157.

48. Dick Vink, "Will Wisconsin Works (W-2) Fit into the Dutch 'Poldermodel?' " *Focus* 19 (Summer–Fall 1998), 41.

49. Levy, "Vice into Virtue?" 258.

50. Vink, "Will Wisconsin Works (W-2) Fit into the Dutch 'Poldermodel?' " 41.

51. Ibid., 41, 45.

52. Ibid., 46.

53. Ibid., 45.

54. Finn, "A Comparison of Local Approaches," 156.

55. Vink, "Will Wisconsin Works (W-2) Fit into the Dutch 'Poldermodel?' " 45.

56. OECD Social Expenditure Database 1980–1997. Accessed at http://www.oecd.org// els/social/nse/index.htm.

57. Olsen, "Half Empty or Half Full?" 246.

58. Ibid., 248.

59. Ramesh Mishra, *Globalization and the Welfare State* (Northhampton, Mass.: Edward Elgar, 1999), 76.

60. Hort, "From a Generous to a Stingy Welfare State?" 205.

61. Anonymous, "Nordic Countries—Farewell, Welfare," *The Economist*, October 23, 1993, 67.

62. Xan Smiley, "Survey: The Nordic Countries: Happy Family?" *The Economist*, January 23, 1999, 1–16.

63. Thomas Omestad, "Norway's Equally Good Life," *U.S. News & World Report*, December 7, 1998, 37.

64. Richard Clayton and Jonas Pontusson, "Welfare-State Retrenchment Revisited: Entitlement Cuts, Public Sector Restructuring, and Inegalitarian Trends in Advanced Capitalist Societies," in *World Politics* 51 (1998), 95.

65. European Union, Delegation of the European Commission to the United States, "What is the European Union?" in *The European Union: A Guide for Americans* (Washington, D.C.: Delegation of the European Commission to the United States, 2000). Accessed at http://www.eurunion.org/infores/euguide/euguide.htm.

66. Mishra, *Globalization and the Welfare State*, 84.

67. Olsen, "Half Empty of Half Full?" 261–262.

68. Guy Backman and Satish Sharma, "Changing Social Welfare Systems in the Nordic Nations: Some Observations and Analysis," in *Journal of International and Comparative Social Welfare* XIV (1998), 37.

69. See, for example, Sune Sunesson, Staffan Blomberg, Per Gunnar Edebalk, Lars Harrysson, Jan Magnusson, Anna Meeuwisse, Jan Petersson, and Tapio Salonen, "The Flight from Universalism," in *European Journal of Social Work* 1 (March 1998), 19–30.

70. Mishra, *Globalization and the Welfare State*, 130; Clayton and Pontusson, "Welfare-State Retrenchment Revisited," 95–96.

71. Ibid., 85.

72. Mark Mitchell and David Russell, "Immigration, Citizenship and Social Exclusion in the New Europe," in *Developments In European Social Policy*, ed. Rob Sykes and Pete Alcock (Bristol, UK. Policy Press, 1998), 81.

73. Warren Hoge, "A Swedish Dilemma: The Immigrant Ghetto," *New York Times*, October 6, 1998, A3.

74. Mishra, *Globalization and the Welfare State*, 76–77.

75. Waldfogel, "Research on Poverty and Anti-Poverty Policies," 9–12.

76. Clayton and Pontusson, "Welfare-State Retrenchment Revisited," 97.

77. Cousins, *Society, Work, and Welfare in Europe*, 145–146.

78. Clayton and Pontusson, "Welfare-State Retrenchment Revisited," 97–98.

79. Omestad, "Norway's Equally Good Life," 37.

80. Walker, "The Americanization of British Welfare," 39.

Appendix

159

Further Research and Chronology

Bibliography of Print Sources

Bane, Mary Jo, and David T. Ellwood. *Welfare Realities*. Cambridge, Mass.: Harvard University Press, 1996.

Blank, Rebecca. *It Takes a Nation*. Princeton: Princeton University Press, 1998.

Blank, Rebecca, and Ron Haskins, ed. *The New World of Welfare*. Washington, D.C.: Brookings Institution Press, 2001.

Cammisa, Anne Marie. *From Rhetoric to Reform?* Boulder, Colo.: Westview Press, 1998.

Danziger, Sandra K., Mary Corcoran, Sheldon Danziger, Colleen Heflin, Ariel Kalil, Judith Levine, Daniel Rosen, Kristin S. Seefeldt, Kristine Siefert, and Richard Tolman. "Barriers to the Employment of Welfare Recipients," in R. Cherry and W. Rodgers, ed., *Prosperity for All?* New York: Russell Sage, 2000.

Danziger, Sheldon, and Peter Gottschalk. *America Unequal*. New York: Russell Sage, 1995.

Danziger, Sheldon, and Ann Chih Lin, eds. *Coping with Poverty: The Social Contexts of Neighborhood, Work, and Family in the African-American Community*. Ann Arbor: University of Michigan Press, 2000.

DeParle, Jason. "Life After Welfare." Ten part series on welfare reform in Wisconsin, appearing in the *New York Times* from February 21 to December 30, 1999.

Ellwood, David. *Poor Support*. New York: Basic Books, 1988.

Liebschutz, Sarah L., ed. *Managing Welfare Reform in Five States: The Challenge of Devolution*. Albany, N.Y.: Rockefeller Institute Press, 2000.

Mead, Lawrence M. *The New Politics of Poverty*. New York: Basic Books, 1992.

———. *Beyond Entitlement*. New York: Free Press, 1986.

Murray, Charles. *Losing Ground*. New York: Basic Books, 1984.

Weaver, R. Kent. *Ending Welfare as We Know It*. Washington, D.C.: Brookings Institution Press, 2000.

Wilson, William Julius. *When Work Disappears*. New York: Knopf, 1996.

———. *The Truly Disadvantaged*. Chicago: University of Chicago Press, 1987.

Bibliography of Internet Sources

U.S. Department of Health and Human Services, Administration for Children and Families   http://www.acf.dhhs.gov.
> Its "Welfare Reform" page has information on TANF policies and statistics related to TANF, and its "Welfare Reform Financial Data" page has information on state TANF expenditures.

U.S. Department of Health and Human Services, Office of the Assistant Secretary for Planning and Evaluation (ASPE)   http://aspe.os.dhhs.gov.
> Its "Human Services Policy" page has links to pages providing summaries of ongoing ASPE-funded research projects on "Welfare & Work" (studies of welfare leavers, family well-being under welfare reform, caseload trends, and state policies and programs); "Family Formation" (studies on fatherhood and teen pregnancy programs); and "Special Populations" (studies on victims of domestic violence, immigrants, and mental health issues).

U.S. General Accounting Office   http://www.gao.gov
> As Congress's investigative arm, the GAO prepares reports at the request of individual members of Congress. Its Health, Education, and Human Services division has issued numerous reports on topics related to welfare reform, ranging from financing to the well-being of recipients.

U.S. House of Representatives, Committee on Ways and Means "Green Book"   http://aspe.os.dhhs.gov/2000gb/index.htm

Welfare Information Network   www.welfareinfo.org
> Welfare Information Network (WIN) is a foundation-funded organization that maintains a comprehensive Web site cataloging reports, events, and organizations related to welfare reform. WIN also periodically produces syntheses of research and state and local "best practices" in welfare reform.
>
> The WIN Web site also provides links to federal and state agencies involved in welfare reform; other agencies and organizations that publish material or provide other resources related to this topic; and thousands of online papers and reports written by public agencies, research organizations, and advocacy groups. These papers are organized topically for convenience.

Bibliography of Other Media

"Checks and Balances," a segment by Maria Shriver for the NBC program *Dateline* on Wisconsin's welfare system that chronicles a year in the life of four Wisconsin welfare recipients. First aired on NBC on April 17, 1998.

"Ending Welfare as We Know It," a documentary by Roger Weisberg, profiling six women living in Florida, New Jersey, and Wisconsin and their experiences with the welfare system. First aired on PBS on June 5, 1998.

Chronology

1988   Congress passes the Family Support Act, which reforms the existing welfare system in a number of ways, in particular, by creating the Job Opportunities and Basic Skills (JOBS) program. JOBS attempts to address unemployment of welfare recipients by encouraging participation in education and training programs, with the ultimate goal of moving recipients from welfare to self-sufficiency.

Early 1990s   States increasingly request waivers from federal welfare and JOBS regulations to test out new rules and policies. Many of these waivers allow states to broaden the categories of recipients required to participate in JOBS and toughen penalties for failure to meet program requirements.

1992   Arkansas governor Bill Clinton is elected president; his campaign platform includes a promise to "end welfare as we know it."

June 1994   Clinton presents his welfare reform plan that calls for recipients to be working within two years of receiving benefits or else be placed in community service jobs. Job training programs and child care assistance are designed to help recipients move into employment. Many Republicans criticized the plan for its provisions of phasing in work requirements and setting time limits for only a portion of the welfare caseload. Many Democrats take issue with any time limits. The plan is introduced into the House but no action is taken.

November 1994   Republicans win control of both houses of Congress in midterm elections. Led by Georgia representative Newt Gingrich, many members had pledged to fulfill the "Contract with America," a conservative agenda that included welfare reform and cuts in federal spending on welfare.

December 9, 1995   President Clinton vetoes Congress's budget reconciliation bill, in part because of the cuts proposed for welfare funding.

December 21–22, 1995   Congress passes HR 4, which would eliminate the existing federal entitlement to cash assistance for eligible families and convert federal welfare spending to block grants, giving states more flexibility in how they allocate funds. Unlike Clinton's plan, HR 4 contains no provision of community service jobs for those who seek work and cannot find it.

January 9, 1996   President Clinton vetoes HR 4.

August 1, 1996   Congress passes the Personal Responsibility and Work Opportunity Reconciliation Act (PRWORA), which abolishes the prior system of welfare benefits (the Aid to Families with Dependent Children-AFDC-program) and replaces it with the Temporary Assistance for Needy Families (TANF) program. TANF ends the federal entitlement to cash assistance; provides funds to states for welfare in the form of a capped block grant; institutes work requirements and a provision that recipients must be in a work activity after two years of benefit receipt; places a five-year lifetime limit on benefit receipt; and gives unprecedented amounts of discretion to states and localities in defining and operating cash assistance programs.

August 31, 1996   Despite his objections to some of the provisions in PRWORA, in particular those that barred most legal immigrants from receiving benefits through food stamps, Medicaid, and the Supplemental Security Income (SSI) program, President Clinton signs PRWORA into law. Several of Clinton's appointees within the Department of Health and Human Services subsequently resign in protest.

October 1, 1996   Many states officially begin implementing PRWORA.

June 2000   The number of families nationwide receiving welfare (2.2 million) is half of what it was when PRWORA was signed into law (4.4 million in August 1996). However, welfare caseloads begin declining in 1995, after reaching a peak of just over five million families on assistance in 1994.

October 2002   Authorization of PRWORA expires unless extended or revised.

Facts, Policies, and Commentary

California and the Wisconsin Welfare Waivers Experiments

Welfare waiver projects in Riverside County, California, and in the state of Wisconsin received a great deal of attention from policy-makers and the media as welfare reform gained prominence as a political issue in the mid-1990s.

Riverside's GAIN program

Riverside County, located in southern California, was one of six test counties selected as a research site for the evaluation of that state's Greater Avenues for Independence (GAIN) program. GAIN was California's JOBS program, but the state sought to test a new method of providing services that placed welfare recipients into different tracks depending on their skill level and education: those with low skills, education, or English proficiency were placed in education programs while more "job ready" individuals received assistance with finding work. However, compared to the other counties in the evaluation, Riverside placed a much stronger emphasis on helping recipients find work, including linking staff performance evaluations to the number of clients that staff placed successfully in employment.

Compared to five other test counties, Riverside achieved greater success, measured in terms of earnings of welfare recipients and savings to the welfare offices. These results were often interpreted to mean that the more effective way to move welfare recipients toward self-sufficiency was to require them to look for work rather than allowing them to participate in education and training programs. However, many recipients in Riverside also participated in training and other educational type programs. Moreover, evaluators of Riverside's GAIN program speculated that it was not any one factor that accounted for the county's success, but rather a combination of welfare office practices and other conditions that might not be replicable in other areas.

Source: James Riccio, Daniel Friedlander, Stephen Freedman, with Mary E. Farrell, Veronica Fellerath, Stacey Fox, and Daniel J. Lehman, "GAIN: Benefits, Costs, and Three-Year Impacts of a Welfare-to-Work Program," (New York, Manpower Demonstration Research Corporation, 1994) xxi–lvii.

Wisconsin's Waivers

Under Gov. Tommy Thompson, Wisconsin submitted numerous waiver requests to the U.S. Department of Health and Human Services. Many of the types of policies that the state sought to implement were included in the final 1996 welfare reform bill. These included provisions to:

- Penalize AFDC parents whose children failed to attend school.
- Pay lower cash AFDC benefits to families who recently moved into the state.
- Discourage out-of-wedlock childbearing by eliminating automatic benefit increases to women on AFDC who give birth to more children.

The Wisconsin legislature also passed legislation during the mid-1990s to end the state's participation in the AFDC program by 1999 (which was rendered unnecessary by the passage of the 1996 law), replacing AFDC with its own program that emphasized immediate placement into jobs. As a way of moving toward its new vision, Wisconsin operated in two counties a waiver program called "Work Not Welfare," which obligated recipients to find work shortly after applying for welfare benefits or be placed in a community service job. In the two test counties, welfare rolls dropped and employment of former recipients increased from levels prior to the start of the program. However, research findings from Work Not Welfare, as well as the other waiver programs, were never released to the public.

Source: Elisabeth Boehnen and Thomas Corbett, "Work-Not-Welfare: Time limits in Fond du Lac County, Wisconsin," Focus 18, (Special Issue 1996). Accessed at http://www.ssc.wisc.edu/irp/pubs/foc181/index.htm; Kristin S. Seefeldt, Laura Kaye, Christopher Botsko, Pamela Holcomb, Kimura Flores, Carla Herbig, and Karen C. Tumlin, *Income Support and Social Services for Low Income People in Wisconsin,* (Washington, D.C.: Urban Institute, 1998).

Examples of State Work First Policies

"WorkFirst" in Washington

In 1989 Washington became one of the first states in the nation to receive a welfare waiver to implement its Family Independence Program (FIP), which placed a heavy emphasis on education and training for welfare recipients. However, in 1997 when the state passed its legislation to implement TANF, its new "WorkFirst" program required an immediate job search for those who were determined to be "work ready" (for example, not disabled or not in a domestic violence situation).

In WorkFirst, welfare office workers first meet with clients to determine eligibility for assistance and to identify potential barriers to participation in the work program. Welfare office workers are responsible for providing assistance with needs such as child care and transportation.

After this initial meeting, clients are referred to a local Employment Security (ES) office, where they attend a thirty-hour "job readiness" workshop. They are then required to search for employment for up to twelve weeks. If clients do not find a job during this time period, they meet with their welfare caseworker for placement in an alternate activity. However, this alternate activity usually has a work focus so that it counts toward the federal work participation requirement. Possible alternate activities include work in a community service job or participation in on the job training, in which a private employer receives a subsidy to train and then hire a welfare recipient.

Source. Janet Looney and Betty Jane Narver, "Washington's WorkFirst Program: Key Policy Challenges," in *Managing Welfare Reform in Five States: The Challenge of Devolution,* ed., Sarah L. Liebschutz (Albany, N.Y.: Rockefeller Institute Press, 2000), 86.

New York City's Workfare

In 1995 New York City embarked on one of the most ambitious welfare-to-work programs in the country. Recipients who are unable to find a job in the private sector are required to work in public jobs in exchange for their welfare benefits. Frequently called "workfare," this practice has not been widely used by states, either before or after passage of PRWORA. Workfare programs are frequently costly, and critics note that recipients often end up performing "make work" jobs. The latter complaint stems from the "nondisplacement" clause usually attached to workfare programs: workfare jobs are designed to not take the place of jobs that would otherwise be held by regular employees. Despite these potential problems, New York City placed more than 200,000 individuals into its program over the course of its first two years.

In recent years labor disputes have arisen in New York City, because of workfare participants allegedly working side by side with city employees, performing tasks such as cleaning city parks, doing clerical work in hospitals, or doing the work of laid-off public employees. Nevertheless, New York City remained committed to workfare as the best first step for helping low-skilled recipients enter the labor market.

Source: Alan Finder, "Evidence Is Scarce That Workfare Leads to Full-Time Jobs," *New York Times,* April 12, 1998) 1; and Steven Greenhouse, "Many Participants in Workfare Take the Place of City Workers," *New York Times,* April 13, 1998, 1.

Maine and Wyoming: Work First Alternative Programs

Although Maine and Wyoming place the majority of their TANF recipients into work first programs, these two states are unique in that they have created separate, state-funded programs for welfare recipients who wish to pursue postsecondary education. With the exception of short-term, vocational education programs, postsecondary education, including pursuit of a college degree, is currently not an allowable activity under TANF.

Maine's program, Parents as Scholars (PaS), allows up to 2,000 adults in families who would otherwise be eligible for TANF to be a part of PaS if they do not already have a bachelor's degree and meet other requirements, such as not having the skills necessary to earn at least 85 percent of the state's median wage. The recipients' course of postsecondary study must be approved by the state, and they must maintain a "C" grade point average. Participants receive a cash grant and other services such as child care assistance. Since PaS is a state program, participants are not subject to the federal time limit; however, the state sets a time limit of two to four years in the program, depending on the degree being pursued.

TANF applicants in Wyoming who are already enrolled in a postsecondary education program may also be eligible to continue their degree and receive a cash grant through a state program. However, fewer than 100 individuals were in this program as of mid-1998, since the state prefers to place most recipients in its work first program.

Source: Marie Cohen, "Post-Secondary Education Under Welfare Reform," (Washington, D.C.: Welfare Information Network, 1998). Accessed at http://www.welfareinfo.org/vocational%20ed.htm; Maine Department of Human Services. Accessed at http://janus.state.me.us/dhs/bfi/pas.htm.

Challenges with Welfare Privatization Policies
Problems with Privatization in Mississippi

In early 1997 Republican Gov. Kirk Fordice of Mississippi signed legislation enabling his state's welfare reform. More important than in enacting Fordice's vision for reform, perhaps, was an earlier move by the state legislature that gave the governor control over appointments to the administration of the Department of Human Services (DHS), Mississippi's TANF agency. Fordice filled DHS management positions with like-minded Republicans who backed his intention to privatize much of the delivery of welfare services in the state.

In Mississippi's initial attempt to privatize welfare services in 1997, the state quickly chose private contractors to provide case management or job-seeking services. Local DHS offices continued to determine eligibility before referring clients to one of the contractors. Private contractors were set up to serve a regional area, however, while local DHS offices continued to be county-based. Because contractors' regions did not always align with county borders, communication problems arose. In addition, county DHS offices were held accountable for results, such as the number of clients placed into jobs. Yet the contractors, who were providing this service, were not accountable to the local DHS offices. Furthermore, contractors were expected to start providing services within a short time period after winning contracts, leading to hastily developed programs.

Because of all these problems, less than two years after Mississippi's privatization efforts began, control for all functions related to TANF was returned to DHS.

Source: David A. Breaux, Christopher M. Duncan, C. Denise Keller, and John C. Morris, "To Privatization and Back: Welfare Reform Implementation in Mississippi," in *Managing Welfare Reform in Five States: The Challenge of Devolution,* ed. Sarah L. Liebschutz (Albany, N.Y.: Rockefeller Institute Press, 2000), 44–45.

Large-Scale Privatization in Texas Scaled Back

Texas hoped to make great use of PRWORA's flexibility in giving power over welfare programs to the states. Texas designed a system to integrate eligibility determination for TANF with those for food stamps and Medicaid, the federal programs that provide food assistance and health care coverage to very low-income individuals, as well as a variety of other assistance programs. Texas's proposed system, the Texas Integrated Enrollment System (TIES), would have revamped the process by which clients are determined eligible for health and human services assistance programs. To improve efficiency and customer service, Texas proposed to invest substantially in new computer systems and to privatize the whole process by contracting out the eligibility determination function.

The task of creating a large automated system, coupled with the $2.8 billion privatization contract, attracted interest from large corporations such as Unisys, Lockheed Martin, IBM, and EDS. However, Texas state workers voiced concerns about job loss because of the proposed privatization, while other critics questioned the appropriateness of giving large private corporations the responsibility for determining eligibility for federal assistance programs. In the end Texas had to scale back on its privatization plans, since the federal government ruled in 1997 that only public, merit-based employees may perform food stamp and Medicaid eligibility functions.

Source: Nancy Pindus, Randy Capps, Jerome Gallagher, Linda Giannerelli, Milda Saunders, and Robin Smith, *Income Support and Social Services for Low Income People in Texas* (Washington, D.C.: Urban Institute), 53.

Compromises in Privatized Welfare in Wisconsin

In the late 1980s and early 1990s, Wisconsin Gov. Tommy Thompson gained a national reputation as one of the more innovative voices in welfare reform. Wisconsin was one of the first states to begin experimenting with a work-focused welfare program and in many ways has gone farther than other states in terms of interpreting PRWORA.

One of the key tenets of Wisconsin's reform agenda was the notion that public bureaucracies should *not* have the presumptive right to run welfare programs. The state embraced competition as crucial in ensuring that clients receive the best services and that outcomes, particularly placement into employment, were achieved. In initial plans for the state's program, called Wisconsin Works or W-2, state officials proposed that county human service agencies, the agencies providing welfare services under AFDC, would have to compete to operate welfare in the future. Presumably, they would be competing against private agencies. County officials balked at this arrangement, and in the end, a compromise was reached. Counties that attained certain performance standards set by the state (which included placing a certain proportion of clients into work activities) would retain the right to operate W-2 if they choose. Counties not meeting these standards could only operate W-2 if they were successful in securing a contract in an open bidding process.

In the vast majority of counties in Wisconsin, a county human service agency runs the state's W-2 program. However, in Milwaukee County, where most of the states' TANF caseload resides, five private agencies run the program. These agencies include four local nonprofit organizations and Maximus, the national for-profit corporation. Private agency staff determine eligibility for W-2 and provide services designed to move recipients into employment. But because of federal prohibitions against private agencies determining eligibility for food stamps and Medicaid, county workers are housed with the W-2 agencies to do this task.

Source: Jennifer Ehrle, Kristin S. Seefeldt, Patricia McMahon and Kathleen Snyder, "Changes to Wisconsin's Welfare and Work, Child Care, and Child Welfare Systems Since 1997," (Washington, D.C.: Urban Institute 2001); David Dodenhoff, "Privatizing Welfare in Wisconsin: Ending Administrative Entitlements—W-2's Untold Story," (Thiensville: Wisconsin Policy Research Institute, 1998).

Charles Murray and *Losing Ground*

In 1984 political scientist Charles Murray published his controversial book, *Losing Ground,* which ten years later had great influence on the welfare reform debates leading up to PRWORA. In *Losing Ground,* Murray concluded that the growth of federal programs, such as AFDC and food stamps, worsened conditions for the poor and increased their number rather than ameliorating poverty. This, he noted, was because of rules and regulations of the welfare system that made it "profitable for the poor to behave in the short term in ways that were destructive in the long term." In Murray's analyses, the increase in out-of-wedlock childbearing was a direct result of the welfare system because it encouraged unwed mothers (especially teenagers), to look for support from welfare (as opposed to a husband), even though doing so increased the chances that their resulting families would remain poor.

In several subsequent articles, such as "The Coming White Underclass," and "Does Welfare Bring More Babies?" Murray developed this theme and also proposed that the solution to the out-of-wedlock "problem" was to end all types of social assistance, including welfare payments, to single mothers and to increase the stigma associated with out-of-wedlock childbearing.

Although Murray's ideas were well-received by many in conservative circles, he was criticized for his analytical methods. For example, in *Losing Ground*, he employed "thought experiments"—exercises in drawing conclusions from hypothetical scenarios—to make a number of his points rather than using widely accepted social science techniques. Murray's reputation for controversy was established when he published in 1994, along with Richard Herrnstein, *The Bell Curve*, which undertook an examination of intelligence, race, and social problems. While the book was a best-seller, it generated a heated debate within academic circles and the media for its assertions of a black-white intellectual gap that explains the overrepresentation, for example, of blacks living in poverty and bearing children out of wedlock.

Source: Charles Murray, *Losing Ground* (New York: Basic Books, 1984); Charles Murray, "The Coming White Underclass," *Wall Street Journal*, October 29, 1993, A14; Charles Murray, "Does Welfare Bring More Babies?" *The Public Interest*, 115 (Spring 1994): 17–30; Tom Morganthau with Pat Wingert, "IQ: Is It Destiny?" *Newsweek*, October 24, 1994, 52.

The following twelve CQ Weekly *articles trace the evolution of the welfare reform legislation that was enacted in 1996 and look ahead toward the issues that could shape welfare policy in coming years, especially during congressional reauthorization of welfare reform in 2002.*

Long-Awaited Welfare Proposal Would Make Gradual Changes

By Jeffrey L. Katz
(Reprinted from CQ Weekly, *June 18, 1994)*

President Clinton, who promised during his presidential campaign "to end welfare as we know it," is trying to phase it out instead.

His proposal, unveiled June 14, takes an incremental approach to such changes as imposing time limits on welfare benefits. While many lawmakers have said Congress is too busy with health care to take up welfare, House Ways and Means Committee leaders said June 17 that they would try to get a bill to the floor this summer.

The long-advertised centerpiece of Clinton's plan is the requirement that recipients would have to work within two years of accepting welfare benefits. Those who could not find a job would be placed in federally subsidized jobs. Because most welfare recipients have little education or job experience, the federal government would ease their transition into the workforce by spending more on job training and child care.

"We propose to offer people on welfare a simple contract," Clinton said in a speech at Kansas City, Missouri. "We will help you get the skills you need, but after two years, anyone who can go to work must go to work—in the private sector if possible, in a subsidized job if necessary. But work is preferable to welfare. And it must be enforced."

Clinton was forced to phase in his proposal—applying it only to people born after 1971—because it would cost too much to include all welfare recipients immediately, and he said in April that he would not suggest new taxes to pay for it. He also decided not to follow the lead of House Republicans and some moderate Democrats to cut off most welfare benefits to immigrants, although he did suggest new restrictions.

The administration outlined an array of financing schemes worth $9.3 billion over five years to pay for the changes, including some restrictions in aid to immigrants, small cuts in some entitlement programs, and fees diverted from unrelated programs.

Besides the financing, the proposal offered few new details from drafts that had been widely circulated. However, it did reflect last-minute decisions to allow states to deny additional benefits to welfare recipients who had more children and to permit recipients to work in subsidized jobs without limit as long as they continued to look for unsubsidized positions.

Critics in Both Parties

Some congressional liberals immediately criticized the plan for dealing too harshly with welfare recipients. But the strongest fire came from Republicans, who complained that Clinton's plan was much more liberal than his campaign rhetoric. They denounced it for encompassing only part of the welfare caseload, for doing too little to discourage illegitimate births, for providing too much flexibility in the time limits and for continuing to give some welfare assistance to immigrants.

"The president is brilliant at describing a Ferrari, but his staff continues to deliver a Yugo," said Newt Gingrich of Georgia, the House Republican whip.

Senate Minority Leader Bob Dole, R-Kan., quipped that the proposal might only represent "the end of welfare reform as we know it."

Clinton had been pressured to reveal his welfare plan by moderate Democrats who were eager to bring a plan before the voters this fall and by Republicans who taunted him for neglecting his campaign pledge.

In the absence of an administration proposal, a number of welfare bills have been introduced recently in Congress. These measures indicate that welfare reform can mean anything from terminating all benefits to unwed teenage mothers to simply giving states a block grant to run their welfare programs as they wish.

Among Democrats, Sen. Tom Harkin of Iowa expressed "serious concerns" about whether Clinton's plan was realistic. Some Hispanic members quickly objected to any cuts in aid to immigrants. But Rep. Robert T. Matsui, D-Calif., called it "a positive step in the sense that the president has made this an issue of national importance and concern, one that we have to deal with, probably in 1995."

Any welfare plan will have difficulty moving people off welfare within a strict time frame and creating jobs for those who cannot find work, said Judith M. Gueron, president of the Manpower Demonstration Research Corp., which evaluates social programs for the disadvantaged.

While Clinton's plan to phase in the work requirements "can be criticized for not changing things fast enough," she said, "it might provide an opportunity to find out whether this can be done and what it's going to cost."

Starting the Plan

As proposed by Clinton, the legislation would take effect October 1, 1995, although states could petition the federal government for a delay. All programs would have to be fully implemented within two years of the plan's start.

The work requirements would apply to those born after 1971. This group would constitute about one-third of the welfare caseload in 1997 and two-thirds of all welfare recipients by 2004. States would have the option of including more of the caseload.

The administration says that focusing on the youngest welfare recipients would encourage teenagers to take more responsibility for their lives. Critics of this approach say it would force mothers with the youngest children into the workforce first and bypass older recipients who might be more in need of work requirements and job assistance.

Time Limits

The plan would limit the amount of time someone could receive benefits to underscore that welfare is meant to be a temporary safety net. Recipients who are capable of working would be limited to two years of government cash assistance throughout their lifetime.

Exemptions would be provided to those who are seriously ill or caring for a disabled or seriously ill child. As they entered the welfare system, recipients would receive a twelve-month deferral from the time limits for their first child. They would receive a twelve-week deferral for another child.

In addition, any time spent on welfare up to age eighteen would not be counted toward the two-year time limit.

States would be permitted to extend the time limit for individuals enrolled in an education or training program and for those who were learning-disabled, illiterate, or faced other "serious obstacles to employment." Extensions also would be given to those who were not given access to the services specified by the state in a written agreement with the applicant. These extensions could not amount to more than 10 percent of the eligible caseload.

Clinton made the two-year limit a cornerstone of his 1992 campaign, and there appears to be strong support for it in Congress. However, many liberals object to what they consider an arbitrary time limit.

Work and Training

All welfare recipients born after 1971 would be required to search for a job during their first twelve weeks on the welfare rolls. Those who could not find a job would be required either to attend school or to undergo job training. Those who could not find jobs within two years would be placed in federally subsidized positions.

Individuals who applied for welfare would have to sign a written agreement that would obligate them to follow plans to increase their employability. These contracts would detail the state's responsibility to provide them with education, training, and job placement services.

The main training component would be expanding the Job Opportunities and Basic Skills (JOBS) program created by the 1988 overhaul (PL 100-485) of federal welfare programs. JOBS gives states funds for education, training, and work for recipients of Aid to Families with Dependent Children (AFDC). The proposal would raise the federal contribution to JOBS from $1 billion in fiscal 1994 to $1.5 billion in fiscal 1996 and increase the federal matching rate to the states.

In all, the plan envisions spending an additional $2.8 billion over five years for more education, training, and job placement assistance for recipients.

Those welfare recipients who were unable to find private sector jobs within two years would be required to participate in a government-sponsored job called the WORK program.

Each state would run a WORK program that would make paid work assignments available to recipients who reached the time limit. States could choose to subsidize nonprofit or private-sector jobs, give employers other financial incentives or hire JOBS graduates for public work.

States would provide child care, transportation, and other services to help individuals participate in the program.

WORK participants generally would be paid the minimum wage. Each WORK assignment would be for fifteen to thirty-five hours per week, at the state's discretion. Participants who did not work the determined number of hours would have their wages reduced correspondingly.

An individual's WORK assignment could last up to twelve months. Recipients then would be required to search for an unsubsidized job, followed, if necessary, by another WORK assignment. States would have to make a comprehensive assessment of anyone who spent two years in the program.

The plan sets aside $1.2 billion over five years for WORK slots. By fiscal 2000, the administration estimates, 394,000 people would be in subsidized jobs under the WORK program.

If a job did not pay as much as AFDC benefits, the worker could receive funds to make up the difference.

Sanctions would be imposed on recipients who did not attend job training programs or refused to work. For example, payment under the WORK program would be by the hour; individuals who skipped work would not get paid for the requisite hours. Those who refused a WORK assignment or an offer for an unsubsidized job would lose their opportunity for pay and any AFDC benefits they might be entitled to for up to six months.

Incentives, Child Care

Forcing poor people off the welfare rolls will require making work more financially rewarding to them, the administration says.

Its plan says one incentive was enacted in last year's budget-reconciliation bill (PL 103-66) with the expansion of the earned-income tax credit (EITC), which reduces the taxes of the working poor and gives them a check if they owe no taxes. The administration plan encourages states to bolster its effect by trying strategies such as paying the EITC in installments throughout the year, rather than at year's end.

The administration said that overhauling the health care system as it has proposed would ensure that welfare recipients remain eligible for health coverage after they move into the workforce.

The administration calls for spending $2.7 billion over five years to pay for child care for those in the mandatory education and training programs, the WORK slots, and for one year after welfare recipients join the workforce. It would add another $1.5 billion to expand child care for working poor families.

Steps also would be taken to encourage welfare recipients to work by letting them keep more of their income. Under current law, AFDC recipients generally lose $1 of benefits for each $1 they earn by working. The administration proposes disregarding at least $120 in earnings per month when calculating an individual's AFDC benefits. States also could let welfare parents keep more than the $50 in child support payments they can retain under current law.

Illegitimacy, Child Support

Saying that illegitimate births make young women more likely to need welfare, Clinton proposes to lead a national campaign, orchestrated by a new nonprofit agency, against teen pregnancy. The plan envisions a national information clearinghouse and grants to local programs to combat teen pregnancy, with a five-year cost of $300 million.

Every school-age parent or pregnant teenager who received or applied for welfare would be required to finish school or enroll in a JOBS program.

Parents who were minors would be required to live with a responsible adult, preferably a parent. States now have the option of requiring these teenage mothers to reside in their parents' household. States also would have the option to limit benefit increases when all welfare recipients, including those born before 1972, have more children, as New Jersey, Georgia, and Arkansas have done.

On the principle that parents should be the first source of support for their children, the plan suggests that more efforts be made to establish paternity at birth, and the administration proposes to spend $600 million over five years to improve enforcement of court orders for child support and related programs.

Mothers who apply for AFDC would be required to cooperate to establish paternity. Once paternity information is given to the states, officials would have one year to establish paternity or risk losing a portion of their federal matching funds for AFDC benefits.

Some children's advocates have called for bolder approaches, such as having the federal government take responsibility for enforcement and adequacy of support awards.

Eligibility Changes

The plan would give states the option of making it easier for two-parent families to be eligible for AFDC payments. Currently, AFDC eligibility for two-parent families is limited to those in which the principal wage earner is unemployed but has worked in six of the last thirteen calendar quarters.

The administration says current law penalizes welfare recipients who want to get married. However, Republicans charge that loosening the laws would encourage married couples to apply for welfare and thereby expand the rolls significantly.

Reconciliation: GOP Produces Welfare Agreement, Urges Clinton to Sign On

By Jeffrey L. Katz
(Reprinted from CQ Weekly, *November 11, 1995)*

Congressional Republicans virtually completed agreement November 10 on legislation to overhaul welfare and said President Clinton ought to support the measure even though it ignores most of his recent suggestions.

Most of the measure will be included in the conference agreement on the deficit-reducing budget-reconciliation bill (HR 2491), which both chambers plan to consider the week of November 13.

The welfare provisions are expected to save about $81.5 billion over seven years. Related savings in the earned-income tax credit (EITC), which provides tax relief to the working poor, would save about $32.5 billion.

The legislation represents a compromise between House and Senate versions of a free-standing welfare bill (HR 4) that would give states broad new authority over welfare policy, create new time limits and work requirements on welfare benefits, and restrict social services for noncitizens, drug addicts, alcoholics, and children.

Among the issues that GOP negotiators settled was to require states to continue spending a certain percentage of their welfare funding and to provide more federal money for child care. Republicans also chose to retain federal control over key aspects of foster care and adoption assistance as well as for nutrition programs for pregnant women and their young children.

But a few major issues were still unresolved by the evening of November 10, including whether to end federal funding of welfare checks to unwed teenage mothers and for children born to welfare recipients.

Several Republicans who negotiated the welfare provisions said they were measures that President Clinton should support.

"This is a bill that the president has no reason not to sign," said Sen. Rick Santorum, R-Pa. "This is well within the parameters he set for welfare when he ran for president."

But an administration spokesman said November 10 that he was discouraged by the Republican negotiations, which he described as "a backroom budget deal" rather than welfare reform.

The administration, under pressure from congressional liberals and advocates for the poor, issued a fresh assertion November 9 that the likely product of Republican efforts would plunge more children into poverty.

An Office of Management and Budget (OMB) study concluded that the welfare bill passed by the Senate—which was less stringent than the House-Senate compromise—

would plunge 1.2 million more children below the poverty line. The House-passed welfare bill would cause 2.1 million children to slip into poverty, it said.

The report exacerbated a split among congressional Democrats, who were largely ignored in the closed-door welfare negotiations. Some liberals on the issue argued that Clinton now has no choice but to veto the measure unless it is completely redrawn. Moderates suggested that Clinton work with Republicans to improve the product.

Key Republicans on the House Ways and Means Committee quickly dismissed the OMB report. Committee Chairman Bill Archer, R-Texas, called it "a road map to another Clinton flip-flop."

White House Press Secretary Michael D. McCurry played down the likelihood of a veto November 9, saying that if Congress sent Clinton the Senate version, he might have to accept it because it would be "within striking distance" of what the president wants. But he added that House-Senate conferees "appear to be moving in the wrong direction."

Tie-in with Reconciliation

Although House and Senate negotiators worked on the free-standing welfare bill, the measure's overall savings were set by broader discussions over the reconciliation bill.

And the welfare measure's fiscal components, at least, will be included in the reconciliation bill to help Republicans meet their balanced-budget targets. Democrats invoked the so-called Byrd rule October 27 to knock out significant welfare provisions from the Senate reconciliation bill.

If some provisions again cannot overcome the procedural hurdle that limits the scope of reconciliation bills and prohibits the inclusion of extraneous issues, Republicans will attach the welfare overhaul's policy provisions to a must-pass spending bill, Santorum said.

But if the reconciliation bill is vetoed—as expected—Republicans would get another chance to pass a free-standing welfare bill that included all financing and policy provisions.

Both the House and Senate welfare bills would end the sixty-year-old federal guarantee of providing welfare checks to eligible low-income mothers and children.

These were the major issues still unresolved late November 10:

- **Restrictions on aid.** Negotiators were considering prohibiting states from using federal funds to give welfare checks to unwed teenage mothers or for children born to welfare recipients. But they would permit states to opt out of this restriction if the states passed legislation to do so.
- **Food stamps.** The legislation would permit states to gain broad authority over their food stamp programs and receive funding in block grants, or predetermined lump sums. Negotiators were still deliberating the criteria for getting a block grant and the number of states that would be permitted to do so.

- **Child nutrition.** House negotiators wanted to give states the option to receive their child nutrition funding as block grants, but senators balked.

These are some issues that GOP welfare negotiators said they had agreed to:

- **State funding.** For the next five years, states would be penalized for spending less than 75 percent of what they previously spent on cash welfare. States could choose to use their welfare spending in fiscal 1995, 1994 or the average of 1992–1994 when making the comparison.
- **Child care.** The measure would provide $2.5 billion of the $3 billion over five years that the Senate included for additional child care funding. Total child care funding would be $12.5 billion over five years.
- **Noncitizens.** Current and future immigrants would be denied food stamps and Supplemental Security Income (SSI), which provides cash benefits to the aged, poor, and disabled. Also, the measure dropped a Senate provision that would have made an immigrant's sponsor financially responsible for that individual even after the immigrant became a citizen.
- **Foster care.** States would continue to be reimbursed for each low-income child they placed in foster care or assisted in adoption, but funding for other child protection programs would be limited.
- **SSI.** The legislation would make it harder for children to qualify as disabled under SSI, but it drops House-passed provisions that would have given medical assistance but not cash to children not considered severely disabled. Instead, negotiators agreed to give these less severely disabled children 25 percent less in cash than the full cash benefit available. Rep. Jim McCrery, R-La., who pushed for tougher restrictions on SSI, said, "We went a long way to solving the problem of abuse of the program."

To Ease the Impact on Poverty

To mitigate the impact of welfare legislation on poverty, the administration's OMB report suggested starting with the Senate bill and adjusting it to:

- Make permanent an increase in child care funding, worth $3 billion over five years, that would otherwise expire after 2000.
- Require states to maintain their current level of welfare spending and set aside more money for states to use if the economy faltered.
- Give more money to states that are most successful in moving people from welfare to work.
- Provide vouchers redeemable for goods and services to children whose parents cannot find work after exhausting their five-year limit on welfare checks.

The report also said Republicans ought to abandon planned cuts in the EITC and raise the minimum wage from $4.25 to $5.15 per hour.

Some liberals on the issue had pressured the administration to analyze the impact of the Senate bill. They said the report issued November 9 should lead to a veto, in part, because Republicans would never agree to Clinton's suggestions.

"There is no possibility that any of these improvements will be made," said Daniel Patrick Moynihan of New York, ranking Democrat on the Finance Committee. Moynihan led a group of Democrats who voted against the Senate welfare bill, which was approved 87–12 on September 19.

But Democratic Sen. John B. Breaux of Louisiana argued that the administration's study used an unusually broad definition of poverty by taking into account proposed cuts in the EITC, food stamps, and housing. Under the official poverty definition, which considers only earned income and government cash assistance, the Senate bill would increase the number of children in poverty—now estimated at 15.5 million—by 300,000, Breaux said.

Another moderate, Sen. Joseph I. Lieberman, D-Conn., said the administration report "is a reason to go forward with bipartisan action to improve the Senate welfare reform bill" and not "an excuse to veto."

Breaux did express disappointment with the administration's timing of the study. "Where was this information before we were called upon to vote?" Breaux asked.

Welfare: Conference Report Highlights

By Jeffrey L. Katz
(Reprinted from CQ Weekly, *December 23, 1995)*

Here are highlights of the conference report on the welfare overhaul bill (HR 4—H Rept 104-430). The House adopted it December 21 and the Senate cleared it December 22. President Clinton has said he will veto it.

Cash Welfare Grants

Benefits and eligibility. The bill would create a block grant to replace Aid to Families with Dependent Children (AFDC), the nation's main cash welfare program, and several related programs.

As a result, low-income people who met the eligibility criteria for AFDC would no longer automatically be entitled to cash benefits. Instead, states would have wide discretion in determining eligibility.

Funding. Federal funding for the block grant would be $16.3 billion annually. Money would be distributed to each state in proportion to its federal funding for AFDC and related programs in either fiscal 1995, fiscal 1994 or the average of fiscal 1992–1994, whichever was higher.

To receive their full share of federal welfare funds, states would have to spend at least 75 percent of the state funds they spent on AFDC and related programs in fiscal 1994.

Several additional funds would be available for states, including $800 million over five years for states with growing populations, a $1.7 billion revolving loan fund, and $1 billion over five years in matching grants to states with high unemployment.

Additional financial bonuses would be available to states that reduced out-of-wedlock birth rates and that were most successful in moving welfare recipients into the workplace.

Restrictions on aid. Federal funds for cash welfare generally could not be provided to any adult for more than five years.

States would also be prohibited from using federal funds to provide welfare checks for children born to welfare recipients. However, states could opt out of this prohibition by passing legislation to do so.

States would have the option to deny welfare checks to unwed teenage parents until they reach age eighteen.

Work requirements. Adults receiving welfare benefits would be required to begin working within two years of receiving aid. States would be required to place at least 50 percent of their overall welfare caseload in jobs by 2002.

Supplemental Security Income

Substance abuse. Drug addiction and alcoholism would no longer be considered disabilities under Supplemental Security Income (SSI), a cash benefit program for the low-income aged, blind, and disabled.

Disabled children. The bill would make it harder for children to be considered disabled to qualify for SSI. Children considered not severely disabled would be eligible for only 75 percent of full SSI benefits.

Child Support Enforcement

Registries. States would be required to create a central case registry to track the status of all child-support orders. Similar federal registries would be created to help track deadbeat parents nationwide.

Enforcement. States would be required to pass laws to suspend driver's licenses of those who owed past-due child support.

Other Issues

Immigration. Legal immigrants who arrived in the United States after the bill was enacted would be denied most low-income federal social services for five years after their arrival. Refugees, veterans, those granted asylum, and immigrants who had worked for at least ten years would be exempt from these restrictions.

Legal immigrants who already resided in the United States would be ineligible for SSI and food stamps, and states could exempt them from more programs.

Child welfare. States would continue to be reimbursed by the federal government for the maintenance—or room and board costs—involved in placing each eligible low-income child in foster care or in adoption.

Other federal funding for child welfare programs would come from two new block grants. One would encompass administration and training costs involved in foster care and adoption, including moving children out of unsafe homes and monitoring foster homes. The other block grant would consolidate child abuse prevention and treatment programs.

Child care. All major federal child care programs—including those for the working poor as well as for welfare recipients—would be folded into the existing Child Care and Development Block Grant. The current block grant would be amended to give states broad authority to run their own programs.

Mandatory, or guaranteed, federal funding for this block grant would be $1.3 billion in fiscal 1997, rising to $2.05 billion in fiscal 2002, for a total of $11 billion. An additional $1 billion in discretionary funding would also be authorized each year through fiscal 2002.

Child nutrition. Spending on child nutrition programs would be reduced by about $3.9 billion over seven years. Up to seven states could opt to receive their school lunch and breakfast programs in the form of a block grant, giving them more control over their programs while getting their federal funding in lump sum payments.

Food stamps. The bill would scale back food stamp benefits by cutting individual allotments and making other formula adjustments. Able-bodied recipients between the ages of eighteen and fifty who do not have dependents would have to work.

States could receive their food stamp assistance as a block grant. Penalties for fraud and abuse would double.

Presidential Veto Message: Welfare-to-Work Provisions Cited in Veto of Overhaul

(Reprinted from CQ Weekly, *January 13, 1996)*

Following is the text of President Clinton's January 9 message to Congress vetoing a bill (HR 4) to overhaul the nation's welfare system:

TO THE HOUSE OF REPRESENTATIVES:

I am returning herewith without my approval HR 4, the "Personal Responsibility and Work Opportunity Act of 1995." In disapproving HR 4, I am nevertheless determined to keep working with the Congress to enact real, bipartisan welfare reform. The current welfare system is broken and must be replaced, for the sake of the taxpayers who pay for it and the people who are trapped by it. But HR 4 does too little to move people from welfare to work. It is burdened with deep budget cuts and structural changes that fall short of real reform. I urge the Congress to work with me in good faith to produce a bipartisan welfare reform agreement that is tough on work and responsibility, but not tough on children and on parents who are responsible and who want to work.

The Congress and the administration are engaged in serious negotiations toward a balanced budget that is consistent with our priorities—one of which is to "reform welfare," as November's agreement between Republicans and Democrats made clear. Welfare reform must be considered in the context of other critical and related issues such as Medicaid and the earned-income tax credit. Americans know we have to reform the broken welfare system, but they also know that welfare reform is about moving people from welfare to work, not playing budget politics.

The administration has and will continue to set forth in detail our goals for reform and our objections to this legislation. The administration strongly supported the Senate Democratic and House Democratic welfare reform bills, which ensured that states would have the resources and incentives to move people from welfare to work and that children would be protected. I strongly support time limits, work requirements, the toughest possible child support enforcement, and requiring minor mothers to live at home as a condition of assistance, and I am pleased that these central elements of my approach have been addressed in HR 4.

We remain ready at any moment to sit down in good faith with Republicans and Democrats in the Congress to work out an acceptable welfare reform plan that is motivated by the urgency of reform rather than by a budget plan that is contrary to America's values. There is a bipartisan consensus around the country on the fundamental elements of real welfare reform, and it would be a tragedy for this Congress to squander this historic opportunity to achieve it. It is essential for the Congress to address shortcomings in the legislation in the following areas:

- Work and Child Care: Welfare reform is first and foremost about work. HR 4 weakens several important work provisions that are vital to welfare reform's success. The final welfare reform legislation should provide sufficient child care to enable recipients to leave welfare for work; reward states for placing people in jobs; restore the guarantee of health coverage for poor families; require states to maintain their stake in moving people from welfare to work; and protect states and families in the event of economic downturn and population growth. In addition, the Congress should abandon efforts included in the budget-reconciliation bill that would gut the earned-income tax credit, a powerful work incentive that is enabling hundreds of thousands of families to choose work over welfare.

- Deep Budget Cuts and Damaging Structural Changes: HR 4 was designed to meet an arbitrary budget target rather than to achieve serious reform. The legislation makes damaging structural changes and deep budget cuts that would fall hardest on children and undermine states' ability to move people from welfare to work. We should work together to balance the budget and reform welfare, but the Congress should not use the words "welfare reform" as a cover to violate the nation's values. Making $60 billion in budget cuts and massive structural changes in a variety of programs, including foster care and adoption assistance, help for disabled children, legal immigrants, food stamps, and school lunch is not welfare reform. The final welfare reform legislation should reduce the magnitude of these budget cuts and the sweep of structural changes that have little connection to the central goal of work-based reform. We must demand responsibility from young mothers and young fathers, not penalize children for their parents' mistakes.

I am deeply committed to working with the Congress to reach bipartisan agreement on an acceptable welfare reform bill that addresses these and other concerns. We owe it to the people who sent us here not to let this opportunity slip away by doing the wrong thing or failing to act at all.

WILLIAM J. CLINTON
THE WHITE HOUSE
January 9, 1996

GOP Prepares to Act on Governors' Plan

By Jeffrey L. Katz
(Reprinted from CQ Weekly, *February 17, 1996)*

The nation's governors have revitalized Congress's quest to overhaul welfare programs and related social services. Congressional Republicans are preparing to modify a welfare proposal put forth by the governors, which they would then consider passing—daring President Clinton to veto a plan that has bipartisan support.

GOP leaders are still assessing what changes to make to the plan unanimously approved February 6 by the National Governors Association (NGA). They also are weighing whether to attach a welfare bill to must-pass legislation raising the $4.9 trillion national debt ceiling. "What the governors did is being perceived around here as providing enormous tail wind to push for a deal," a House leadership aide said February 13.

The NGA plan is based on the GOP welfare bill (HR 4—H Rept 104-430) that Clinton vetoed January 9. The governors endorsed many key aspects of the bill, including ending the sixty-year-old federal guarantee of providing cash to all eligible low-income mothers and children. But the governors called for easing the bill's work requirements and many of its proposed restrictions on social services. The NGA also asked for more federal child care money to help welfare recipients get jobs.

Congressional Republicans seem likely to scale back some of the governors' suggestions, largely in an attempt to save more federal money.

Both parties have much at stake as they seek to fulfill their campaign promises to overhaul welfare.

Revamping the nation's welfare programs is a top priority for House Republicans—who included it in their "Contract with America"—and they consider it an important element in cutting federal spending. It is also important to Clinton, who vowed in 1992 to "end welfare as we know it."

But the two sides had different ideas about how to fulfill their goals. Republicans passed a welfare bill drawn largely on conservative terms and with little Democratic support. Clinton vetoed it twice—on December 6 as part of the deficit-reducing budget-reconciliation bill (HR 2491), then a month later as a free-standing welfare bill.

Moderates in both parties are eager to compromise and enact a welfare bill. So are most of the nation's governors, who would gain more flexibility to run their own welfare programs no matter what version passes.

But the NGA proposal is troubling to core supporters of both parties. Among Democrats, many liberals adamantly oppose any bill that would end a low-income family's entitlement to welfare. Among Republicans, many conservatives disapprove of the governors' attempt to loosen the bill's language regarding work requirements and curtailing out-of-wedlock births. Some Republicans are also reluctant to give Clinton another chance to sign a bill and claim a key legislative victory.

But the prevailing view for the moment seems to have been captured by Rep. E. Clay Shaw Jr., R-Fla., chairman of the Ways and Means Human Resources Subcommittee: "We may have finally found a way to do business."

Panel Hearings

Congressional Republicans are expected to decide on a strategy soon. The two panels with prime responsibility for welfare legislation will hold hearings on the NGA proposal the week of February 19. The Human Resources Subcommittee plans to begin February 20, followed two days later by the Senate Finance Committee.

With a relatively compressed legislative schedule this year, neither House nor Senate leaders are likely to plan for another protracted debate on welfare. GOP leaders have said they will act on the debt ceiling by February 29. Failing that, they could try to move a free-standing welfare bill.

Any revised bill would probably begin in the House, where conservatives hold more sway than in the Senate. Some of those conservatives are already objecting to the governors' moderating influence.

A Split Over Overhaul

Republicans generally amassed solid support among their ranks for their welfare overhaul efforts last year, though they had to resolve disagreements between Senate moderates and conservatives. But further moderating the plan along the lines of the NGA proposal could prompt deeper GOP splits.

The pressure points include:

- **Politics.** Some Republicans, especially campaign strategists, would prefer not to move another welfare bill. They think Clinton will be haunted by his vetoes as he tries to explain why he failed to follow through on a popular campaign promise. These Republicans do not want to give Clinton another chance to fulfill that promise. Others maintain that the GOP would gain by giving the issue another try regardless of what Clinton does.

  If Clinton signed the welfare bill, he would anger his party's liberals while Republicans boasted of a key legislative accomplishment drawn largely on their terms. If Clinton vetoed the welfare bill—especially one supported by Democratic moderates—Republicans would have fresh evidence of Clinton's allegiance to the left.

  House Speaker Newt Gingrich, R-Ga., is said to be leaning toward another attempt to overhaul welfare. Shaw said, "I think the majority of the people would like to take another run at it, even if it means that the president's going to regain some of the credibility he lost on it with a veto."

- **Finances.** A main Republican motive for overhauling welfare was to help balance the federal budget in seven years. They have abandoned balanced-budget legislation this year, but they still want to cut federal spending. And the governors proposed to save considerably less with their welfare plan than congressional Republicans.

  The Congressional Budget Office estimated that HR 4 would save $64.1 billion, over seven years, including $4 billion in Medicaid. The NGA handled Medicaid separately. Its welfare plan would save about $44 billion, according to unofficial estimates. A GOP source predicted that the governors' proposal would be altered to save at least $50 billion.

- **Policy.** The governors' plan exacerbates differences among those Republicans who believe that states should be free to do as they like on welfare and those who believe that certain policies—especially those designed to reduce out-of-wedlock births—ought to be set in Washington.

Two aspects of the governors' proposal are particularly troubling to conservatives. One would make it easier for states to meet requirements that they move a certain percentage of welfare recipients into the workplace. The other would let states decide whether to use federal money to provide welfare checks for children born to welfare recipients. This latter point, known as the family cap, has been an emotional issue throughout the welfare debate.

Conservatives preferred the original House version of HR 4, which would have prohibited states from using federal funds to provide welfare checks for children born to welfare recipients. The Senate version would have let states decide whether to do so. The conference report would have imposed the prohibition, but enabled states to opt out by passing legislation to do so.

Two Republican members who have pushed for the family cap—James M. Talent of Missouri and Tim Hutchinson of Arkansas—distributed a letter to their GOP colleagues deriding the NGA proposal as "simply unacceptable. It completely misses the point of what real welfare reform is all about."

Democrats' Dissension

The NGA welfare plan also seems destined to cause dissension among Democrats. Liberals are wary of any plan that removes a poor family's entitlement for welfare checks. Civil rights groups denounced the plan at a February 13 news conference and called for more education, training, and child care for welfare recipients.

However, moderate Democrats were encouraged. Rep. Sander M. Levin, D-Mich., said the governors "had moved the ball a step forward. . . . But there needs to be considerably more work on key ingredients." Levin said that would include more federal oversight and more assurances that states would maintain welfare funding.

Clinton's Changing Welfare Views

By Jeffrey L. Katz
(Reprinted from CQ Weekly, July 27, 1996)

President Clinton's views on welfare have evolved over the years, as follows:

- **1988:** Clinton, then governor of Arkansas, plays a key role as a leader of the National Governors Association in pushing Congress to move what was then considered a dramatic welfare measure. The Family Support Act (PL 100-485), which has strong bipartisan support, emphasizes education and training for welfare recipients as a way to prepare them to get jobs.

- **1992:** In his presidential campaign, Clinton promises to "end welfare as we know it." He says welfare recipients should be required to work within two years of receiving benefits. The issue helps define him as a "New Democrat" unbeholden to the party's liberal wing; it is a key plank in his successful effort to gain support from middle class and suburban voters.

- **1994:** The administration puts the welfare issue aside to focus on its health care proposal. Finally, after intense negotiations within the administration, Clinton unveils his proposal in June. The centerpiece is the work requirement, which would apply only to people born after 1971. Those who could not find work would be placed in federally subsidized jobs. The federal government would continue to play a key role in the welfare system, spending more money on job training and child care for welfare recipients and continuing to guarantee a check to all eligible low-income mothers and children. Clinton never seriously pushes the plan and Congress never acts on it.

- **1995:** Buoyed by the November 1994 election in which they wrested control of Congress from the Democrats, Republicans swiftly move a conservative welfare overhaul (HR 4) through the House in March. Clinton joins most Democrats in condemning it. "A narrow, partisan Republican majority passed a bill that is weak on work and tough on children," he says.

  The Senate passes a more moderate version in September, drawing Clinton's praise. He said if the effort remains bipartisan, "we will have welfare reform this year, and it will be a very great thing. But if the Congress gives in to extremist pressure . . . they will kill welfare reform."

  But Democratic support wanes as Republicans combine the House and Senate versions, and the administration releases a study that says the legislation would push more than 1 million children below the poverty line. Clinton vetoes the deficit-reducing budget-reconciliation bill (HR 2491) that includes many welfare provisions December 6.

- **1996:** Clinton vetoes the separate welfare bill January 9, saying, "it does too little to move people from welfare to work." He then tries to put the onus on Republicans in his January 23 State of the Union address, urging them to send him a bipartisan welfare plan and promising to "sign it immediately."

  The National Governors Association recommends a variation of HR 4, mainly to give states more flexibility and gain more federal child care assistance. Neither Clinton nor Senate Majority Leader Bob Dole, R-Kan., the likely GOP presidential nominee, immediately endorses the proposals, though Clinton calls them "encouraging."

  But on February 28, Health and Human Services Secretary Donna E. Shalala tells the Senate Finance Committee that Clinton cannot support the NGA proposal without significant changes.

Republicans prepare to send Clinton another welfare bill that would also revamp Medicaid. Clinton says the Medicaid provisions are unacceptable and terms them a "poison pill" that would doom the welfare measures.

Clinton infuriates Republicans during his May 18 radio address, in which he praises a dramatic new welfare plan proposed by Wisconsin that Republicans say goes far beyond anything Clinton supports. Wisconsin cannot begin the program without waivers of federal laws and regulations. When the administration does not immediately grant them, House Republicans take the unusual step of promoting legislation to allow Wisconsin to put the plan in place. The measure (HR 3562) passes the House on June 6, but languishes in the Senate.

After Republicans move the joint welfare-Medicaid plan through House and Senate committees, they succumb the week of July 8 to pressure from within their ranks to drop the Medicaid provisions. "We now stand on the verge of having a welfare reform proposal that can get bipartisan support and the president's signature," says White House spokesman Mike McCurry. He says Clinton would seek changes, which he describes as "not insurmountable hurdles."

On July 16, with floor action about to begin in both chambers on the welfare legislation, Clinton says: "I think we have now reached a real turning point, a breakthrough for welfare reform."

The following day, Senate Minority Leader Tom Daschle, D-S.D., tries to debunk the idea that Clinton will sign whatever welfare bill Congress sends to him, saying, "He will veto a bad bill."

Presidential News Conference: Clinton Says Welfare Bill Is a 'Real Step Forward'

(Reprinted from CQ Weekly, *August 3, 1996)*

Following is a transcript of President Clinton's July 31 news conference during which he announced that he would sign the welfare overhaul bill (HR 3734). The transcript was provided by the White House.

President Clinton: Good afternoon. When I ran for president four years ago, I pledged to end welfare as we know it.

I have worked very hard for four years to do just that. Today, the Congress will vote on legislation that gives us a chance to live up to that promise—to transform a broken system that traps too many people in a cycle of dependence to one that emphasizes work and independence; to give people on welfare a chance to draw a paycheck, not a welfare check.

It gives us a better chance to give those on welfare what we want for all families in America, the opportunity to succeed at home and at work. For those reasons I will sign it into law.

The legislation is, however, far from perfect. There are parts of it that are wrong, and I will address those parts in a moment.

But, on balance, this bill is a real step forward for our country, our values, and for people who are on welfare. For fifteen years I have worked on this problem, as governor and as a president. I've spent time in welfare offices, I have talked to mothers on welfare who desperately want the chance to work and support their families independently. A long time ago I concluded that the current welfare system undermines the basic values of work, responsibility, and family, trapping generation after generation in dependency and hurting the very people it was designed to help.

'Historic Opportunity'

Today we have an historic opportunity to make welfare what it was meant to be—a second chance, not a way of life. And even though the bill has serious flaws that are unrelated to welfare reform, I believe we have a duty to seize the opportunity it gives us to end welfare as we know it.

Over the past three and one-half years I have done everything in my power as president to promote work and responsibility, working with forty-one states to give them sixty-nine welfare reform experiments. We have also required teen mothers to stay in school, required federal employees to pay their child support, cracked down on people who owe child support and crossed state lines.

As a result, child support collections are up 40 percent, to $11 billion, and there are 1.3 million fewer people on welfare today than there were when I took office. From the outset, however, I have also worked with members of both parties in Congress to achieve a national welfare reform bill that will make work and responsibility the law of the land. I made my principles for real welfare reform very clear from the beginning.

First and foremost, it should be about moving people from welfare to work. It should impose time limits on welfare. It should give people the child care and the health care they need to move from welfare to work without hurting their children. It should crack down on child support enforcement, and it should protect our children.

This legislation meets these principles. It gives us a chance we haven't had before—to break the cycle of dependency that has existed for millions and millions of our fellow citizens, exiling them from the world of work that gives structure, meaning, and dignity to most of our lives.

Different Priorities

We've come a long way in this debate. It's important to remember that not so very long ago, at the beginning of this very Congress, some wanted to put poor children in orphanages and take away all help for mothers simply because they were poor, young, and unmarried. Last year the Republican majority in Congress sent me legislation that had its priorities backward. It was soft on work and tough on children. It failed to provide child care and health care. It imposed deep and unacceptable cuts in school lunches, child welfare, and help for disabled children. The bill came to me twice and I vetoed it twice.

The bipartisan legislation before the Congress today is significantly better than the bills I vetoed. Many of the worst elements I objected to are out of it. And many of the improvements I asked for are included. First, the new bill is strong on work. It provides $4 billion more for child care so that mothers can move from welfare to work and protects their children by maintaining health and safety standards for day care. These things are very important. You cannot ask somebody on welfare to go to work if they're going to neglect their children in doing it.

It gives states powerful performance incentives to place people in jobs. It requires states to hold up their end of the bargain by maintaining their own spending on welfare. And it gives states the capacity to create jobs by taking money now used for welfare checks and giving it to employers as income subsidies as an incentive to hire people or (using it) to create community service jobs.

Second, this new bill is better for children than the two I vetoed. It keeps the national nutritional safety net intact by eliminating the food stamp cap and the optional block grant. It drops the deep cuts and devastating changes in school lunch, child welfare and help for disabled children. It allows states to use federal money to provide vouchers for children whose parents can't find work after the time limits expire. And it preserves the national guarantee of health care for poor children, the disabled, pregnant women, the elderly and people on welfare.

Just as important, this bill continues to include the child support enforcement measures I proposed two years ago, the most sweeping crack down on deadbeat parents in history. If every parent paid the child support they should, we could move 800,000 women and children off welfare immediately. With this bill we say to parents, if you don't pay the child support you owe, we will garnish your wages, take away your driver's license, track you across state lines and, as necessary, make you work off what you owe. It is a very important advance that could only be achieved in legislation. I did not have the executive authority to do this without a bill.

So I will sign this bill. First and foremost because the current system is broken. Second, because Congress has made many of the changes I sought. And, third, because even though serious problems remain in the nonwelfare reform provisions of the bill, this is the best chance we will have for a long, long time to complete the work of ending welfare as we know it by moving people from welfare to work, demanding responsibility, and doing better by children.

However, I want to be very clear. Some parts of this bill still go too far. And I am determined to see that those areas are corrected.

Nutrition Cuts

First, I am concerned that although we have made great strides to maintain the national nutritional safety net, this bill still cuts deeper than it should in nutritional assistance, mostly for working families with children. In the budget talks, we reached a tentative agreement on $21 billion in food stamp savings over the next several years. They are included in this bill.

However, the congressional majority insisted on another cut we did not agree to, repealing a reform adopted four years ago in Congress, which was to go into effect next year. It's called the Excess Shelter Reduction, which helps some of our hardest pressed working families. Finally, we were going to treat working families with children the same way we treat senior citizens who draw food stamps today.

Now, blocking this change, I believe—I know—will make it harder for some of our hardest pressed working families with children. This provision is a mistake, and I will work to correct it.

Effect on Immigrants

Second, I am deeply disappointed that the congressional leadership insisted on attaching to this extraordinarily important bill a provision that will hurt legal immigrants in America, people who work hard for their families, pay taxes, serve in our military. This provision has nothing to do with welfare reform. It is simply a budget-saving measure, and it is not right.

These immigrant families with children who fall on hard times through no fault of their own—for example because they face the same risks the rest of us do from accidents, from criminal assaults, from serious illnesses—they should be eligible for medical and other help when they need it.

The Republican majority could never have passed such a provision standing alone. You see that in the debate in the immigration bill, for example, over the Gallegly amendment and the question of education of undocumented and illegal immigrant children.

This provision will cause great stress for states, for localities, for medical facilities that have to serve large numbers of legal immigrants. It is just wrong to say to people, we'll let you work here, you're helping our country, you'll pay taxes, you serve in our military, you may get killed defending America—but if somebody mugs you on a street corner or you get cancer or you get hit by a car or the same thing happens to your children, we're not going to give you assistance any more.

I am convinced this would never have passed alone, and I am convinced when we send legislation to Congress to correct it, it will be corrected.

In the meantime, let me also say that I intend to take further executive action directing the INS to continue to work to remove the bureaucratic roadblocks to citizenship to all eligible, legal immigrants. I will do everything in my power, in other words, to make sure that this bill lifts people up and does not become an excuse for anyone to turn their backs on this problem or on people who are generally in need through no fault of their own.

This bill must also not let anyone off the hook. The states asked for this responsibility, now they have to shoulder it and not run away from it. We have to make sure that in the coming years reform and change actually result in moving people from welfare to work.

The business community must provide greater private sector jobs that people on welfare need to build good lives and strong families. I challenge every state to adopt the reforms that Wisconsin, Oregon, Missouri, and other states are proposing to do, to take the money that used to be available for welfare checks and offer it to the private sector as wage subsidies to begin to hire these people, to give them a chance to build their families and build their lives.

All of us have to rise to this challenge and see that—this reform, not as a chance to demonize or demean anyone, but instead as an opportunity to bring everyone fully into the mainstream of American life, to give them a chance to share in the prosperity and the promise that most of our people are enjoying today.

And we here in Washington must continue to do everything in our power to reward work and to expand opportunity for all people. The earned-income tax credit, which we expanded in 1993 dramatically, is now rewarding the work of 15 million working families.

I am pleased that congressional efforts to gut this tax cut for the hardest pressed working people have been blocked. This legislation preserves the EITC and its benefits for working families. Now we must increase the minimum wage, which also will benefit millions of working people with families and help them to offset the impact of some of the nutritional cuts in this bill.

Through these efforts, we all have to recognize, as I said in 1992, the best antipoverty program is still a job. I want to congratulate the members of Congress in both parties who worked together on this welfare reform legislation. I want to challenge them to put politics aside and continue to work together to meet our other challenges and to correct the problems that are still there with this legislation.

I am convinced that it does present an historic opportunity to finish the work of ending welfare as we know it, and that is why I have decided to sign it.

Effect on Children

Question: Mr. President, some civil rights groups and children's advocacy groups still say that they believe that this is going to hurt children. I wonder what your response is to that. And, also, it took you a little while to decide whether you would go along with this bill or not. Can you give us some sense of what you and your advisers kind of talked about and the mood in the White House over this?

Clinton: Sure. Well, first of all, the conference was not completed until late last evening, and there were changes being made in the bill right up to the very end. So when I went to bed last night, I didn't know what the bill said. And this was supposed to be a day off for me, and when I got up and I realized that the conference had completed its work late last night and that the bill was scheduled for a vote late this afternoon, after I did a little work around the house this morning, I came in and we went to work I think about 11:00.

And we simply—we got everybody in who had an interest in this and we went through every provision of the bill, line by line, so that I made sure that I understood exactly what had come out of the conference. And then I gave everybody in the administration who was there a chance to voice their opinion on it and to explore what their views were and what our options were. And as soon as we finished the meeting, I went in and had a brief talk with the vice president and with (White House Chief of Staff Leon E.) Panetta, and I told them that I had decided that, on balance, I should sign the bill. And then we called this press conference.

Question: And what about the civil rights groups?

Clinton: I would say to them that there are some groups who basically have never agreed with me on this, who never agreed that we should do anything to give the states much greater flexibility on this if it meant doing away with the individual entitlement to the welfare check. And that is still, I think, the central objection to most of the groups.

My view about that is that for a very long time it's hard to say that we've had anything that approaches a uniform AFDC (Aid to Families With Dependent Children) system when the benefits range from a low of $187 a month to a high of $655 a month for a family of three or four. And I think that the system we have is not working. It works for half the people who just use it for a little while and get off. It will continue to work for them. I think the states will continue to provide for them.

For the other half of the people who are trapped on it, it is not working. And I believe that the child support provisions here, the child care provisions here, the protection of the medical benefits—indeed, the expansion of the medical guarantee now from 1998 to 2002, mean that on balance these families will be better off. I think the problems in this bill are in the nonwelfare reform provisions, in the nutritional provisions that I mentioned and especially in the legal immigrant provisions that I mentioned.

Credit or Blame

Question: Mr. President, it seems likely there will be a kind of political contest to see who gets the credit or the blame on this measure. Sen. (Bob) Dole is out with a statement calling—saying that you've been brought along to sign his bill. Are you concerned at all that you will be seen as having been kind of dragged into going along with something that you originally promised to do and that this will look like you signing onto a Republican initiative?

Clinton: No. First of all, because I don't—you know, if we're doing the right thing there will be enough credit to go around. And if we're doing the wrong thing there will be enough blame to go around. I'm not worried about that. I've always wanted to work with Senator Dole and others. And before he left the Senate, I asked him not to leave the budget negotiations. So I'm not worried about that.

But that's a pretty hard case to make, since I vetoed their previous bills twice and since while they were talking about it we were doing it. It's now generally accepted by everybody who has looked at the evidence that we effected what the *New York Times* called a quiet revolution in welfare. There are 1.3 million fewer people on welfare today than there were when I took office.

But there are limits to what we can do with these waivers. We couldn't get the child support enforcement. We couldn't get the extra child care. Those are two things that we had to have legislation to do. And the third thing is we needed to put all the states in a position where they had to move right now to try to create more jobs. So far—I know that we had Wisconsin and earlier, Oregon, and I believe Missouri. And I think those are the only three states, for example, that had taken up the challenge that I gave to the governors in Vermont a couple of years ago to start taking the welfare payments and use it for wage subsidies to the private sector to actually create jobs. You can't tell people to go to work if there is no job out there.

So now they all have the power and they have financial incentives to create jobs, plus we've got the child care locked in and the medical care locked in and the child support enforcement locked in. None of this could have happened without legislation. That's why I thought this legislation was important.

Question: Mr. President, some of the critics of this bill say that the flaws will be very hard to fix because that will involve adding to the budget, and, in the current political climate, adding to the expenditures is politically impossible. How would you respond to that?

Clinton: Well, it just depends on what your priorities are. For one thing, it will be somewhat easier to balance the budget now in the time period because the deficit this year is $23 billion less than it was the last time we did our budget calculations. So we've lowered that base $23 billion this year. Now, in the out years it still comes up, but there's some savings there that we could turn around and put back into this.

Next, if you look at—my budget corrects it right now. I had $42 billion in savings, this bill has about $57 billion in savings. You could correct all these problems that I mentioned with money to spare in the gap there. So when we get down to the budget negotiations, either at the end of this year or at the beginning of next year, I think the American people will say we can stand marginally smaller tax cuts, for example, or cut somewhere else to cure this problem of immigrants and children, to cure the nutritional problems. We're not talking about vast amounts of money over a six year period. It's not a big budget number, and I think it can easily be fixed, given where we are in the budget negotiations.

Question: The last couple days in these meetings among your staff and this morning, would you say there was no disagreement among people in the administration about what you should do? Some disagreement? A lot of disagreement?

Clinton: No, I would say that there was—first of all, I have rarely been as impressed with the people who work in this administration on any issue as I have been on this. There was significant disagreement among my advisers about whether this bill should be signed or vetoed, but 100 percent of them recognized the power of the arguments on the other side. It was a very moving thing. Today the conversation was almost 100 percent about the merits of the bill and not the political implications of it. Because I think those things are very hard to calculate anyway. I think they're virtually impossible.

I have tried to thank all of them personally, including those who are here in the room and those who are not here, because they did have differences of opinion about whether we should sign or veto, but each side recognized the power of the arguments on the other side. And 100 percent of them, just like 100 percent of the Congress, recognized that we needed to change fundamentally the framework within which welfare operates in this country. The only question was whether the problems in the nonwelfare reform provisions were so great that they would justify a veto and giving up what might be, what I'm convinced is, our last best chance to fundamentally change the system.

Democratic Legacy

Question: Mr. President, even in spite of all the details of this, you as a Democrat are actually helping to dismantle something that was put in place by Democrats sixty years ago. Did that give you pause, that overarching question?

Clinton: No. No, because it was put in place sixty years ago when the poverty population of America was fundamentally different than it is now. As Sen. (Daniel Patrick) Moynihan (D-N.Y.)—you know, Sen. Moynihan strongly disagrees with me on this—but as he has pointed out repeatedly, when welfare was created, the typical welfare recipient was a miner's widow with no education, small children, husband dies in the mine, no expectation that there was a job for the widow to do or that she ever could do it, very few out-of-wedlock pregnancies and births. The whole dynamics were different then.

So I have always thought that the Democratic Party should be on the side of creating opportunity and promoting empowerment and responsibility for people, and a system that was in place sixty years ago that worked for the poverty population then is not the one we need now. But that's why I have worked so hard too to veto previous bills. That does not mean, I think, we can walk away from the guarantee that our party gave on Medicaid, the guarantee our party gave on nutrition, the guarantee our party gave in school lunches, because that has not changed. But the nature of the poverty population is so different now that I am convinced we have got to be willing to experiment, to try to work to find ways to break the cycle of dependency that keeps dragging folks down.

And I think the states are going to find out pretty quickly that they're going to have to be willing to invest something in these people to make sure that they can go to work in the ways that I suggested.

Yes, one last question.

Question: Mr. President, you have mentioned Senator Moynihan. Have you spoken to him or other congressional leaders, especially congressional Democrats? And what was the conversation and reaction to your indication?

Clinton: Well, I talked to him as recently, I think, as about a week ago. When we went up to meet with the TWA families, we talked about it again. And, you know, I have an enormous amount of respect for him. And he has been a powerful and cogent critic of this whole move. I'll just have to hope that in this one case I'm right and he's wrong—because I have an enormous regard for him. And I've spoken to a number of other Democrats, and some think I'm right and some don't.

This is a case where, you know, I have been working with this issue for such a long time—a long time before it became—to go back to Mr. Hume's question—a long time before it became a cause celebre in Washington or anyone tried to make it a partisan political issue. It wasn't much of a political hot potato when I first started working on it. I just was concerned that the system didn't seem to be working. And I was most concerned about those who were trapped on it and their children and the prospect that their children would be trapped on it.

I think we all have to admit here—we all need a certain level of humility today. We are trying to continue a process that I've been pushing for three and a half years. We're trying to get the legal changes we need in federal law that will work to move these folks to a position of independence where they can support their children, and their lives as workers and in families will be stronger.

But if this were an easy question, we wouldn't have had the two and a half hour discussion with my advisers today and we'd all have a lot more answers than we do. But I'm convinced that we're moving in the right direction. I'm convinced it's an opportunity we should seize. I'm convinced that we have to change the two problems in this bill that are not related to welfare reform, that were just sort of put under the big shade of the tree here, that are part of this budget strategy with which I disagree. And I'm convinced when we bring those things out into the light of day we will be able to do it. And I think some Republicans will agree with us, and we'll be able to get what we need to do to change it.

Special Report/Social Policy—Issue: Welfare

(Reprinted from CQ Weekly, *August 31, 1996)*

Legislation replacing six decades of federal welfare policy with a new reliance on the states gained bipartisan congressional approval after President Clinton announced that he would sign it despite his reservations. The legislation gives states broad authority over their own welfare programs, though recipients are required to work within two years and are limited to five years of benefits. The measure is expected to save $54.1 billion through fiscal 2002, mainly by cutting the food stamp program and denying a variety of federal benefits to legal aliens.

When the year began, the outlook for the legislation was murky. Clinton had twice vetoed GOP welfare plans—on December 6, 1995, as part of the deficit-reducing budget-reconciliation bill (HR 2491), then on January 9, as a free-standing welfare bill (HR 4). He branded them as too harsh, more likely to hurt children than to help welfare recipients get jobs.

Clinton challenged Congress in his January 23 State of the Union address to send him a bipartisan welfare plan, promising to "sign it immediately." But there was little enthusiasm for the idea until the National Governors Association endorsed legislation February 6 to overhaul welfare and Medicaid, the federal-state health insurance program for the poor.

GOP leaders began to warm to the notion of combining a welfare and Medicaid overhaul, but Democrats quickly objected. Clinton referred to the Medicaid provisions as a "poison pill" that would prompt him to veto the welfare legislation if the two matters were linked. Although Clinton had signaled his willingness to end the federal guarantee of welfare checks, as the GOP proposed, he wanted to retain the Medicaid entitlement.

Senate Majority Leader Bob Dole, R-Kan., insisted that Republicans would move the welfare legislation only with the Medicaid changes. Clinton's veto threat seemed to matter little to Dole. As the likely GOP presidential nominee, Dole was eager to blast Clinton's vetoes and reluctant to send him a bill he might sign.

Republican leaders unveiled the welfare-Medicaid legislation May 22. They had narrowed and modified the scope of the welfare portion since February 1995, when Republicans released their revised version of the proposal contained in the House's "Contract with America."

But the centerpiece remained unchanged: The federal government would end its sixty-one-year-old guarantee of providing welfare checks to all eligible low-income mothers and children. Federal funding would be sent to states in predetermined lump-sum payments known as block grants, giving states almost complete control over eligibility and benefits.

Because of the savings, Republicans designated it a budget-reconciliation bill, which gave it protection from a Senate filibuster. Nevertheless, Clinton's opposition to the Medicaid provisions seemed to doom it.

But to an increasing number of GOP lawmakers, especially in the House, that seemed like an unsatisfactory ending. They began to urge the leadership to try to accommodate Clinton. Many of them wanted to be part of historic changes in the nation's welfare laws, and they were eager to tout that as an accomplishment for their reelection campaigns. And, they reasoned, if Clinton did veto the GOP welfare plan for the third time, he should not be allowed to cite his objections to the Medicaid provisions as an excuse.

Republicans moved the welfare and Medicaid legislation through House and Senate committees in June. But in July, a month after Dole left the Senate to campaign for president full time, GOP leaders bowed to internal pressure and dropped the Medicaid provisions.

That permitted Democratic support for the welfare measure to grow, especially in the Senate. A House-Senate conference committee then borrowed enough from the generally more moderate Senate bill to make Clinton and many congressional Democrats comfortable.

Clinton resisted a last-ditch appeal from liberals to veto the bill. After a dramatic meeting in the White House with top aides and some Cabinet members July 31, Clinton announced that he would sign the bill despite misgivings about the food stamp savings and cuts in aid to legal immigrants. Democrats in both chambers split on the measure, but Republicans supported it nearly unanimously.

Provisions: Welfare Overhaul Law

By Jeffrey L. Katz
(Reprinted from CQ Weekly, *September 21, 1996)*

The welfare legislation signed into law by President Clinton on August 22 replaces six decades of federal policy with a new reliance on the states.

Clinton signed the "Personal Responsibility and Work Opportunity Reconciliation Act of 1996" (HR 3734—PL 104-193), despite his objections to cuts in the food stamp program and to denial of various federal benefits to legal aliens. These and related federal savings are expected to amount to $54.6 billion through fiscal 2002, according to the Congressional Budget Office.

The legislation's focus remained unchanged after Republicans seized control of Congress—and the welfare issue—in January 1995. They decided that the federal government would end its sixty-one-year-old guarantee of providing welfare checks to all eligible low-income mothers and children. Federal funding instead will be sent to states in predetermined lump-sum payments, known as block grants, giving states almost complete control over eligibility and benefits.

Several significant federal restrictions will apply. Among the most prominent: welfare recipients will be required to work within two years of receiving benefits and they will be limited to five years of aid.

The legislation's scope is narrower than many Republicans once envisioned, but its provisions extend far beyond cash welfare programs. Besides the food stamps and immigration measures, the act will also make it harder for disabled children to qualify for federal aid, reorganize federal child care assistance programs, and toughen enforcement of child support orders.

Republicans endorsed the final legislation almost unanimously, while Democrats ultimately split on the issue. The House adopted the conference report (H Rept 104-725), 328–101, on July 31. The Senate did so the following day, 78–21, clearing the bill.

Ending Welfare

Clinton had raised the profile of the welfare issue during his 1992 presidential campaign, when he promised to "end welfare as we know it." But he largely deferred action on the idea during his first two years in office, mainly to focus on his ultimately unsuccessful effort to overhaul the nation's health care system.

Clinton found little to like in the initial GOP welfare efforts. He vetoed them twice—on December 6, 1995, as part of the deficit-reducing budget-reconciliation bill (HR 2491), then on January 9, as a free-standing welfare bill (HR 4). He branded them as too harsh, more likely to hurt children than to help welfare recipients get jobs.

Prospects for enacting a welfare overhaul seemed dim at the beginning of 1996, but were revitalized after the National Governors Association endorsed legislation February 6 to overhaul welfare and Medicaid, the federal-state health insurance program for the poor.

Although Clinton and some Democrats were encouraged by signs of moderation on welfare, they objected to the Medicaid provisions Clinton had signaled his willingness to end the federal guarantee of welfare checks, as the GOP proposed, but he wanted to retain the Medicaid entitlement.

Senate Majority Leader Bob Dole, R-Kan., insisted that Republicans would move the welfare legislation only in conjunction with the Medicaid changes. As the likely GOP presidential nominee, Dole was reluctant to send Clinton a welfare bill that he might sign.

Republican leaders unveiled the welfare-Medicaid legislation May 22. The bill's projected savings enabled Republicans to designate it as a budget-reconciliation bill, giving it protection from a Senate filibuster.

Clinton's opposition to the Medicaid provisions seemed to doom it. But a growing number of GOP lawmakers, especially in the House, urged the leadership to compromise a bit with Clinton. They were eager to campaign for reelection with a GOP law toppling the nation's unpopular welfare system. And, they reasoned, if Clinton did veto a welfare plan for the third time, he should not be allowed to cite his objections to the Medicaid provisions as an excuse.

Republicans moved the welfare and Medicaid legislation through House and Senate committees in June. In July, a month after Dole left the Senate to campaign for president full time, GOP leaders bowed to internal pressure and dropped the Medicaid provisions.

That permitted Democratic support for the welfare measure to grow, especially in the Senate. A House-Senate conference committee then borrowed just enough from the generally more moderate Senate bill to make Clinton and many congressional Democrats comfortable.

Clinton resisted a last-ditch appeal from liberals to veto the bill. After a dramatic meeting in the White House with top aides and some Cabinet members July 31, Clinton announced that he would sign the bill despite misgivings about the food stamp savings and cuts in aid to legal immigrants.

Following are provisions of the law:

Welfare

The legislation will end the federal guarantee of providing welfare checks to all eligible mothers and children and let states largely create their own welfare programs. New work requirements and time limits on welfare benefits will be imposed.

State Plans

Block grants for temporary assistance for needy families (TANF) will be created to replace Title IV-A of the Social Security Act, which provides Aid to Families with Dependent Children (AFDC). Individuals and families will no longer be entitled to benefits if they meet the existing eligibility requirements.

Each state must file a plan with the secretary of Health and Human Services (HHS) every two years that:

- Explains how it will serve all of the state's political subdivisions.
- Explains how it will require and ensure that parents and caretakers who receive block grant assistance engage in work activities within two months of receiving benefits.
- Establishes goals to prevent and reduce out-of-wedlock pregnancies.
- Explains whether and how the state intends to treat families moving into the state differently from other residents.
- Explains whether it intends to provide aid to noncitizens.
- Establishes criteria for delivering benefits and determining eligibility, and for providing fair and equitable treatment. It must also explain how the state will provide an administrative appeals process for recipients.
- Requires a parent or caretaker who is not engaged in work or exempt from work requirements and who has received assistance for more than two months to participate in community service. A state may opt out of this requirement if the governor sends a letter to the HHS secretary.
- Provides education and training on statutory rape and expands teenage pregnancy prevention programs to include men.
  Each state also must certify that it will:
- Operate a child support enforcement program.
- Operate a foster care and adoption assistance program and ensure medical assistance for the children involved.
- Specify which state agencies will administer the welfare plan, and provide assurances that local governments and private sector organizations have been consulted on it.
- Provide Native Americans with equitable access to assistance.
- Establish standards to combat fraud and abuse.
- At state option, establish procedures to identify recipients with a history of domestic violence, and refer them to counseling and supportive services.

Funding

Federal funds. Federal funding for the new block grant will be $16.4 billion annually from fiscal 1996 through fiscal 2001. States must convert to block grants by July 1, 1997, and can choose to do so earlier.

Money will be distributed to each state based on its federal funding for AFDC benefits and administration, emergency assistance, and the Job Opportunities and Basic Skills (JOBS) program in either fiscal 1995, fiscal 1994 or the average of fiscal 1992–1994, whichever is higher.

State spending. To receive their full share of federal welfare funds in fiscal 1997–2001, states must spend at least 75 percent of the state funds they spent in fiscal 1994 on AFDC benefits and administration, emergency assistance, JOBS, AFDC-related child care, and at-risk child care. States that do not place the required percentage of welfare recipients into the workforce—as stipulated by the legislation—will have to spend at least 80 percent of their funds. States will lose $1 in federal funding for each $1 they fall short of this requirement.

Expenditures that count toward the requirement are:

- State spending on programs created by the block grant for eligible families for cash and child care assistance; educational activities designed to increase self-sufficiency, job training and work (excluding most expenditures on public education); administrative costs (up to 15 percent of total qualified state expenditures), and any other funds used to accomplish the block grant's purposes. This also applies to state spending on block grant programs for those who lose their welfare eligibility because of the five-year time limit or the legislation's treatment of noncitizens.
- Spending on other state or local programs that benefit families who are eligible for the above activities—if the amount spent exceeds the 1994 level.

Transferring funds. States may transfer up to 30 percent of funds paid under this block grant to the child care block grant or the social services block grant. However, states may transfer no more than 10 percent of the welfare block grant to the social services block grant. Also, money transferred into the social services block grant must be spent on services to children and families whose incomes do not exceed 200 percent of the poverty level, as determined annually by the Office of Management and Budget.

Use of funds. States may use their welfare block grant funds "in any manner reasonably calculated to accomplish the purposes" of the program. That includes activities now authorized under AFDC and the Job Opportunities and Basic Skills program for welfare recipients, as well as those that help low-income households with heating and cooling costs.

States may also opt to:

- Carry over funds to provide assistance in future years under the block grant.
- Pay or give vouchers to job placement services.
- Use an electronic benefits transfer (EBT) system for distributing welfare benefits.
- Fund individual development accounts established by recipients for postsecondary education expenses, first-home purchases and business capitalization.
- Provide newcomers from another state the same benefits the families would have received in their former state for up to twelve months.

Administrative expenses. States may not spend more than 15 percent of their welfare block grant on administration. Money for information technology and computerization needed to monitor the program is exempted from this cap.

Additional federal funds. Several additional sources of federal funds will be available to states. They are:

- **Out-of-wedlock births.** Financial incentives will be provided to the states that demonstrate the largest decline in the proportion of out-of-wedlock births without increasing abortions. Between fiscal 1999 and 2002, the five states that best meet this criterion will receive $20 million each. If fewer than five states are eligible for this bonus, the grant will be $25 million each.

- **Supplemental grant.** States with above-average population growth and below-average welfare benefits per recipient will be entitled to a supplemental grant between fiscal 1998 and 2001. States that had particularly low welfare benefit payments in fiscal 1994 or particularly high population growth between April 1, 1990, and July 1, 1994, automatically qualify for the grant. Eligible states will receive an additional 2.5 percent of the federal funds they received in fiscal 1994 for AFDC and related programs. The bill appropriates $800 million over four years for this fund. If that is insufficient, pro rata reductions will be made to each qualifying state.

- **High performance grants.** States that are most successful in meeting the legislation's goals (such as moving welfare recipients into the workplace and reducing out-of-wedlock birth rates) will be eligible for a total of $1 billion in bonuses from fiscal 1999 to 2003. The formula for measuring state performance and making the awards will be developed by the HHS secretary after consulting with the National Governors' Association and the American Public Welfare Association.

- **Contingency fund.** States with high unemployment or rapidly growing food stamp rolls will be eligible for a total of $2 billion from fiscal 1997 to 2001. Eligible states must continue to maintain 100 percent of their fiscal 1994 welfare expenditures. They must also meet one of the following two criteria: 1) An unemployment rate that is at least 6.5 percent in the most recent three-month period and at least 10 percent higher than the comparable quarter in either of the two preceding years; 2) The number of food stamp recipients in the most recent three-month period is at least 10 percent higher than the average number of recipients in the comparable quarter of fiscal 1994 or fiscal 1995 (whichever is lower). Adjustments in the calculation will be made to account for the legislation's impact on the food stamp caseload.

- **Loan fund.** States will be permitted to draw from a $1.7 billion revolving loan fund from fiscal 1997 though 2001. States will have to repay the loans, with interest, within three years. They will be permitted to borrow up to 10 percent of their annual block grant. States that incur penalties under the cash welfare block grant would be ineligible for a loan.

Work Requirements

Adults receiving benefits under the block grant will be required to begin working within two years of receiving aid.

States may develop individual responsibility plans that set employment goals, the individual's obligations and services the state will provide. States may reduce assistance to families that include an individual who does not comply with these plans.

Work participation rates. States will be required to have a certain percentage of their welfare caseload participating in work activities, starting at 25 percent in fiscal 1997 and rising to 50 percent in fiscal 2002.

A state's annual participation rate will be set at the average participation rate for each month in the fiscal year. The state's monthly participation rate will be the number of families receiving assistance that include an adult or minor head of household who is working, divided by the number of families receiving assistance (excluding those who have been subject to a recent penalty for refusing to work).

A state's required participation rate for a year will be reduced by the same percentage that it reduces its average monthly welfare caseload below fiscal year 1995 levels. However, those caseload reductions will not be considered if they are required by federal law—such as when recipients exceed the five-year time limit on benefits—or result from changes in state eligibility criteria.

The work participation rates for the entire caseload are:

- Fiscal 1997: 25 percent.
- Fiscal 1998: 30 percent.
- Fiscal 1999: 35 percent.
- Fiscal 2000: 40 percent.
- Fiscal 2001: 45 percent.
- Fiscal 2002 and thereafter: 50 percent.

States also must meet higher participation rates for two-parent families that receive cash assistance. The following apply:

- Fiscal 1996: 50 percent.
- Fiscal 1997–1998: 75 percent.
- Fiscal 1999 and thereafter: 90 percent.

State options. A state may:

- Count those who receive assistance under tribal family assistance in the work participation calculation.
- Count toward meeting the work requirement single parents with a child under age six, if the parent works at least twenty hours per week.
- Exempt from the work requirement and the participation rates a parent of a child under age one. However, a parent could receive this exemption only for a total of twelve months, regardless of whether they were consecutive.

Work activities. Individuals must engage in one or more of the following activities for a state to count them toward the work participation rate:

- Unsubsidized employment.
- Subsidized private sector employment.
- Subsidized public sector employment.
- Work experience if sufficient private sector employment is unavailable.
- On-the-job training.
- Job search and job readiness assistance for up to six weeks, no more than four weeks of which may be consecutive. Individuals in states with unemployment rates at least 50 percent above the national average may engage in these activities for up to twelve weeks.
- Community service programs.
- Vocational educational training, for up to one year. (No more than 20 percent of all families may count toward the work rate by participating in vocational education.)
- Jobs skills training directly related to employment.
- Education directly related to employment, for a recipient who lacks a high school diploma or equivalency and is under age twenty.
- Satisfactory attendance at a secondary school, for a recipient who has not completed high school and is under age twenty.
- Providing child care to another welfare recipient who is engaged in community service programs.

No more than 20 percent of all families may count toward the work rate by participating in vocational education, education directly related to employment, or secondary school.

Hours. To count toward the work participation rate, individuals must work a minimum number of hours per week:

- Fiscal 1996–1998: twenty hours.
- Fiscal 1999: 25 hours.
- Fiscal 2000 and thereafter: thirty hours.

The primary wage earner in a two-parent family must work at least thirty-five hours per week to count toward the work participation rate.

Both parents in a two-parent family must engage in work activities if they also receive federally funded child care. Exceptions would be granted in cases where one parent is disabled or caring for a severely disabled child.

Penalties against individuals. A state must reduce assistance to a family by at least the same pro rata percentage that an adult family member refused to work as required under the welfare block grant. In other words, someone who misses work 20 percent of the time will receive 20 percent less aid. A state may waive the penalty for good cause and other reasons established by the state.

A state may also terminate assistance to adults who refuse to work, and end their Medicaid coverage—though Medicaid coverage would continue for their children.

A state may not penalize a single parent caring for a child under age six if the parent proves he or she failed to work because child care was unavailable.

Penalties against states. States that fail to meet the work requirements will have their block grant reduced by 5 percent. Subsequent failures would result in an additional 2 percent reduction per year, reaching 7 percent the second year and 9 percent the third year, rising to a maximum deduction of 21 percent. However, the HHS secretary may reduce the penalty based on the degree of noncompliance, or if the state has a high unemployment rate or rapidly growing food stamp rolls as defined in criteria for the contingency fund.

Restrictions on Aid

Children. Only families with a minor child (who resides with a custodial parent or other adult relative) or a pregnant woman may receive assistance from the grant.

Time limit. Block grant funds cannot be used for adults who have received welfare for more than five years, although those who exceed the time limit can still qualify for other federal, state, and local funds. The time limit applies only to those who are the head of a household or the spouse of a household head. (Children could qualify later for five years of aid as parents, no matter how many years they got as children.) The time limit also applies only to benefits received after the state accepts its welfare block grant.

States can exempt up to 20 percent of their caseload from the five-year time limit. They can also opt to impose a shorter time limit.

Paternity. Parents who do not cooperate in establishing paternity or in assisting a child support enforcement agency will have their family's benefit reduced by at least 25 percent. States can choose to eliminate their benefit entirely. States can also exempt parents from these responsibilities for good cause.

Drug abuse. Individuals convicted of a felony offense for possessing, using, or distributing an illegal drug will be denied welfare benefits and food stamps. Family members or dependents of the individual will still be eligible for aid. Those penalized for drug abuse will still be eligible for emergency benefits, including emergency medical services. States could opt out of this prohibition if they passed legislation to do so.

Fraud. Any person convicted of fraudulently misrepresenting his or her residence to obtain benefits in two or more states from the welfare grant, Medicaid, food stamps, or Supplemental Security Income will be ineligible for aid from the family assistance grant for ten years.

Unwed teenagers. Unmarried parents under age eighteen could qualify for block grant funds only if they attend high school or an alternative educational or training program and if they live with a parent or in an adult-supervised setting.

State options. States can choose to:

- Deny welfare assistance to children born to welfare recipients.
- Deny welfare to all unwed parents under age eighteen.
- Provide newcomers from another state the same benefits the families would have received from their former state for up to twelve months.

State Penalties

If a state's welfare block grant is reduced because of one of the following penalties, it must replace the penalized federal funds during the next fiscal year with state funds. The penalties are:

- Unauthorized use of block grant funds: repay amount used and, if the violation was intentional, repay an additional 5 percent of the state's quarterly block grant payments.
- Failure to submit a required report within one month of the end of each fiscal quarter: 4 percent of the annual block grant, to be rescinded if the state submits the report before the end of the next fiscal quarter.
- Failure to satisfy minimum work participation rates: 5 percent of the block grant, plus an additional 2 percent each year for consecutive failures, up to a maximum of 21 percent.
- Failure to use an income and eligibility verification system: up to 2 percent of the annual block grant.
- Failure to enforce penalties sought by a child support agency: up to 5 percent of the block grant.
- Failure to repay a federal loan in a timely fashion: a reduction of the block grant by the amount of the outstanding loan, plus interest.
- Failure to maintain the proper percentage of state spending as required by the legislation: $1 reduction in the block grant for each $1 the state falls below the requirement for state spending.
- Failure of a state child support enforcement program to comply with federal law: for the first finding of noncompliance, a reduction of between 1 and 2 percent of a quarterly block grant payment; for the second consecutive finding of noncompliance, between 2 and 3 percent of the next quarterly payment; for the third or subsequent findings, between 3 and 5 percent.
- Failure to maintain 100 percent of state fiscal 1994 welfare expenditures when receiving money from the contingency fund: repay money received.
- Failure to provide benefits to single adult parents who have custody over their children but cannot obtain child care for them, up to age six: up to 5 percent of the block grant.
- Failure to comply with the five-year time limit on benefits: 5 percent of the annual block grant.

Related Provisions

Medicaid. States must continue to offer Medicaid coverage for one year to welfare recipients who lose their welfare benefits because of increased earnings if their income remains below the poverty line.

States also will have to continue to provide Medicaid to those who would have been eligible for AFDC if that program were still in effect.

Federal waivers. States that previously received waivers of federal laws and regulations to conduct experimental welfare programs can continue those programs until the waivers expire.

Work force reduction. HHS must reduce the number of positions within the department by 245 full-time equivalent positions—including sixty managerial positions—related to the conversion of several federal programs into the block grant.

Charitable and religious organizations. States are allowed to provide family assistance services (as well as services under SSI, foster care, adoption assistance, and independent living programs) by contracting with charitable, religious, or private organizations.

Supplemental Security Income

Disabled children will find it more difficult to qualify for Supplemental Security Income (SSI), which provides cash assistance to the low-income aged, blind, and disabled.

Disabled Children

The bill will make it harder for children to be considered disabled to qualify for SSI. The Congressional Budget Office estimates that about 315,000 children—or 22 percent—who would be receiving SSI in 2002 will lose their eligibility as a result of the legislation.

Definition. A child under age eighteen with an impairment of "comparable severity" to what would be considered a work disability in an adult will no longer be eligible for SSI benefits.

The bill redefines a childhood disability to add that the child must have a "medically determinable physical or mental impairment, which results in marked and severe functional limitations." As in current law, this disability must be expected to result in death or to last more than twelve months.

Assessments. Children will no longer qualify for SSI under an Individualized Functional Assessment (IFA).

Under existing law, the Social Security Administration first determines whether a child is eligible for SSI by deciding whether he or she meets or exceeds a "Listing of Impairments." A child who does not meet that test can still qualify for SSI through an easier-to-reach determination, known as an IFA, that analyzes whether a child's mental, physical, and social functioning is substantially lower than children of the same age.

By ending the IFA as a standard, children will only be able to qualify for SSI through the more stringent "Listing of Impairments." The legislation also eliminates references to "maladaptive behavior" when determining a child's personal and behavioral functioning.

Effective date. The Social Security Administration has one year after the law's enactment to decide whether children now on SSI meet the new, more restrictive standard for determining SSI eligibility. Current recipients will continue receiving SSI benefits until either July 1, 1997, or the date of redetermination, whichever is later.

Redeterminations. The Social Security Administration will generally be required to reevaluate the eligibility of each child who receives SSI at least once every three years. Children whose medical condition is not expected to improve are generally exempted from a redetermination. At the time of the review, the child's parent or guardian must present evidence showing that the child is receiving treatment that is medically necessary.

For children who qualify for SSI based on a low birthweight, reviews must occur one year after birth.

Children who qualify for SSI must have their eligibility redetermined using the criteria for an adult within one year after their eighteenth birthday.

The legislation authorizes an additional $150 million in fiscal 1997 and $100 million in 1998 to help the Social Security Administration conduct more continuing disability reviews and redeterminations. The legislation also lifts the limits on discretionary spending to allow for the additional money.

Savings account. A child's parent or guardian will be required to establish a separate savings account for any past-due SSI payments that exceed six times the maximum monthly payment. The money may be used to cover specific expenses such as education or job skills training, special equipment, or housing modifications and medical treatment.

Private insurance. Children who are hospitalized and whose medical costs are covered by private insurance will receive no more than the $30 monthly SSI benefit paid to children whose medical bills are covered by Medicaid.

Other SSI Provisions

Multistate benefits. Anyone convicted of fraudulently trying to get benefits from two or more states for several social service programs—including food stamps, welfare, and SSI—will be ineligible for SSI benefits for ten years.

Fugitive felons. Anyone fleeing to avoid prosecution, custody or confinement after being convicted of a felony or who violates probation or parole will be ineligible for SSI.

Prisoners. State and local prisons and jails will receive financial incentives to report to the Social Security Administration any information on inmates who are fraudulently receiving SSI. The correctional institution will receive $400 for each such prisoner who loses eligibility if the information is provided within thirty days of the inmate's arrival. The institution will receive $200 if the information is provided within thirty to ninety days.

Large past-due payments. An individual eligible for past-due SSI benefits that exceed twelve times the maximum monthly benefit payable to an eligible individual (currently $470) or couple (currently $705) generally will be paid in three installments at six-month intervals rather than in a lump sum. The first and second installments may not exceed twelve times the maximum monthly payable benefit.

Child Support Enforcement

New procedures will be put in place to establish paternity and enforce child support orders.

Distribution of Payments

The legislation changes the way child support payments—and overdue payments known as arrearages—are disbursed to welfare recipients.

Currently, welfare recipients must assign to the state the right to collect child support payments and any past-due payments on their behalf. The first $50 collected of monthly child support payments is required to be given to the family as a "pass-through," without affecting the family's welfare eligibility or benefits. Next, the federal and state governments are reimbursed for their AFDC benefits paid to the family that month. If there is any money left, the family receives it up to the amount of the current month's child support. Any money beyond that pays arrearages, first to the state and federal governments, then to the family.

The legislation changes this structure in several ways. First, beginning October 1, 1997, child support received for arrearages that accumulate after the family leaves welfare will be paid to the family before the state can use that money to reimburse itself or the federal government.

Second, beginning October 1, 2000, child support received for arrearages that accumulate before the family went on welfare will also be paid to the family before the state can use the money to reimburse itself or the federal government. However, this provision will be rescinded if Congress decides, based on an HHS study, that providing the money to the family first has not helped to keep people off welfare.

Exempted from both of these changes are child support arrearages collected by intercepting tax refunds.

The legislation gives states the option to "pass-through" the first $50 of any child support collected on behalf of a family on welfare, but no longer requires it. And if states choose this option, the federal government will still have to be paid its share of the child support.

Locating and Tracking Cases

State registries. States will be required to create a central case registry to track the status of all child-support orders created or modified after October 1, 1998. This will record basic information about both parents involved in a child support order, including their names, Social Security numbers, dates of birth and case identification numbers. Information will be regularly updated and shared with other entities such as a federal case registry.

State disbursement units. States will be required to operate a centralized disbursement unit by October 1, 1998. This entity will collect child support from employers (who withhold an employee's child support obligations), noncustodial parents, and other states (that are collecting money from a parent in their state). The unit will also distribute the money to custodial parents.

State directory of new hires. States generally will be required to establish a "new hire" registry by October 1, 1997, to which employers will have to send the name, address, and Social Security number of all new employees. States will compare information on new hires with the state and national registries of child support orders. The information must also be used to establish paternity as well as to create, modify, and enforce child support obligations. And it must also be shared with the state agency administering welfare, Medicaid, unemployment compensation, food stamps, and SSI to verify individuals' income eligibility.

Income withholding. States must enact laws to ensure that child support orders issued or modified before October 1, 1996, that are not otherwise subject to income withholding immediately become subject to income withholding if arrearages occur.

Federal Parent Locator Service. The Federal Parent Locator Service, which helps states and parents enforce support orders, will be expanded to include a federal registry of child support orders and a national directory of new hires. Information in these two registries will be provided by states. It will be used to identify and locate parents who are subject to child support orders and to establish paternity. The legislation calls for confidentiality in cases involving domestic violence or child abuse.

Social Security numbers. To assist in tracking child support orders, Social Security numbers must be listed on applications for professional licenses, commercial driver's licenses, occupational licenses, and marriage licenses. States must also list Social Security numbers in divorce decrees, child support orders, paternity determinations, and death notices.

Uniform Procedures

State laws. States will be required to adopt a model state law for handling interstate child support cases. The Uniform Interstate Family Support Act, developed in 1992 by the

National Conference of Commissioners on State Uniform Laws, was designed to deal with desertion and nonsupport cases across state lines. It ensures that only one child support order from a court or agency will be in effect at any given time and helps eliminate jurisdictional disputes between states.

Interstate cases. The legislation revises a federal law that restricts a state court's ability to modify a support order issued by another state unless the child and the custodial parent have moved there or have agreed to the modification. Among the revisions are those that clarify the definition of a child's home state and clarify the rules regarding which child support orders states must honor when there is more than one order.

Forms. The HHS secretary must issue standardized forms that states must use for income withholding, imposing liens, and issuing administrative subpoenas in interstate cases.

Expedited procedures. The legislation requires states to adopt procedures that would give the state child support agency the authority to enforce an order without having to first obtain an order from a court or other administrative entity.

States must be able to: order genetic testing; issue subpoenas to obtain necessary information; require all entities in the state to provide information on employment, compensation, and benefits of any employee or contractor; obtain access to a series of public and private records; change the name of the payee on the order or require income withholding when appropriate; intercept unemployment or workers' compensation, other state benefits, settlements, lottery winnings, assets held by financial institutions, and public and private retirement funds; gain access to public and private retirement funds to help pay past-due support; impose liens to force the sale of property, and automatically increase the monthly support due to include past-due payments.

Establishing Paternity

State laws. The legislation amends laws to improve states' ability to establish paternity. Among changes are those that require:

- States to permit paternity establishment at least until the child reaches age eighteen.
- The child and other parties to undergo genetic testing if a party involved in the case requests it and circumstances warrant it.
- Procedures in each state that allow men to voluntarily acknowledge paternity through a simple civil process and through hospitals.
- The HHS secretary to issue regulations governing services whereby fathers can voluntarily acknowledge paternity. States must include the basic elements in their own such forms.
- Procedures in each state under which a signed acknowledgment of paternity is considered a legal judgment after sixty days. Beyond that date, the paternity acknowledgment can be challenged only on the basis of fraud, duress, or mistake of fact.

- File voluntary acknowledgments and adjudications of paternity with the state registry of birth records and compare that information with the child support case registry.
- The Social Security numbers of both parents to be used on voluntary acknowledgments of paternity.

Welfare recipients. The legislation expands existing requirements that individuals applying for welfare cooperate with the state in establishing paternity and child support orders. If the individual does not cooperate, states must reduce the family's cash assistance benefit by at least 25 percent and may choose to eliminate it.

Administration

Funding. The legislation continues the practice of reimbursing state child support expenses so that the federal government pays 66 percent and states spend 34 percent. However, it directs the HHS secretary to revise the current system of incentive payments in which states earn an additional six to ten percent of federal matching aid, depending on the effectiveness of their child support enforcement.

Central unit. States will have to begin operating a centralized system to collect and disburse child support and to monitor and enforce child support collections by October 1, 1998. States that process payments though local courts may continue to do so until September 30, 1999.

Technical assistance. The HHS secretary can set aside 1 percent of the federal share of child support collections obtained from families on welfare and use it to provide technical assistance to states.

Case reviews. States must review—and, where appropriate, adjust—child support orders at least once every three years or when either parent requests it. States may choose to review the orders on an individual basis, adjust them for inflation or use automated methods.

Health care coverage. The legislation tries to help custodial parents get their children covered by health plans provided by a noncustodial parent's employer. It requires health insurance plans governed by the Employee Retirement Income Security Act (ERISA) to recognize child support orders issued by administrative agencies as well as by courts.

The legislation also requires that new employers of a noncustodial parent be notified by a state agency if the noncustodial parent was, as part of a support order, providing health care coverage of the child in the previous job. This notice will be used to enroll the child in the noncustodial parent's new health plan.

Visitation. Up to $10 million is authorized annually to help states provide access and visitation programs for noncustodial parents. Potential programs include mediation, counseling, education, and visitation enforcement.

Enforcement

Federal employees. The legislation clarifies that federal employees are covered by federal child support laws. It also makes a wider range of income sources subject to being used to satisfy child support obligations, including insurance benefits, retirement pay, survivor's benefits, veteran's benefits, and workers' compensation.

Armed forces. The secretary of Defense must keep an updated central record of addresses of military personnel. The information must be shared with the Federal Parent Locator Service. The secretary of each military department must also issue regulations to grant leave to military personnel so that they can attend hearings related to paternity establishment or child support orders.

Work requirement. States must adopt procedures so that they have the authority to order (or request that a court order) an individual who owes past-due child support for a child on welfare to either pay the overdue support according to a plan approved by the court or child support agency or to participate in work activities.

Licenses. States must adopt procedures so that they have the authority to suspend driver's licenses, professional licenses, occupational licenses, and recreational licenses of anyone who owes past-due child support.

Passports. The federal government must have procedures to deny, revoke, or restrict the passport of anyone who owes more than $5,000 in past-due child support as of October 1, 1997.

International cases. The secretary of State, after consulting with the secretary of HHS, may enter into cooperative agreements with other countries to establish and enforce support orders.

Financial institutions. States must enter into agreements with financial institutions doing business in the state to automatically search their files every three months to provide the name, address, Social Security number, and other identifying information for each noncustodial parent who has an account at the institution and owes past-due child support.

Grandparents. States have the option to enforce a child support order against the grandparents (the parents of the minor noncustodial parent) if the custodial parent is receiving assistance from the welfare block grant.

Native American tribes. States and Native American tribes may enter into cooperative agreements regarding paternity establishment and child support orders.

Immigration

Legal immigrants generally will face new restrictions on receiving SSI, food stamps, and other benefits.

Illegal Aliens

Restrictions. The legislation restricts the federal benefits for which illegal aliens and legal nonimmigrants—such as travelers and students—can qualify. The benefits specifically denied are those provided by a federal agency or by federal funds for:

- Any grant, contract, loan, professional license, or commercial license.
- Any retirement, welfare, health, disability, food assistance, or unemployment benefit.

Exceptions. Illegal aliens and legal nonimmigrants are eligible for:

- Emergency medical services under Medicaid. The conference report specifically denies coverage for prenatal or delivery care assistance that is not an emergency.
- Short-term, noncash emergency disaster relief.
- Immunizations and testing and treatment for the symptoms of communicable diseases.
- Noncash programs identified by the attorney general that are delivered by community agencies—such as soup kitchens, counseling, and short-term shelter—that are not conditioned on the individual's income or resources and are necessary for the protection of life or safety.
- Certain housing benefits (for current recipients only).
- Licenses and benefits directly related to work for which a nonimmigrant has been authorized to enter the United States.
- Certain Social Security retirement benefits protected by treaty or statute.

State and local programs. States are prohibited from providing state or local benefits to most illegal aliens, unless a state law is enacted after August 22, 1996 (the day the bill was enacted) that explicitly makes illegal aliens eligible for the aid.

However, illegal aliens are entitled to receive a school lunch and/or breakfast if they are eligible for a free public education under state or local law. A state may also opt to provide certain other benefits related to child nutrition and emergency food assistance.

Legal Immigrants

Current immigrants. Most legal immigrants, including those already in the United States, will be ineligible for SSI and food stamps until they become citizens. Current recipients must have an eligibility review by August 1997.

Those exempted from this ban are:

- Refugees, those granted asylum and aliens whose deportation has been withheld. (Withholding of deportation is a form of relief in immigration law that is similar to asylum.) Immigrants in this category will be eligible for SSI and food stamps only for the first five years of residence in the United States—including any time they were here before the law was enacted.

- Those who have worked in the United States for the equivalent of ten years.
- Veterans and those on active military duty, as well as their spouse and unmarried dependent children.

Future immigrants. Legal immigrants who arrive in the United States after August 22 will be denied most low-income federal benefits for five years after arrival.

Individuals exempted from this ban are:

- Refugees, those granted asylum and aliens whose deportation has been withheld. Cuban and Haitian entrants may also be exempted.
- Veterans and those on active military duty, as well as their spouse and unmarried children.

Programs exempted from this ban are:

- Emergency medical services under Medicaid.
- Short-term, noncash emergency disaster relief.
- Child nutrition, including school lunches, and the special supplemental nutrition program for Women, Infants and Children (WIC).
- Immunization and testing and treatment of symptoms of communicable diseases.
- Foster care and adoption assistance.
- Noncash programs identified by the attorney general that are delivered by community agencies—such as soup kitchens, counseling and short-term shelter—that are not conditioned on the individual's income or resources and are necessary for the protection of life or safety.
- Loans and grants for higher education.
- Elementary and secondary education.
- The Head Start program for preschool children.
- Assistance from the Job Training Partnership Act.

State options. States may choose to deny most legal immigrants—including those who are already in the United States—benefits from the welfare block grant, Medicaid, and social services block grant. The same exemptions apply as those for SSI and food stamps. Future immigrants are first subject to the five-year ban noted above.

Current recipients must continue to receive the benefits until January 1, 1997.

States may generally determine the eligibility of legal immigrants, including those who are already in the United States, for benefits funded entirely by state or local money. Current recipients must continue to receive the benefits until January 1, 1997. Exemptions are granted to refugees, those granted asylum and aliens whose deportation has been withheld; those who have worked in the United States for the equivalent of ten years; and veterans and those on active military duty, as well as their spouse and unmarried dependent children.

Sponsors. The bill will increase the circumstances under which an immigrant's sponsor will be considered financially responsible for that individual. This generally affects those who enter the United States because they have been sponsored by a member of their immediate family.

Until now, when an immigrant applied for AFDC, food stamps, or SSI, the sponsor's income and other resources were taken into account or "deemed" when determining the applicant's eligibility. The sponsor's finances are generally considered for three years after the immigrant arrives in the United States, and for five years for SSI. These terms will still apply to legal immigrants who are already in the United States and receiving the aid.

Most legal immigrants who arrive in the United States after August 22 will first be subject to the five-year ban noted above. After five years, the sponsor's finances will be considered for most federal programs to which the immigrant applies.

By February 1997, the new terms will also apply to immigrants who are already in the United States but who were not receiving the benefits when the bill was enacted.

The sponsor's financial responsibility will extend until the immigrant has worked in the United States for ten years or has become an American citizen.

The affidavits of support will be legally enforceable against the sponsor by the sponsored immigrant as well as by federal, state, and local agencies for up to ten years after the immigrant last receives benefits.

Programs exempted from deeming are the same as those exempted from the five-year ban on benefits to future legal immigrants.

Reporting and verifying. Agencies that administer SSI, housing assistance or the welfare block grant must report quarterly to the Immigration and Naturalization Service the names and addresses of people they know are unlawfully in the United States.

Within eighteen months after enactment, the attorney general must issue regulations requiring that anyone applying for federal benefits is in the United States legally. States administering federal benefits must comply with the verification system within twenty-four months after they have been issued.

Child Protection

The legislation makes modest changes to child protection programs, but generally retains their current structure.

Eligibility. The legislation continues the current eligibility criteria for child protection programs. Under existing law, children qualify for federal foster care and adoption assistance if they meet AFDC eligibility requirements. The legislation continues those eligibility guidelines for foster care and adoption assistance even though AFDC is being eliminated.

Information systems. The deadline for providing 75 percent federal funding for the Statewide Automated Child Welfare Information Systems is extended from October 1, 1996, to October 1, 1997. This program helps states collect automated data on children in foster care and other child welfare services.

For-profit providers. States will be permitted to use federal foster care funds under Title IV-E of the Social Security Act to enable for-profit providers to care for children in foster care.

Preference to relatives. States are to give preference to an adult relative when determining a child's placement, provided that the relative meets all relevant state child protection standards.

Child Care

Most federal child care funding will be provided to states through a revised block grant.

Funding

Block grant. Several federal child care programs will be folded into the existing Child Care and Development Block Grant to the states. That block grant provides child care services for low income families and activities to improve the quality and availability of child care.

The legislation ends the guarantee of providing federal matching funds to states without limits for families that participate in two of the child care programs to be consolidated. Those programs help welfare recipients participate in work or training programs and help welfare recipients keep their jobs for a year after they leave the welfare rolls. A third program to be consolidated, which provides child care for those at risk of needing welfare, has not been subject to a federal guarantee.

The effective date for the consolidated block grant is October 1, 1996.

Mandatory funding. Total mandatory or entitlement funding to the states for child care will be $13.85 billion from fiscal 1997 through fiscal 2002. The money will come from two accounts:

- **Base allocation.** States will share a basic annual allocation of $1.2 billion, amounting to $7.2 billion over six years. Each state will receive the amount of funds it received for child care for AFDC recipients, those who are making the transition from welfare and those at risk of needing welfare in fiscal 1994, fiscal 1995, or the average amount in fiscal 1992- 1994, whichever is higher.
- **Matching funds.** Another $6.7 billion will be available over six years in matching grants to qualified states. That includes $760 million in fiscal 1997, $860 million in fiscal 1998,

$960 million in fiscal 1999, $1.16 billion in fiscal 2000, $1.36 billion in fiscal 2001, and $1.51 billion in fiscal 2002. To qualify for these funds, states must have spent all of their basic child care allocation. They must also continue spending at least as much of their own funds on child care that they spent on AFDC-related child care in fiscal 1994 or fiscal 1995, whichever is higher. Funds will be distributed to states based on their proportion of children under age thirteen. Unused funds will be redistributed to other states.

Discretionary funds. The legislation authorizes $1 billion annually through fiscal 2001 in discretionary spending, based on the current Child Care and Development Block Grant formula.

Use of Funds

Native American tribes. HHS must set aside between 1 percent and 2 percent of the child care funds annually for Native American tribes and organizations.

Targeted population. States must spend at least 70 percent of the mandatory funds to provide child care to help welfare recipients, those attempting to leave the welfare rolls and those at risk of needing welfare.

Quality. At least 4 percent of the new consolidated block grant must be used for consumer education and improving the quality and availability of child care. The law previously required that 25 percent of state allotments from discretionary funds be reserved for improving quality, increasing the availability of early childhood development and expanding before- and after-school care.

Administrative costs. States may spend no more than 5 percent of the block grant on administrative costs.

Lead agency. States are required to designate a lead agency for the block grant, which may be a government or nongovernment entity.

Penalties. States that do not comply with the legislation may be required to reimburse HHS for improperly spent funds. The HHS secretary may deduct from the administrative portion of the state allotment for the following fiscal year an amount equal to or less than the misspent funds. The legislation repeals a requirement that the secretary withhold further child care block grant payments to a state until noncompliance is corrected.

State Plan

States must certify that they have licensing requirements for child care services and describe how these requirements are enforced. They must also detail how they are meeting the specific child care needs of welfare recipients, those attempting to leave the welfare rolls and those at risk of needing welfare.

Child Nutrition

The legislation generally retains the current structure of child nutrition programs, including the federal guarantees of coverage. But spending will be reduced in specified ways.

Summer Food Service and school breakfasts. Federal subsidies will be reduced for the Summer Food Service Program for Children.

The reimbursements, which will first apply to the summer of 1997, will be adjusted for inflation on January 1, 1997, and each year thereafter. Assuming a 3 percent inflation adjustment in both the new and old reimbursement rates, the subsidy levels for 1997 will be an estimated $2.02 for each lunch or supper (down from a projected $2.23), $1.16 for each breakfast (down from $1.24) and 47 cents for each snack (down from 58 cents).

The legislation deletes funds set aside to help states initiate or expand the school breakfast and summer food service programs.

Child and Adult Care Food Program. Federal subsidies will be reduced for meals and snacks served in family day-care homes in all but low-income neighborhoods. The existing rates generally will continue to apply to family day-care homes located in areas that meet at least one of these criteria:

- At least half of the children are in households that are below 185 percent of the poverty level;
- At least half the elementary school students in the area qualify for free or reduced price school meals;
- The day-care provider's income is below 185 percent of the poverty level.

The new subsidy structure for nonpoor homes will begin on July 1, 1997. It will be adjusted for inflation on that date and each year thereafter. Assuming a 3 percent inflation adjustment, the expected subsidies in nonpoor homes beginning July 1 will be an estimated 97 cents for each lunch (down from a projected $1.62), 27 cents for each breakfast (down from 88 cents) and 13 cents for snacks (down from 48 cents).

The legislation eliminates the option of reimbursing a child care center for serving a fourth meal or snack to children who are there for more than eight hours a day. Also eliminated are requirements that states expand the availability of the child and adult care food program, and that they provide training and technical assistance to help day care home sponsors increase participation in the program. And child care centers will no longer be required to provide information about WIC.

Women, Infants and Children. The legislation deletes specific requirements that states show how they plan to serve women in prisons and juvenile detention facilities with WIC, which provides infant formula, milk, and other basic foods to pregnant women, infants, and young children. The legislation also deletes a requirement that the Agriculture secretary promote WIC in specific ways.

Subsidy rates. Federal subsidy rates will be rounded down to the nearest cent—rather than quarter cent—when indexing for full-priced meals in the school breakfast and lunch programs, full-priced meals in child care centers and all subsidies to family day care homes and summer food service providers.

Food Stamps

The food stamp program will remain largely intact, though the legislation makes significant cuts in benefits and imposes a new work requirement on certain recipients.

Benefits and Eligibility

The legislation will continue to give benefits to anyone who meets food stamp eligibility requirements, enabling the program to expand or contract with demand.

However, it will reduce individual allotments to 100 percent of the Agriculture Department's "Thrifty Food Plan," rather than 103 percent. The Thrifty Food Plan is intended to reflect the benefits needed to purchase food for minimal nutrition requirements.

Benefits will be reduced by changing various deductions that recipients are allowed to count against their income or their assets, which are used to calculate benefits and eligibility. Among the changes:

- The standard deduction—applied to all food stamp applicants to help determine benefit levels—generally will be kept at $134 per month. It had previously been indexed to inflation.
- State and local energy assistance will be considered as income when determining allotment levels (though federal energy assistance will continue to be excluded).
- Earnings from students will be considered as part of the family's income once the person reaches age eighteen (instead of age twenty-two, as has been the case).
- The minimum monthly allotment of $10 in food stamp benefits for a one- or two-person household will no longer be indexed to inflation.
- The threshold above which the fair market value of a vehicle is counted as an asset will be set at $4,650 and frozen at that level. The vehicle allowance had been $4,600. It was scheduled to increase to an estimated $5,150 on October 1, 1996, and subsequently to be adjusted for inflation.
- The maximum shelter expense deduction generally will be kept at $247 per month through December 31, when it will increase to $250 per month. It will be $275 per month

in fiscal 1999 and 2000, and $300 per month in fiscal 2001 and thereafter. The limits on the deduction had been scheduled to expire on January 1, 1997.

- All parents and children twenty-one years of age or younger living together must apply for food stamps as a single household. The legislation eliminates the exception that has allowed children who are married or have children of their own to apply as a separate household from their parents when living together.

Work Requirements

Able-bodied food stamp recipients between the ages of eighteen and fifty who do not have dependents will have to work an average of at least twenty hours per week or participate in a state-approved work, training or workfare program. Otherwise, they will be eligible to receive no more than three months of food stamps out of every three years, plus an additional three months if they reenter the program and then are laid off.

If a state requests it, the Agriculture secretary can waive this work requirement in an area where the unemployment rate is more than 10 percent or where there are not enough jobs to employ food stamp recipients.

The new work requirements also do not apply to pregnant women and to those otherwise exempt from work registration requirements (such as those caring for incapacitated people).

The legislation will gradually increase federal funding for food stamp employment and training programs from $79 million in fiscal 1997 to $90 million in fiscal 2002. States will also get more leeway in running these work and training programs.

Certain states will be permitted to require parents of children as young as age one to work. States qualify for this if the state had requested the option as a waiver from federal rules and had had the waiver denied as of August 1, 1996. This age may be lowered to below age six for not more than three years. The law otherwise exempts parents of children up to age six from the food stamp work requirements.

State Flexibility

Waivers. The Agriculture secretary is given broader authority to waive federal food stamp requirements to encourage state experiments. State projects must be consistent with the goal of providing food assistance to raise nutrition levels among low-income people. They must also include an evaluation.

Permissible projects are those that improve administration, increase self-sufficiency of food stamp participants, test innovative welfare overhaul plans or allow more conformity with the rules of other social service programs.

However, if the secretary concludes that a project would reduce benefits by more than 20 percent for more than 5 percent of households in the project (excluding those whose benefits are reduced because they failed to comply with work or other conduct-related requirements), then the project:

- Cannot include more than 15 percent of the state's food stamp population.
- Is limited to five years, unless an extension is approved.

The secretary may not approve a waiver that:

- Involves the payment of food stamp allotments in cash (unless the project was approved before enactment).
- Substantially transfers food stamp funds to services or benefits provided through another public assistance program.
- Uses food stamp funds for anything but food, program administration, or an employment or training program.
- Gives or increases housing expense deductions to households with either no out-of-pocket housing expenses or housing expenses that represent a low percentage of their income.
- Absolves the state from the responsibility of acting promptly to reported changes in income or household size.
- Is not limited to a specific time period.
- Waives a provision in a "simplified food stamp program," which states may set up for households in which all members receive food stamps and cash assistance.

The legislation also prohibits waivers from some provisions that were in effect before the legislation was enacted. These include:

- A general ban against providing benefits to people in institutions.
- The requirement to provide food stamp assistance to all who are eligible, as long as they meet the program's rules.
- The income eligibility limit for households without elderly or disabled members.
- The rule that no parent or caretaker of a child under age six will be subject to work and training requirements (except as provided for above).
- The rule that employment or workfare programs be subject to the minimum wage.
- The requirement that food stamps not be considered income for other purposes.

Unified rules. States will be permitted to create a "simplified food stamp program" for households in which all members are also receiving welfare cash assistance. States could establish a single set of benefit rules for food stamps, welfare checks, and other programs.

States that choose this option will still have to follow certain food stamp rules, including calculating benefits by assuming 30 percent of household income is available for food purchases as determined under rules set by the state.

Cash-out options. States can convert food stamp benefits to wage subsidies for employers who hire food stamp recipients. The recipients will then receive wages instead of food stamps. This option cannot be used to displace nonsubsidized workers. Also, states that choose this option must have a plan that shows how they are helping to move the recipients into unsubsidized jobs.

Also, certain states can choose to issue food stamps in cash to households that participate in the welfare block grant and in the food stamp program, if a member of the household has been working for at least three months and earns at least $350 a month in unsubsidized employment.

Electronic Benefits

The legislation encourages states to shift to an electronic benefit transfer system (EBT) and requires them to do so by October 1, 2002, unless they receive a waiver from the Agriculture secretary. Under EBT, food coupons are replaced by automatic teller machine cards.

Food stamp card holders will not be protected by the same federal regulation that protects credit card holders from losses stemming from stolen cards. The legislation directs that regulations regarding lost EBT benefits be similar to those regarding lost food stamp coupons.

Penalties

Fraud. Basic penalties for fraud and abuse will double. Those who intentionally violate food stamp program requirements the first time will be disqualified for one year instead of six months. The penalty for the second intentional violation—and first involving a controlled substance—will be two years instead of one year.

Trafficking. People convicted of trafficking in food stamp benefits of $500 or more will be permanently disqualified from receiving food stamps. Also, property involved in or gained by food stamp trafficking must be forfeited.

Work requirements. Individuals who refuse to cooperate with a state in determining their job status or availability or who refuse to work without good cause will be disqualified for food stamps.

Those who violate the work requirements will be disqualified for at least one month for the first violation and up to three months at state option. The second violation will draw a minimum disqualification of three months and a maximum of six months. For the third violation, individuals will be disqualified for six months—or permanently, if a state chooses.

Violations of other programs. States are barred from increasing food stamp benefits for a recipient who loses welfare benefits for failing to comply with the rules of welfare programs. States may reduce food stamp allotments by up to 25 percent for failure to comply with another low-income benefit program's rules. Stiffer penalties are possible for a recipient who violates rules regarding the welfare block grant.

Multiple locations. Individuals will be ineligible for food stamps for ten years if a state agency (or federal or state court) concludes that they have fraudulently tried to receive food stamp benefits in more than one location at the same time.

Fleeing felons. Individuals will be ineligible for food stamps while fleeing to avoid prosecution, custody, or confinement for a felony or attempted felony or violating a condition of probation or parole.

Businesses. The Agriculture Department will have more authority to penalize retailers and wholesalers who are considered likely to permit program violations—such as those who have been disqualified from WIC.

Child support. States are permitted to disqualify from the food stamps program:

- The custodial parents of children under age eighteen who have an absent parent, unless the parent cooperates with the state child support agency to establish paternity and obtain support for the child. Cooperation is not required if the state finds there is good cause.
- The noncustodial parents of children under eighteen if they refuse to cooperate with the state child support agency in establishing paternity and obtaining support for the child.
- Anyone who is delinquent in court-ordered child support payments, unless the court allows a delay or the individual complies with a payment plan approved by the court or a state child support agency.

Commodity Food Programs

The Emergency Food Assistance Program (TEFAP), which distributes commodities to emergency food operations, will be consolidated with similar programs for soup kitchens and food banks. The legislation sets aside $100 million annually in food stamp funds from fiscal 1997 to 2002 to buy commodities for the revised TEFAP. Commodities will be distributed to states based on the current formula, which considers poverty and unemployment rates.

Other Provisions

State legislatures. The legislation clarifies that federal aid for the family assistance and child care block grants will be appropriated through state legislatures and will not be controlled exclusively by governors.

Public housing. Anyone who is fleeing prosecution after being convicted of a felony will be ineligible for public housing or subsidized housing assistance. This prohibition also extends to those who violate probation or parole.

Also, anyone whose low-income assistance benefits are reduced because of an act of fraud cannot receive additional public or subsidized housing aid to compensate for the penalty.

Teenage pregnancies. The HHS secretary is required, by January 1, 1997, to begin implementing a plan to prevent out-of-wedlock teenage pregnancies and assure that at least 25 percent of the nation's communities have programs in place to prevent teenage pregnancy.

Electronic benefits. The legislation generally exempts those who receive low-income assistance through automatic teller machine cards from the same federal regulation that protects credit card holders from losses stemming from stolen cards. The legislation specifically exempts from this protection any low-income assistance program created under state or local law or administered by a state or local government.

Social services. The social services block grant, which provides money to states for services such as child care, will be reduced by 15 percent from the previously approved level of $2.8 billion annually. As a result, $2.4 billion annually will be set aside from fiscal 1997 through 2002. The $2.8 billion appropriation will be reinstated in fiscal 2003 and thereafter.

The legislation explicitly permits states to use social services block grant funds to provide noncash vouchers for children whose parents exceed the five-year time limit on welfare benefits and for children who are born to welfare recipients.

Earned-Income Tax Credit. The legislation makes modest changes to scale back the Earned-Income Tax Credit, which provides tax relief for low-income workers. The provisions generally aim to tighten compliance with tax rules and make it harder for some people to qualify for the credit. The measures:

- Require use of a valid taxpayer identification number to allow the Internal Revenue Service to more closely track claimants' identity and income.
- Include additional categories of income—such as capital gains—to disqualify a taxpayer for the credit. It also lowers the threshold of disqualified income—which also includes interest, dividends, and rent—above which an individual cannot qualify for the tax credit from $2,350 to $2,200, and indexes it for inflation.
- Exclude certain losses—such as net capital losses—that are considered when determining whether a worker's adjusted gross income is low enough to qualify for the credit.

Abstinence education. The legislation sets aside $50 million annually from fiscal 1998 through 2002 to promote abstinence from sexual activity as one of the services provided under the Maternal and Child Health block grant. This block grant helps state and local health agencies provide services aimed at reducing infant mortality and improving the health of young children.

Parties Differ Over Success of '96 Welfare Law

By Sue Kirchhoff
(Reprinted from CQ Weekly, *May 29, 1999)*

Three years after Congress approved a broad welfare overhaul that set tight limits on benefits, Democrats and Republicans are divided about whether to label it a historic success or a still-unproven experiment.

Led by House Speaker J. Dennis Hastert, R-Ill., Republicans on May 26 held a news conference to press their case that the 1996 welfare law (PL 104-193), largely a GOP initiative, had been a triumph.

Republicans pointed to a dramatic 45 percent reduction in welfare rolls since 1994 and released a General Accounting Office (GAO) study finding that 61 percent to 87 percent of adults leaving welfare in seven states having been employed for at least some period of time. "What works is work," said Ways and Means Committee Chairman Bill Archer, R-Texas.

Later, at a hearing before the Ways and Means Subcommittee on Human Resources, Democrats questioned the GOP members' conclusions. Benjamin L. Cardin, D-Md., expressed concern that even though caseloads were down, many individuals leaving welfare had not moved out of poverty.

The same GAO study, for example, found that many former welfare recipients were moving into low-paying jobs and that from 19 percent to 30 percent of those studied who left welfare moved back onto the rolls.

President Clinton has also boasted about the falling caseload, but called for additional aid such as job training assistance and restoration of benefits cut under the law.

At the subcommittee hearing, some experts pointed to gains in income of some leaving welfare, while others warned of a troubling decline in income among the poorest, single-mother families. Congress is expected to make only modest changes to the welfare law this session, including creating outreach programs to get fathers more involved with their children. Hearings examining dramatic drops in the Medicaid and food stamp rolls are also likely.

As Welfare Caseloads Decline, Parties Disagree Over Whether to Reach Out or Cut Back

By Sue Kirchhoff
(Reprinted from CQ Weekly, *August 7, 1999)*

Republicans and Democrats agree on one point regarding the landmark 1996 welfare law—income assistance and food stamp caseloads have plummeted further and faster than anyone anticipated when it was signed by President Clinton. But even after a spate of new studies on the impact of the law (PL 104-193), the two parties still have far different views about whether the decline is cause for celebration or concern.

A General Accounting Office (GAO) study released February 2 said that food stamp rolls, which have declined nearly 30 percent since 1996, have fallen faster than can be explained by the combination of a booming economy and changes in the welfare law, which restricted benefits to legal immigrants and working-age individuals with no dependents.

The GAO study, requested by Rep. Sander M. Levin, D-Mich., and Rep. William J. Coyne, D-Pa., suggested that many eligible recipients did not know they qualified for aid and that some states have purposely made it difficult for low-income people to sign up for nutrition assistance.

The Clinton administration, alarmed about the nearly 30 percent reduction in food stamp rolls since 1996, has begun an outreach effort to persuade eligible families to sign up.

Officials' concerns are heightened by the fact that children account for about half the caseload reduction. The GAO said that in fiscal year 1997 the number of children living in poverty dropped by 3 percent, but the number of children receiving food stamps fell by 10 percent.

Efforts to restore benefits are opposed by key lawmakers such as Rep. Robert W. Goodlatte, R-Va., chairman of the Agriculture Subcommittee on Department Operations, Oversight, Nutrition and Forestry.

"I think that the food stamp rolls are responding to a very healthy economy and changes in the welfare law. . . . It's a positive thing," Goodlatte said August 4. "It restores dignity to millions of people."

Goodlatte's subcommittee, with prodding from ranking member Eva Clayton, D-N.C., held a hearing on the issue August 5.

"Food stamps are not welfare, they are a means to escape it," Shirley R. Watkins, Agriculture undersecretary for food, nutrition and consumer affairs, told the subcommittee. "They are not a lifestyle. Most people are off the rolls within a year."

Fine-Tuning Welfare?

A parallel drop in caseloads has fueled a similar debate about whether the welfare law needs fine-tuning. The outlook is complicated by a split between governors and House leaders.

The 1996 law limited cash assistance to five years, required recipients to work after two years and replaced a six-decade entitlement with an annual $16.4 billion block grant to states. Because caseloads have fallen faster than expected, governors have built up a healthy surplus of funds—$4.2 billion as of last December.

At the same time, congressional Republicans find themselves short of money to finance must-pass spending bills and a $792 billion, ten-year tax cut. To raise cash, House Speaker J. Dennis Hastert, R-Ill., and other House leaders want governors to refund unused welfare payments.

States have angrily rejected the plan, and Democrats have tried to capitalize on the dispute.

"There are some in Congress who want to cut the welfare block grant we give to the states and take some of that money back—because the welfare rolls are so low—to finance a big tax cut. I think that would be a mistake," Clinton told a welfare-to-work conference in Chicago on August 3.

Welfare caseloads have fallen from 11.4 million in January 1997 to 7.3 million in March 1999.

Nancy L. Johnson, R-Conn., chairwoman of the House Ways and Means Subcommittee on Human Resources, which oversees welfare, is also fighting the GOP leaders' effort. "I unequivocally oppose it," Johnson said on August 4. "I don't think it will have enough support, but I am tracking every murmur carefully." For months, Johnson has been urging states to spend more of their block grant money.

Governors contend they have made enormous efforts to move welfare recipients to work. That was borne out August 2 when the Department of Health and Human Services announced that all fifty states and the District of Columbia had met the law's requirements that 30 percent of participants work at least twenty hours a week in 1998. Despite the healthy economy, however, only twenty-eight of forty-one states met a requirement that 75 percent of recipients in two-parent families work thirty-five hours a week. The statistics reflect the first full year of reporting on the welfare work provisions.

Separately, the nonpartisan Urban Institute released its study of the well-being of women who had left welfare. It found that most women who had left welfare were working in low-wage jobs; nearly 20 percent had reported problems paying rent and one-third to one-half had struggled to buy food.

Clinton's fiscal 2000 budget requested billions of dollars for job training, housing, and child care subsidies to ensure that families moving off welfare could become self-sufficient.

The House's fiscal 2000 spending for the Veterans Affairs and Housing and Urban Development departments would provide $2 billion less for subsidized housing than Clinton requested. Johnson has rejected calls for more child care funding this year, pointing to state welfare surpluses. She added that some states—including Connecticut—have used all available child care funds and Congress may provide more aid next year. The GOP tax bill includes a two-year extension of a welfare-to-work tax credit.

Welfare Overhaul's Next Wave

By David Nather
(Reprinted from CQ Weekly, *March 17, 2001)*

It was just a sentence buried under a mountain of budget proposals, but that one line in President Bush's first budget may have captured the essence of the coming debate in Congress over the future structure of the welfare system.

In the fiscal 2002 outline he sent to Capitol Hill on Feb. 28, Bush said states should be encouraged to set up tax credits to reward people who give money to private charities. No problem so far; lawmakers from both parties say charities should get more help.

The catch is how Bush proposed paying for the tax credits. He wants to let states dip into a pot of money that used to be politically untouchable: the funds for Temporary Assistance for Needy Families (TANF), the program commonly known as "welfare."

With that proposal, Bush stepped squarely into the heart of the congressional debate over the upcoming reauthorization of the 1996 law (PL 104-193) that wiped out the old welfare system and built a new, time-limited one in its place.

Congress is just starting to turn to the task, but the outlines of the debate are already clear as lawmakers take a good hard look at the biggest social policy change of the 1990s.

Many Republicans will argue that the battle against welfare dependency is essentially over—caseloads have dropped by more than 50 percent, and there are 6.9 million fewer people on the rolls—and that lawmakers should feel free to spend TANF money on other things. Democrats and some moderate Republicans will argue the opposite: The remaining welfare recipients have more serious problems that will require just as much federal spending, if not more, to help them leave.

Without saying a word officially, Bush may have picked an early fight with Democrats.

By allowing states to spend welfare funds on other initiatives, the Bush proposal would set "a dangerous precedent," said Benjamin L. Cardin of Maryland, the ranking Democrat on the House Ways and Means Subcommittee on Human Resources. "We should be moving in the opposite direction." Administration officials did not respond to requests for comment on the proposal.

Five years ago, the welfare overhaul produced a flood of emotional and bitter exchanges. Rep. John Lewis, D-Ga., called it "mean" and "downright lowdown." House Majority Whip Tom DeLay, R-Texas, called the criticisms "one last, desperate attempt by the minority to cling to the status quo."

Those kinds of exchanges are unlikely to be repeated this time, because welfare has largely disappeared from the political debate. When Bush first ran for governor of Texas in 1994, "welfare reform" was one of his biggest themes. In his presidential campaign last year, he barely mentioned it.

But the question Congress faces is still important to millions of poor families: What comes next?

Among Republicans, the ideas include toughening work requirements, encouraging marriage, curbing out-of-wedlock births, and creating a greater role for faith-based social services. The faith-based proposals are in keeping with the direction Bush has signaled, but they come at a time of growing doubts on Capitol Hill.

Democrats, meanwhile, will try to ease the program's time limits and shift the emphasis to reducing poverty, not just caseloads.

The reauthorization will be many lawmakers' first look back at the decision to end welfare as an entitlement, available to all families poor enough to qualify, and replace it with a block grant that limits every poor family to five years of federal assistance—after which adults are expected to go to work.

For both parties, the terms of the debate have changed. For Republicans, the task will be to preserve and build upon a welfare overhaul that they consider one of their greatest successes.

"If it ain't broke, don't fix it," said Rep. Wally Herger, R-Calif., the new chairman of the Human Resources Subcommittee, which has jurisdiction over TANF and held its first reauthorization hearing March 15.

"I think it's exceeded everybody's expectations as the most successful legislation in memory," said Rep. E. Clay Shaw Jr., R-Fla., one of the authors of the 1996 law.

For Democrats, the goal is no longer to fight time limits or work requirements, but to make sure poor families are being treated fairly within the boundaries of the new system. They want to call attention to the story they see behind the plummeting caseloads and declining poverty rates: the single mothers who have been unable to leave welfare or thrive in their new jobs.

"The best you can say is that some people are doing as well as can be expected under the circumstances, and others are doing worse," said Sen. Paul Wellstone, D-Minn., who voted against the 1996 overhaul.

Already, some state and local welfare-to-work programs are experimenting with new ways to help "hard-to-serve" welfare recipients—those who have no high school diploma, little or no work history, little knowledge of English, or more serious problems such as mental illness or substance addiction. The lessons of these programs could become important as Congress looks for ways to deal with the changing face of welfare.

They could be particularly important to moderate Republicans, who appreciate the overhaul's successes, but are mindful that many poor families have not shared in them.

"We definitely want them to get into the workforce. We're not going to go back on that," said Nancy L. Johnson, R-Conn., who chaired the Human Resources Subcommittee in the 106th Congress and remains on the panel. "But we want them to move out of that minimum wage job and up the economic ladder. Not enough states are paying attention to that."

The Other Strands

The TANF reauthorization must be done by October 2002, when the program expires. At the same time, lawmakers will be debating what to do about the other major strands of the safety net for poor families. Food stamps, child-care assistance, and transitional Medicaid health insurance coverage for welfare recipients who have gone to work all must be renewed by the same date.

Smaller pieces of the 1996 welfare law, including a contingency fund for states with high unemployment rates and grants to help states with rapid population growth, must be reauthorized by October 2001.

The broad numbers have made the overhaul look like an unqualified success. Those numbers, however, do not tell the whole story.

Overall poverty rates are lower than they have been since 1979. In 1996, 13.7 percent of Americans were officially classified as poor, with an income of no more than $13,874 for a family of three; by 1999, that had fallen to 11.8 percent. The trend held up for children and for every major racial and ethnic category.

Most low-income mothers who have left welfare have found jobs, and never-married single mothers—the people most likely to stay on welfare for long periods, according to numerous studies—are moving into the workforce in record numbers and earning more than ever.

"The good news is that we have a program that even the critics would admit has worked very well," said Herger.

But some critics say the overhaul left too many people behind. "I think people feel like the problem has been solved—which they shouldn't, because a lot of people have been hurt," said Peter Edelman, one of three Department of Health and Human Services (HHS) officials who resigned in protest in 1996 when President Bill Clinton decided to sign the legislation.

Edelman and other foes of the 1996 law say their greatest fear has been realized: Many families that have left welfare are still struggling. They cite a December study by the Urban Institute, a Washington think tank, that said about a third of former welfare recipients had to skip meals or eat less. About 46 percent said they had been unable to pay rent or utility bills at some point within the previous twelve months.

Many other former recipients have not found jobs. Pamela Loprest, a senior research associate at the Urban Institute and the author of the study, said about a quarter of former welfare recipients had no earnings after leaving the system. Some probably shifted to disability payments, she said, but about 17 percent could not be found.

Those people "are the big concern," said Loprest. "We don't have a good picture of what's happened to these people and how they're surviving."

Even employers who are trying to make the new system work warn Congress not to declare victory too quickly.

"It's easy to gloss over the fact that there are still some major challenges," said Dorian Friedman, vice president of policy at the Welfare to Work Partnership, a national coalition of businesses that promise to hire former recipients. "A lot of the people who have left the rolls and gone to work are still poor."

The biggest unknown is what will happen as more families start running into the time limits on federal TANF benefits. So far, an estimated 60,000 people have hit time limits in twenty-one states.

No studies have looked specifically at how those people have fared, because the limits have kicked in too recently, but news reports from those states suggest many recipients have gotten extensions. Some mothers who lost their benefits ended up "broke, sick and depressed," according to a report in *The Tampa Tribune* in October 1999, a year after Florida's limit on welfare benefits took effect.

Over the next two years, the first time limits will kick in for families in another twenty-seven states and the District of Columbia. States can continue benefits to children and even entire families if the states pick up the tab themselves, but it is not clear how many will do so.

It is also not clear how much of the welfare overhaul's statistical success has been due to the booming economy. Supporters say prosperity alone cannot explain the drops in welfare caseloads or poverty rates, because neither declined in the mid-1980s, when the economy was also strong.

"This has very little to do with the economy," said Rep. Shaw, "and everything to do with the tremendous success of welfare reform."

Still, "there's a concern that an economic downturn could reverse a lot of the gains that we've achieved," said Elaine M. Ryan, acting executive director of the American Public Human Services Association, which represents state human services administrators.

Moderate Republicans, Democrats, and state officials all believe they will have a battle on their hands to prevent conservative Republicans from cutting TANF funds.

Ever since former House Budget Committee Chairman John R. Kasich, R-Ohio (1983–2001), wrote a nonbinding budget resolution for fiscal 1999 that called for TANF cuts, the money has been tempting fiscal conservatives.

"I don't think the states are going to get a pass on [TANF cuts]," warned one Senate Republican aide. "Obviously, state budgets have been relatively healthy."

But state officials say they need the funding because the people still on welfare are more likely to have multiple problems, such as mental illness and substance abuse, and thus will be more expensive to move off the rolls.

"The people who are left on the rolls have a lot of problems, and they need help," said Rep. Johnson, who vowed to fight any TANF budget cuts.

The Players

When welfare legislation begins moving in committee, it will be handled by a cast that is relatively new to welfare policy.

In the House, Herger plans to focus the hearings on "ways to make welfare reform work even better." That could include deciding what to do for welfare recipients who have not been able to find jobs, he said, and ways to "help families stay together and make sure children have two parents."

Herger also brings a longtime pet cause to the debate: eliminating welfare fraud. He is likely to revive a 1999 proposal to crack down on prison inmates who "illegally receive hundreds of millions of dollars in welfare payments each year."

In the Senate, the Finance Committee has a new chairman, Republican Charles E. Grassley of Iowa, who says the question of how ex-welfare recipients are doing will be critical when the panel starts to write its reauthorization plan.

"We need to know as much as possible about how these former welfare recipients got back in the workforce, if they stayed on the job, and how far they've moved to self-sufficiency," Grassley said in a statement.

Johnson and Cardin, who are well-versed in the complexities of welfare policy, and Shaw, who has the institutional knowledge of the debates that shaped the 1996 law, also are expected to play important roles in any discussions of welfare overhaul.

There are also some lawmakers who may not be centrally involved in the committee work but are likely to take an active role in floor debate. They include Sen. Sam Brownback, R-Kan., who believes reauthorization efforts should focus on faith-based organizations that could set up mentoring programs for people who are having the hardest time leaving the rolls.

"This is part of compassionate conservatism," said Brownback. "I would hope we would see more of these steps taken, because we've reduced the welfare rolls a lot."

Lawmakers also will hear from a colleague who has seen welfare firsthand: Rep. Lynn Woolsey, D-Calif., who relied on government aid to supplement her wages when she was a single mother raising three children in the 1970s.

"My fear is that the debate will be about, 'Well, who are these people who are still on welfare? Maybe we should punish them more,'" said Woolsey. "You know what? We're just going to hurt children."

The fact that Bush has not given more clues about his ideas could be a problem for Republicans, who are working with a GOP White House for the first time in eight years and are trying to coordinate their policies with the new administration.

Bush indicated that welfare will not be a back-burner issue when he selected former Wisconsin Gov. Tommy G. Thompson to run HHS, which oversees TANF. As governor, Thompson imposed strict time limits on welfare, but he also argued that states should spend more on services such as child care, health care, and transportation that low-income mothers need when they join the workforce.

However, in testimony at a March 14 hearing of the Ways and Means Committee, Thompson had little to say about the subject. "We really haven't put that much emphasis on TANF reauthorization yet," he said. Thompson is not the only one keeping his silence. One House GOP leadership aide said welfare overhaul is "not on our radar screen yet."

Democrats have no shortage of ideas for smoothing the rough edges they see in the new system. Among other things, they want bonuses to states that reduce poverty and exemptions from time limits for welfare recipients who work part time.

They say they are more focused on welfare than Republicans because they expected to take the House back in 2000. "We had to figure out what we were going to do," said Jim McDermott, D-Wash., a member of the Ways and Means Human Resources Subcommittee. House Republicans "can't do anything because they haven't heard what [Bush] wants."

The Issues

Democrats have begun to accept the general idea of time limits, and Republicans have promised to look more closely at people who are not faring well under the new rules. All signs, however, indicate that the two sides will continue to talk past each other on most of the issues. These areas are likely to be the biggest flashpoints:

- **Funding.** The biggest concern of moderate Republicans, Democrats, and state officials will be to maintain the current funding for the TANF block grant, set at $16.5 billion a year through fiscal 2002.

  Democrats also are likely to push for more child care funding, a move that is likely to be resisted by both conservative Republicans and moderates such as Johnson. New workers need to be helped with transitional services, Johnson said, but "all of this should be able to be done with the resources we're already providing."
- **Work requirements.** For conservative Republicans, one goal will be to strengthen employment guidelines.

  Under the 1996 law, states had to move at least 50 percent of their welfare recipients into jobs or "work activities" such as subsidized employment, on-the-job-training, and community service by fiscal 2002. But they could also satisfy the requirement if people simply left the rolls—and so many did so that those who remained did not have to work.

As a matter of principle, however, Republicans believe people should work in exchange for welfare benefits—so they may push for new work requirements for those who have not left.

"Just the threat of a work requirement was moving people off of welfare" even before the 1996 law took effect, said one House Republican aide.

- **Stopping the clock.** One major goal for Democrats will be to change the time limit for people who are working. In 1999, 28 percent of welfare recipients were working but did not earn enough to get by without TANF benefits. Under the 1996 law, that assistance counts against their five-year time limit.

  Another likely Democratic objective will be to create more exceptions to the five-year limit for people who have been unable to leave welfare and are about to lose their benefits.

  The 1996 law allows states to exempt 20 percent of their caseloads from the time limit because of "hardship." But some Democrats and advocates for the poor believe if the remaining welfare recipients have more serious problems than the ones who left, the 20 percent exemption will not be enough.

  "Some people in that other 80 percent are going to be pushed off a cliff," said Wellstone.

- **Faith-based initiatives.** The debate will offer Republicans a chance to expand on Bush's call for more faith-based initiatives.

  The welfare overhaul already allows federal funds to be used for welfare-to-work programs run by religious groups, a concept Bush wants to expand to a broader range of social services. When Bush outlined his faith-based initiatives proposal during the presidential campaign, he called it "the next bold step of welfare reform."

  Brownback sees it the same way. "We need to do more than just say, "Go get a job,'" he said. "But we don't think the old way helped either—just give them a little bit of money and hope everything works out. You've got to work with them on the inside, and then you've got to hold their hand when they get on the outside."

- **Reducing poverty.** Democrats want to do more to reduce poverty. Cardin said the reauthorization proposal he plans to introduce later this year will include bonus payments to states that do the best job of lowering poverty rates.

  "Yes, we want people to move off of welfare. Yes, we want two-parent families. Yes, we want families to stay together," said Cardin. "But we also want families out of poverty, and right now that is not an objective of welfare reform."

- **Reducing out-of-wedlock births.** Some conservatives believe the key to trimming welfare dependency further is to keep low-income women off the rolls. They say that means doing a better job of reducing births among unmarried women and promoting marriage.

"What we have is a kind of national neurosis where we don't talk about why child poverty exists or why the welfare state exists," said Robert Rector, a senior research fellow at the Heritage Foundation, a conservative think tank. "Both of them exist because of the erosion of marriage."

Such statements make some conservative Republicans nervous because they fear efforts to encourage marriage could lead to new government programs. Others, however, say there is nothing wrong with the message itself.

"What would be the single biggest thing we could do to reduce child poverty? Maintain intact homes," said Sen. Jeff Sessions, R-Ala. "When you split up a family, there will never be as much money as when families stay together."

- **The needs of Hispanics.** One significant change in the welfare rolls since 1996 has been the growing proportion of Hispanic women receiving aid.

  The reason Hispanic women are not leaving the rolls as quickly as white and African-American women is that many lack basic job skills, said Eric Rodriguez, director of the Economic Mobility Project at the National Council of La Raza, an advocacy group. And they are often sent to English classes instead of skills training programs.

  To address the issue, La Raza wants Congress to shift away from the 1996 law's "work first" philosophy and put more emphasis on education, training, and better access to transitional services.

  "The job isn't done," said Friedman of the Welfare to Work Partnership. "There's still a lot more that lawmakers can do."

Primary Documents

Following are texts of selected legislative documents and a Supreme Court case that have played prominent roles in welfare reform in the United States during the past two decades.

Selected Sections of Family Support Act of 1988 (Public Law 100-485)

The Family Support Act (FSA), signed by President Ronald Reagan on October 13, 1988, partly modified the welfare program by creating the Job Opportunities and Basic Skills (JOBS) program. JOBS attempted to address unemployment of welfare recipients by encouraging participation in education and training programs as well as direct employment.

TITLE II — JOB OPPORTUNITIES AND BASIC SKILLS TRAINING PROGRAM

SEC. 201. ESTABLISHMENT AND OPERATION OF PROGRAM.

(a) STATE PLAN REQUIREMENT. — Section 402(a)(19) of the Social Security Act <42 USC 602> is amended to read as follows:

(19) provide —

(A) that the State has in effect and operation a job opportunities and basic skills training program which meets the requirements of part F;

(B) that —

[**2357](i) the State will (except as otherwise provided in this paragraph or part F), to the extent that the program is available in the political subdivision involved and State resources otherwise permit —

(I) require all recipients of aid to families with dependent children in such subdivision with respect to whom the State guarantees child care in accordance with section 402(g) to participate in the program; and 403(l)(2);

239

(C) that an individual may not be required to participate in the program if such individual —

(i) is ill, incapacitated, or of advanced age;

(ii) is needed in the home because of the illness or incapacity of another member of the household;

(iii) subject to subparagraph (D) —

(I) is the parent or other relative of a child under 3 years of age (or, if so provided in the State plan, under any age that is less than 3 years but not less than one year) who is personally providing care for the child, or

(II) is the parent or other relative personally providing care for a child under 6 years of age, unless the State assures that child care in accordance with section 402(g) will be guaranteed and that participation in the program by the parent or relative will not be required for more than 20 hours a week;

(iv) works 30 or more hours a week;

(v) is a child who is under age 16 or attends, fulltime, an elementary, secondary, or vocational (or technical) school;

(vi) is pregnant if it has been medically verified that the child is expected to be born in the month in which such participation would otherwise be required or within the 6-month period immediately following such month; or

[**2358] (vii) resides in an area of the State where the program is not available;

(D) that, in the case of a family eligible for aid to families with dependent children by reason of the unemployment of the parent who is the principal earner, subparagraph (C)(iii) shall apply only to one parent, except that, in the case of such a family, the State may at its option make such subparagraph inapplicable to both of the parents (and require their participation in the program) if child care in accordance with section 402(g) is guaranteed with respect to the family;

(E) that —

(i) to the extent that the program is available in the political subdivision involved and State resources otherwise permit, in the case of a custodial parent who has not attained 20 years of age, has not successfully completed a high-school education (or its equivalent), and is required to participate in the program (including an individual who would otherwise be exempt from participation in the program solely by reason of subparagraph (C)(iii)), the State agency (subject to clause (ii)) will require such parent to participate in an educational activity; and

(ii) the State agency may —

(I) require a parent described in clause (i) (notwithstanding the part-time requirement in subparagraph (C)(iii)(II)) to participate in educational activities directed toward the attainment of a high school diploma or its equivalent on a fulltime (as defined by the educational provider) basis,

(II) establish criteria in accordance with regulations of the Secretary under which custodial parents described in clause (i) who have not attained 18 years of age may be exempted from the school attendance requirement under such clause, or

(III) require a parent described in clause (i) who is age 18 or 19 to participate in training or work activities (in lieu of the educational activities under such clause) if such parent fails to make good progress in successfully completing such educational activities or if it is determined (prior to any assignment of the individual to such educational activities) pursuant to an educational assessment that participation in such educational activities is inappropriate for such parent;

(F) that —

(i) if the parent or other caretaker relative or any dependent child in the family is attending (in good standing) an institution of higher education (as defined in section 481(a) of the Higher Education Act of 1965), or a school or course of vocational or technical training (not less than half time) consistent with the individual's employment goals, and is making satisfactory progress in such institution, school, or course, at the time he or she would otherwise commence participation in the program under this section, such attendance may constitute satisfactory participation in the program [**2359] (by that caretaker or child) so long as it continues and is consistent with such goals;

(ii) any other activities in which an individual described in clause (i) participates may not be permitted to interfere with the school or training described in that clause;

(iii) the costs of such school or training shall not constitute federally reimbursable expenses for purposes of section 403; and

(iv) the costs of day care, transportation, and other services which are necessary (as determined by the State agency) for such attendance in accordance with section 402(g) are eligible for Federal reimbursement;

(G) that —

(i) if an individual who is required by the provisions of this paragraph to participate in the program or who is so required by reason of the State's having exercised the option under subparagraph (D) fails without good cause to participate in the program or refuses without good cause to accept employment in which such individual is able to engage which is offered through the public employment offices of the State, or is otherwise offered by an employer if the offer of such employer is determined to be a bona fide offer of employment —

(I) the needs of such individual (whether or not section 407 applies) shall not be taken into account in making the determination with respect to his or her family under paragraph (7) of this subsection, and if such individual is a parent or other caretaker relative, payments of aid for any dependent child in the family in the form of payments of the type described in section 406(b)(2) (which in such a case shall be without regard to clauses (A) through (D) thereof) will be made unless the State agency, after making reasonable efforts, is unable to locate an appropriate individual to whom such payments can be made; and

(II) if such individual is a member of a family which is eligible for aid to families with dependent children by reason of section 407, and his or her spouse is not participating in the program, the needs of such spouse shall also not be taken into account in making such determination;

(ii) any sanction described in clause (i) shall continue —

(I) in the case of the individual's first failure to comply, until the failure to comply ceases;

(II) in the case of the individual's second failure to comply, until the failure to comply ceases or 3 months (whichever is longer); and

(III) in the case of any subsequent failure to comply, until the failure to comply ceases or 6 months (whichever is longer);

(iii) the State will promptly remind any individual whose failure to comply has continued for 3 months, in [**2360] writing, of the individual's option to end the sanction by terminating such failure; and

(iv) no sanction shall be imposed under this subparagraph —

(I) on the basis of the refusal of an individual described in subparagraph (C)(iii)(II) to accept employment, if the employment would require such individual to work more than 20 hours a week, or

(II) on the basis of the refusal of an individual to participate in the program or accept employment, if child care (or day care for any incapacitated individual living in the same home as a dependent child) is necessary for an individual to participate in the program or accept employment, such care is not available, and the State agency fails to provide such care; and

(H) the State agency may require a participant in the program to accept a job only if such agency assures that the family of such participant will experience no net loss of cash income resulting from acceptance of the job; and any costs incurred by the State agency as a result of this subparagraph shall be treated as expenditures with respect to which section 403(a)(1) or 403(a)(2) applies;

(b) ESTABLISHMENT AND OPERATION OF PROGRAM. — Title IV of such Act is further amended by adding at the end the following new part:

PART F — JOB OPPORTUNITIES AND BASIC SKILLS TRAINING PROGRAM PURPOSE AND DEFINITIONS

SEC. 481. ‹42 USC 681›

(a) PURPOSE. — It is the purpose of this part to assure that needy families with children obtain the education, training, and employment that will help them avoid long-term welfare dependence.

(b) MEANING OF TERMS. — Except to the extent otherwise specifically indicated, terms used in this part shall have the meanings given them in or under part A.

ESTABLISHMENT AND OPERATION OF STATE PROGRAMS

SEC. 482. ‹42 USC 682›

(a) STATE PLANS FOR JOB OPPORTUNITIES AND BASIC SKILLS TRAINING PROGRAMS. — (1)(A) As a condition of its participation in the program of aid to families with dependent children under part A, each State shall establish and operate a job opportunities and basic skills training program (in this part referred to as the 'program') under a plan approved by the Secretary as meeting all of the requirements of this part and section 402(a)(19), and shall, in accordance with regulations prescribed by the Secretary, periodically (but not less frequently than every 2 years) review and update its plan and submit the updated plan for approval by the Secretary.

(B) A State plan for establishing and operating the program must describe how the State intends to implement the program during the period covered by the plan, and must indicate, through cross references to the appropriate provisions of this part and part A, that the program will be operated in accordance with such provision of law. In addition, such plan must contain (i) an estimate of the [**2361] number of persons to be served by the program, (ii) a description of the services to be provided within the State and the political subdivisions thereof, the needs to be addressed through the provision of such services, the extent to which such services are expected to be made available by other agencies on a nonreimbursable basis, and the extent to which such services are to be provided or funded by the program, and (iii) such additional information as the Secretary may require by regulation to enable the Secretary to determine that the State program will meet all of the requirements of this part and part A.

(C) The Secretary shall consult with the Secretary of Labor on general plan requirements and on criteria to be used in approving State plans under this section.

(D)(i) Not later than October 1, 1992, each State shall make the program available in each political subdivision of such State where it is feasible to do so, after taking into account the number of prospective participants, the local economy, and other relevant factors.

(ii) If a State determines that it is not feasible to make the program available in each such subdivision, the State plan must provide appropriate justification to the Secretary.

(2) The State agency that administers or supervises the administration of the State's plan approved under section 402 shall be responsible for the administration or supervision of the administration of the State's program.

(3) Federal funds made available to a State for purposes of the program shall not be used to supplant non-Federal funds for existing services and activities which promote the purpose of this part. State or local funds expended for such purpose shall be maintained at least at the level of such expenditures for the fiscal year 1986.

(d) SERVICES AND ACTIVITIES UNDER THE PROGRAM. — (1)(A) In carrying out the program, each State shall make available a broad range of services and activities to aid in carrying out the purpose of this part. Such services and activities —

(i) shall include —

(I) educational activities (as appropriate), including high school or equivalent education (combined with training as needed), basic and remedial education to achieve a basic literacy level, and education for individuals with limited English proficiency;

(II) job skills training;

(III) job readiness activities to help prepare participants for work; and

(IV) job development and job placement; and

(ii) must also include at least 2 of the following:

[**2363] (I) group and individual job search as described in subsection (g);

(II) on-the-job training;

(III) work supplementation programs as described in subsection (e); and

(IV) community work experience programs as described in subsection (f) or any other work experience program approved by the Secretary.

(B) The State may also offer to participants under the program (i) postsecondary education in appropriate cases, and (ii) such other education, training, and employment activities as may be determined by the State and allowed by regulations of the Secretary.

(2) If the State requires an individual who has attained the age of 20 years and has not earned a high school diploma (or equivalent) to participate in the program, the State agency shall include educational activities consistent with his or her employment goals as a component of the individual's participation in the program, unless the individual demonstrates a basic literacy level, or the employability plan for the individual identifies a long-

term employment goal that does not require a high school diploma (or equivalent). Any other services or activities to which such a participant is assigned may not be permitted to interfere with his or her participation in an appropriate educational activity under this sub-paragraph.

(c) SEPARATE FUNDING FOR JOBS PROGRAM; FEDERAL FINANCIAL PARTICIPA-TION. — (1) Section 403 of such Act <42 USC 603> is amended by adding at the end the fol-lowing new subsection:

[**2373] (k)(1) Each State with a plan approved under part F shall be entitled to pay-ments under subsection (l) for any fiscal year in an amount equal to the sum of the applica-ble percentages (specified in such subsection) of its expenditures to carry out the program under part F (subject to limitations prescribed by or pursuant to such part or this section on expenditures that may be included for purposes of determining payment under subsec-tion (l)), but such payments for any fiscal year in the case of any State may not exceed the limitation determined under paragraph (2) with respect to the State.

(2) The limitation determined under this paragraph with respect to a State for any fiscal year is —

(A) the amount allotted to the State for fiscal year 1987 under part C of this title as then in effect, plus

(B) the amount that bears the same ratio to the amount specified in paragraph (3) for such fiscal year as the average monthly number of adult recipients (as defined in paragraph (4)) in the State in the preceding fiscal year bears to the average monthly number of such recipients in all the States for such preceding year.

(3) The amount specified in this paragraph is —

(A) $ 600,000,000 in the case of the fiscal year 1989,

(B) $ 800,000,000 in the case of the fiscal year 1990,

(C) $ 1,000,000,000 in the case of each of the fiscal years 1991, 1992, and 1993,

(D) $ 1,100,000,000 in the case of the fiscal year 1994,

(E) $ 1,300,000,000 in the case of the fiscal year 1995, and

(F) $ 1,000,000,000 in the case of the fiscal year 1996 and each succeeding fiscal year, re-duced by the aggregate amount allotted to all the States for fiscal year 1987 pursuant to part C of this title as then in effect.

(4) For purposes of this subsection, the term 'adult recipient' in the case of any State means an individual other than a dependent child (unless such child is the custodial parent of another dependent child) whose needs are met (in whole or in part) with payments of aid to families with dependent children.

(5) None of the funds available to a State for purposes of the programs or activities conducted under part F shall be used for construction.

(2) Section 403 of such Act (as amended by paragraph (1) of this subsection) is further amended by adding at the end the following new subsection:

(l)(1)(A) In lieu of any payment under subsection (a), the Secretary shall pay to each State with a plan approved under section 482(a) (subject to the limitation determined under section 482(i)(2)) with respect to expenditures by the State to carry out a program under part F (including expenditures for child care under section 402(g)(1)(A), but only in the case of a State with respect to which section 1108 applies), an amount equal to —

(i) with respect to so much of such expenditures in a fiscal year as do not exceed the State's expenditures in the fiscal year 1987 with respect to which payments were made to such State from its allotment for such fiscal year pursuant to part C of this title as then in effect, 90 percent; and

(ii) with respect to so much of such expenditures in a fiscal year as exceed the amount described in clause (i) —

(I) 50 percent, in the case of expenditures for administrative costs made by a State in operating such a program for [**2374] such fiscal year (other than the personnel costs for staff employed full-time in the operation of such program) and the costs of transportation and other work-related supportive services under section 402(g)(2), and

(II) the greater of 60 percent or the Federal medical assistance percentage (as defined in section 1118 in the case of any State to which section 1108 applies, or as defined in section 1905(b) in the case of any other State), in the case of expenditures made by a State in operating such a program for such fiscal year (other than for costs described in subclause (I)).

(B) With respect to the amount for which payment is made to a State under subparagraph (A)(i), the State's expenditures for the costs of operating a program established under part F may be in cash or in kind, fairly evaluated.

(2)(A) Notwithstanding paragraph (1), the Secretary shall pay to a State an amount equal to 50 percent of the expenditures made by such State in operating its program established under part F (in lieu of any different percentage specified in paragraph (1)(A)) if less than 55 percent of such expenditures are made with respect to individuals who are described in subparagraph (B).

(B) An individual is described in this paragraph if the individual —
(i)(I) is receiving aid to families with dependent children, and
(II) has received such aid for any 36 of the preceding 60 months;
(ii)(I) makes application for aid to families with dependent children, and

(II) has received such aid for any 36 of the 60 months immediately preceding the most recent month for which application has been made;

(iii) is a custodial parent under the age of 24 who (I) has not completed a high school education and, at the time of application for aid to families with dependent children, is not enrolled in high school (or a high school equivalency course of instruction), or

(II) had little or no work experience in the preceding year; or

(iv) is a member of a family in which the youngest child is within 2 years of being ineligible for aid to families with dependent children because of age.

(C) This paragraph may be waived by the Secretary with respect to any State which demonstrates to the satisfaction of the Secretary that the characteristics of the caseload in that State make it infeasible to meet the requirements of this paragraph, and that the State is targeting other long-term or potential long-term recipients.

(D) The Secretary shall biennially submit to the Congress any recommendations for modifications or additions to the groups of individuals described in subparagraph (B) that the Secretary determines would further the goal of assisting long-term or potential long-term recipients of aid to families with dependent children to achieve self-sufficiency, which recommendations shall take into account the particular characteristics of the populations of individual States.

(3)(A) Notwithstanding paragraph (1), the Secretary shall pay to a State an amount equal to 50 percent of the expenditures made by such State in a fiscal year in operating its program established under part F (in lieu of any different percentage specified in paragraph [**2375] (1)(A)) if the State's participation rate (determined under subparagraph (B)) for the preceding fiscal year does not exceed or equal —

(i) 7 percent if the preceding fiscal year is 1990;

(ii) 7 percent if such year is 1991;

(iii) 11 percent if such year is 1992;

(iv) 11 percent if such year is 1993;

(v) 15 percent if such year is 1994; and

(vi) 20 percent if such year is 1995.

(B)(i) The State's participation rate for a fiscal year shall be the average of its participation rates for computation periods (as defined in clause (ii)) in such fiscal year.

(ii) The computation periods shall be —

(I) the fiscal year, in the case of fiscal year 1990,

(II) the first six months, and the seventh through twelfth months, in the case of fiscal year 1991,

(III) the first three months, the fourth through sixth months, the seventh through ninth months, and the tenth through twelfth months, in the case of fiscal years 1992 and 1993, and

(IV) each month, in the case of fiscal years 1994 and 1995.

(iii) The State's participation rate for a computation period shall be the number, expressed as a percentage, equal to —

(I) the average monthly number of individuals required or allowed by the State to participate in the program under part F who have participated in such program in months in the computation period, plus the number of individuals required or allowed by the State to participate in such program who have so participated in that month in such period for which the number of such participants is the greatest, divided by

(II) twice the average monthly number of individuals required to participate in such period (other than individuals described in subparagraph (C)(iii)(I) or (D) of section 402(a)(19) with respect to whom the State has exercised its option to require their participation).

For purposes of this subparagraph, an individual shall not be considered to have satisfactorily participated in the program under part F solely by reason of such individual being registered to participate in such program.

(C) Notwithstanding any other provision of this paragraph, no State shall be subject to payment under this paragraph (in lieu of paragraph (1)(A)) for failing to meet any participation rate required under this paragraph with respect to any fiscal year before 1991.

(D) For purposes of this paragraph, an individual shall be determined to have participated in the program under part F, if such individual has participated in accordance with such requirements, consistent with regulations of the Secretary, as the State shall establish.

(E) If the Secretary determines that the State has failed to achieve the participation rate for any fiscal year specified in the numbered clauses of subparagraph (A), he may waive, in whole or in part, the reduction in the payment rate otherwise required by such subparagraph if he finds that —

(i) the State is in conformity with section 402(a)(19) and part F;

(ii) the State has made a good faith effort to achieve the applicable participation rate for such fiscal year; and

[**2376] (iii) the State has submitted a proposal which is likely to achieve the applicable participation rate for the current fiscal year and the subsequent fiscal years (if any) specified therein.

(4)(A)(i) Subject to subparagraph (B), in the case of any family eligible for aid to families with dependent children by reason of the unemployment of the parent who is the principal earner, the State agency shall require that at least one parent in any such family participate, for a total of at least 16 hours a week during any period in which either parent is required to participate in the program, in a work supplementation program, a community work experience or other work experience program, on-the-job training, or a State designed work program approved by the Secretary, as such programs are described in section 482(d)(1). In the case of a parent under age 25 who has not completed high school or an equivalent course of education, the State may require such parent to participate in educational activities directed at the attainment of a high school diploma (or equivalent) or another basic education program in lieu of one or more of the programs specified in the preceding sentence.

(ii) For purposes of clause (i), an individual participating in a community work experience program under section 482 shall be considered to have met the requirement of such clause if he participates for the number of hours in any month equal to the monthly payment of aid to families with dependent children to the family of which he is a member, divided by the greater of the Federal or the applicable State minimum wage (and the portion of such monthly payment for which the State is reimbursed by a child support collection shall not be taken into account in determining the number of hours that such individual may be required to work).

(B) The requirement under subparagraph (A) shall not be considered to have been met by any State if the requirement is not met with respect to the following percentages of all families in the State eligible for aid to families with dependent children by reason of the unemployment of the parent who is the principal earner:

(i) 40 percent, in the case of the average of each month in fiscal year 1994,

(ii) 50 percent, in the case of the average of each month in fiscal year 1995,

(iii) 60 percent, in the case of the average of each month in fiscal year 1996, and

(iv) 75 percent in the case of the average of each month in each of the fiscal years 1997 and 1998.

(C) The percentage of participants for any month in a fiscal year for purposes of the preceding sentence shall equal the average of —

(i) the number of individuals described in subparagraph (A)(i) who have met the requirement prescribed therein, divided by

(ii) the total number of principal earners described in such subparagraph (but excluding those in families who have been recipients of aid for 2 months or less if, during the period that the family received aid, at least one parent engaged in intensive job search).

(D) If the Secretary determines that the State has failed to meet the requirement under subparagraph (A) (determined with respect to the percentages prescribed in subparagraph (B)), he may waive, in whole or in part, any penalty if he finds that —

(i) the State is operating a program in conformity with section 402(a)(19) and part F,

[**2377] (ii) the State has made a good faith effort to meet the requirement of subparagraph (A) but has been unable to do so because of economic conditions in the State (including significant numbers of recipients living in remote locations or isolated rural areas where the availability of work sites is severely limited), or because of rapid and substantial increases in the caseload that cannot reasonably be planned for, and

(iii) the State has submitted a proposal which is likely to achieve the required percentage of participants for the subsequent fiscal years.

Selected Sections of Personal Responsibility and Work Opportunity Reconciliation Act of 1996 (Public Law 104-193)

The Personal Responsibility and Work Opportunity Reconciliation Act (PRWORA), signed by President Bill Clinton on August 22, 1996, dramatically overhauled the nation's welfare system, in particular by creating the Temporary Assistance for Needy Families (TANF) block grant program. Important features of TANF include provisions that tie welfare receipt to participation in work-related activities and place a lifetime limit of sixty months on these benefits. The following are selected excepts from the law.

PART A—BLOCK GRANTS TO STATES FOR TEMPORARY ASSISTANCE FOR NEEDY FAMILIES

SEC. 401. PURPOSE.

(a) IN GENERAL- The purpose of this part is to increase the flexibility of States in operating a program designed to-

(1) provide assistance to needy families so that children may be cared for in their own homes or in the homes of relatives;

(2) end the dependence of needy parents on government benefits by promoting job preparation, work, and marriage;

(3) prevent and reduce the incidence of out-of-wedlock pregnancies and establish annual numerical goals for preventing and reducing the incidence of these pregnancies; and

(4) encourage the formation and maintenance of two-parent families.

(b) NO INDIVIDUAL ENTITLEMENT- This part shall not be interpreted to entitle any individual or family to assistance under any State program funded under this part.

SEC. 407. MANDATORY WORK REQUIREMENTS.

(a) PARTICIPATION RATE REQUIREMENTS-

(1) ALL FAMILIES- A State to which a grant is made under section 403 for a fiscal year shall achieve the minimum participation rate specified in the following table for the fiscal year with respect to all families receiving assistance under the State program funded under this part:

The minimum participation
If the fiscal year is— rate is:
1997 —25
1998 —30
1999 —35
2000 —40
2001 —45
2002 or thereafter —50.

(2) 2-PARENT FAMILIES- A State to which a grant is made under section 403 for a fiscal year shall achieve the minimum participation rate specified in the following table for the fiscal year with respect to 2-parent families receiving assistance under the State program funded under this part:

The minimum participation
If the fiscal year is—rate is:
1997 —75
1998 —75
1999 or thereafter —90.

(b) CALCULATION OF PARTICIPATION RATES-

(1) ALL FAMILIES-

(A) AVERAGE MONTHLY RATE- For purposes of subsection (a)(1), the participation rate for all families of a State for a fiscal year is the average of the participation rates for all families of the State for each month in the fiscal year.

(B) MONTHLY PARTICIPATION RATES- The participation rate of a State for all families of the State for a month, expressed as a percentage, is—

(i) the number of families receiving assistance under the State program funded under this part that include an adult or a minor child head of household who is engaged in work for the month; divided by

(ii) the amount by which—

(I) the number of families receiving such assistance during the month that include an adult or a minor child head of household receiving such assistance; exceeds

(II) the number of families receiving such assistance that are subject in such month to a penalty described in subsection (e)(1) but have not been subject to such penalty for more than 3 months within the preceding 12-month period (whether or not consecutive).

(2) 2-PARENT FAMILIES-

(A) AVERAGE MONTHLY RATE- For purposes of subsection (a)(2), the participation rate for 2-parent families of a State for a fiscal year is the average of the participation rates for 2-parent families of the State for each month in the fiscal year.

(B) MONTHLY PARTICIPATION RATES- The participation rate of a State for 2-parent families of the State for a month shall be calculated by use of the formula set forth in paragraph (1)(B), except that in the formula the term 'number of 2-parent families' shall be substituted for the term 'number of families' each place such latter term appears.

(c) ENGAGED IN WORK-

(1) GENERAL RULES-

(A) ALL FAMILIES- For purposes of subsection (b)(1)(B)(i), a recipient is engaged in work for a month in a fiscal year if the recipient is participating in work activities for at least the minimum average number of hours per week specified in the following table during the month, not fewer than 20 hours per week of which are attributable to an activity described in paragraph (1), (2), (3), (4), (5), (6), (7), (8), or (12) of subsection (d), subject to this subsection:

The minimum participation

If the month is —average number of in fiscal year: —hours per week is:

1997 —20

1998 —20

1999 —25

2000 or thereafter —30.

(B) 2-PARENT FAMILIES- For purposes of subsection (b)(2)(B), an individual is engaged in work for a month in a fiscal year if—

(i) the individual is making progress in work activities for at least 35 hours per week during the month, not fewer than 30 hours per week of which are attributable to an activity described in paragraph (1), (2), (3), (4), (5), (6), (7), (8), or (12) of subsection (d), subject to this subsection; and

(ii) if the family of the individual receives federally-funded child care assistance and an adult in the family is not disabled or caring for a severely disabled child, the individual's spouse is making progress in work activities during the month, not fewer than 20 hours per week of which are attributable to an activity described in paragraph (1), (2), (3), (4), (5), or (7) of subsection (d).

(2) LIMITATIONS AND SPECIAL RULES-

(A) NUMBER OF WEEKS FOR WHICH JOB SEARCH COUNTS AS WORK-

(i) LIMITATION- Notwithstanding paragraph (1) of this subsection, an individual shall not be considered to be engaged in work by virtue of participation in an activity described in subsection (d)(6) of State program funded under this part, after the individual has participated in such an activity for 6 weeks (or, if the unemployment rate of the State is at least 50 percent greater than the unemployment rate of the United States, 12 weeks), or if the participation is for a week that immediately follows 4 consecutive weeks of such participation.

(B) SINGLE PARENT WITH CHILD UNDER AGE 6 DEEMED TO BE MEETING WORK PARTICIPATION REQUIREMENTS IF PARENT IS ENGAGED IN WORK FOR 20

HOURS PER WEEK- For purposes of determining monthly participation rates under sub-section (b)(1)(B)(i), a recipient in a 1-parent family who is the parent of a child who has not attained 6 years of age is deemed to be engaged in work for a month if the recipient is engaged in work for an average of at least 20 hours per week during the month.

(C) TEEN HEAD OF HOUSEHOLD WHO MAINTAINS SATISFACTORY SCHOOL ATTENDANCE DEEMED TO BE MEETING WORK PARTICIPATION REQUIREMENTS- For purposes of determining monthly participation rates under sub-section (b)(1)(B)(i), a recipient who is a single head of household and has not attained 20 years of age is deemed, subject to subparagraph (D) of this paragraph, to be engaged in work for a month in a fiscal year if the recipient—

(i) maintains satisfactory attendance at secondary school or the equivalent during the month; or

(ii) participates in education directly related to employment for at least the minimum average number of hours per week specified in the table set forth in paragraph (1)(A) of this subsection.

(D) NUMBER OF PERSONS THAT MAY BE TREATED AS ENGAGED IN WORK BY VIRTUE OF PARTICIPATION IN VOCATIONAL EDUCATION ACTIVITIES OR BEING A TEEN HEAD OF HOUSEHOLD WHO MAINTAINS SATISFACTORY SCHOOL ATTENDANCE- For purposes of determining monthly participation rates under paragraphs (1)(B)(i) and (2)(B) of subsection (b), not more than 20 percent of individuals in all families and in 2-parent families may be determined to be engaged in work in the State for a month by reason of participation in vocational educational training or deemed to be engaged in work by reason of subparagraph (C) of this paragraph.

(d) WORK ACTIVITIES DEFINED- As used in this section, the term 'work activities' means—

(1) unsubsidized employment;

(2) subsidized private sector employment;

(3) subsidized public sector employment;

(4) work experience (including work associated with the refurbishing of publicly assisted housing) if sufficient private sector employment is not available;

(5) on-the-job training;

(6) job search and job readiness assistance;

(7) community service programs;

(8) vocational educational training (not to exceed 12 months with respect to any individual);

(9) job skills training directly related to employment;

(10) education directly related to employment, in the case of a recipient who has not received a high school diploma or a certificate of high school equivalency;

(11) satisfactory attendance at secondary school or in a course of study leading to a certificate of general equivalence, in the case of a recipient who has not completed secondary school or received such a certificate; and

(12) the provision of child care services to an individual who is participating in a community service program.

SEC. 408. PROHIBITIONS; REQUIREMENTS.

(a) IN GENERAL-

(7) NO ASSISTANCE FOR MORE THAN 5 YEARS-

(A) IN GENERAL- A State to which a grant is made under section 403 shall not use any part of the grant to provide assistance to a family that includes an adult who has received assistance under any State program funded under this part attributable to funds provided by the Federal Government, for 60 months (whether or not consecutive) after the date the State program funded under this part commences, subject to this paragraph.

(C) HARDSHIP EXCEPTION-

(i) IN GENERAL- The State may exempt a family from the application of subparagraph (A) by reason of hardship or if the family includes an individual who has been battered or subjected to extreme cruelty.

(ii) LIMITATION- The number of families with respect to which an exemption made by a State under clause (i) is in effect for a fiscal year shall not exceed 20 percent of the average monthly number of families to which assistance is provided under the State program funded under this part.

Selected Sections of the Personal Responsibility Act (Welfare Reform), as Found in the "Contract with America"

When Republicans won control of Congress in 1994, many members had signed on to the "Contract with America," an agenda outlining conservatives' positions on many different policy areas including welfare reform. Similar to PRWORA, the "Personal Responsibility Act" in the contract called for increased participation in work activities and time limits for welfare recipients, but it also included measures designed as deterrence against out-of-wedlock childbearing. The following are selected excerpts from the Personal Responsibility Act.

The Personal Responsibility Act overhauls the American welfare system to reduce government dependency, attack illegitimacy, require welfare recipients to enter work programs and cap total welfare spending. The bill's main thrust is to give states greater control over the benefits programs, work programs, and Aid to Families with Dependent Children (AFDC) payments and requirements.

Under the bill, the structure for AFDC payments will drastically change. Mothers under the age of 18 may no longer receive AFDC payments for children born out of wedlock and mothers who are ages 18, 19, and 20 can be prohibited by the states from receiving AFDC payments and housing benefits. Mothers must also establish paternity as a condition for receiving AFDC payments, except in cases of rape and incest. Also, in order to reduce the amount of time families are on welfare, states must begin moving welfare recipients into work programs if they have received welfare for two years. States are given the option to drop families from receiving AFDC benefits after they have received welfare for two years if at least one year has been spent in a work program. To further limit the length of time on AFDC, states must drop families from the program after they have received a total of five years of AFDC benefits.

The bill allows states to design their own work programs and determine who will be required to participate. Welfare recipients must work an average of 35 hours a week or enroll in work training programs. By the year 2001, 1.5 million AFDC recipients will be required to work.

The bill caps the spending growth of several major welfare programs (AFDC, Supplemental Security Income (SSI) and public housing) and consolidates 10 nutrition programs, including food stamps, WIC and the school lunch program, into one discretionary block grant to states.

Finally, the bill grants greater flexibility to states allowing them to design their own work programs and determine who participates in them and can choose to opt out of the current AFDC program by converting their share of AFDC payments into fixed annual block grants.

Background

In the mid-1960s President Lyndon Johnson launched a war on poverty with the hope of creating a "Great Society." The federal government was mobilized to fight poverty by creating a slew of new federal programs and expanding existing ones, such as AFDC. Established in 1935 under the Social Security Act, AFDC was created to help widows care for their children. It now serves divorced, deserted and never-married individuals and their children. AFDC continues to be the major cash welfare program for families. Federal funds pay at least 50 percent of each state's benefits and administrative costs. In June 1994, enrollment reached 5,028,000 families, just below the record of 5,083,000 set in March 1994. Individual recipients numbered 14.2 million and unemployed two-parent families totaled 362,000. Also, food stamp enrollment in June 1994 was 27.4 million persons—a record high. Although almost half of the mothers who enter AFDC can be expected to leave within 2 years, most return. Long-term users often are young, never-married, and high school dropouts; and most AFDC families begin with a birth to a teenager.

In the past few years, the federal governments and state governments have tried to change and improve the welfare system. The Clinton Administration campaigned to "end welfare as we know it," though, to date, Congress has not held a vote on its proposal. The administration proposal limits AFDC benefits to two years, during which employment services would be provided to recipients. Nearly 20 welfare reform bills have been introduced in the 103d Congress, including three major proposals offered by Republican members:

The GOP Leadership Welfare Reform Bill (H.R. 3500). After two years on AFDC (or less at a state's option), welfare recipients must work 35 hours per week in a private or public sector job. It also requires mothers to establish paternity before receiving AFDC benefits, denies AFDC benefits to parents under age 18, and denies increased AFDC benefits for having additional children while on welfare—unless a state enact laws to exempt itself from any of these requirements.

The Real Welfare Reform Act (H.R. 4566). This measure prohibits AFDC, food stamps, and public housing to unmarried mothers under age 21 (the age limit is raised to 25 in 1998); requires paternity to be established as a condition for receiving AFDC, food stamps and public housing; provides a $1,000 pro-marriage tax credit, requires 50 percent of AFDC recipients to work by 1996; requires single able-bodied food stamp recipients to work for benefits; and freezes the rate of growth in several welfare programs at 3.5 percent per year.

The Welfare and Teenage Pregnancy Reduction Act (H.R. 1293). This measure freezes AFDC at current funding levels and returns the program to the states in the form of block grants, giving states maximum discretion to design their own welfare-to-work programs. The bill also prohibits AFDC benefits to parents under age 18 and requires that paternity be established in order to receive AFDC benefits.

Provisions

Reducing Illegitimacy

The bill is designed to diminish the number of teenage pregnancies and illegitimate births. It prohibits AFDC payments and housing benefits to mothers under age 18 who give birth to out-of-wedlock children. The state has the option of extending this prohibition to mothers ages 18, 19, and 20. The savings generated from this provision to deny AFDC to minor mothers (and to mothers age 18 to 20 if the state elects that option) is returned to the states in the form of block grants to provide services—but not cash payments—to help these young mothers with illegitimate children. The state will use the funds for programs to reduce out-of-wedlock pregnancies, to promote adoption, to establish and operate orphanages, to establish and operate residential group homes for unwed mothers, or for any purpose the state deems appropriate. None of the funds may be used for abortion services or abortion counseling.

The bill also includes a number of other provisions to reduce illegitimacy. While AFDC is prohibited to mothers ages 17 and younger who have children out of wedlock, mothers age 18 who give birth to illegitimate children must live at home in order to receive aid—unless the mother marries the biological father or marries an individual who legally adopts the child. Mothers already receiving AFDC will not receive an increase in benefits if additional children are born out of wedlock. Finally, the bill requires mothers to establish paternity as a condition for receiving AFDC. Exceptions are provided for cases of rape and incest and if the state determines that efforts to establish paternity would result in physical danger to the mother. The bill requires states to establish paternity in 90 percent of their cases. Also, states are encouraged to develop procedures in public hospitals and clinics to determine paternity and establish legal procedures that help pinpoint paternity in a reasonable time period.

Requiring Work

States are allowed to establish their own work training and education programs to help recipients move from the welfare program to paid employment as soon as possible. The training programs require recipients to work for an average of 35 hours a week or 30 hours per week plus five hours engaged in job search activities. One parent in a two-parent family is required to work 32 hours a week plus eight hours of job searching. States may not provide the work programs for more than two years to any individual or family which receives welfare benefits. States have the option of ending AFDC to families that have been on the welfare rolls for two years, if at least one year was spent in a work program. All states must terminate AFDC payments to families who have received a total of five years of welfare benefits—regardless of whether or not the AFDC recipient has participated in a jobs program.

As long as states meet the participation requirements, the federal government will not advise other parts of the program. States will design their own work programs and determine who will be required to participate in them. Part of the participation requirement is requiring a certain number of recipients to participate in the job program. Starting in 1996, 100,000 AFDC recipients will be required to work; in 1997, 200,000 recipients will be required; in 1998, 400,000 will be required; in 1999, 600,000 recipients will be required; in 2000, 900,000 will be required; and by 2001, 1.5 million recipients will be required to work.

Identified non-parents, usually men, who receive food stamp benefits are required to work—eight hours per week for those benefits.

Capping the Growth of Welfare Spending

The bill caps the spending growth of AFDC, SSI and numerous public housing programs, and the mandatory work program established under the bill. The cap equals the amount spent the preceding year for these programs with an adjustment for inflation plus growth in poverty population. The entitlement status of these programs is ended.

The bill also consolidates a number of nutrition programs into a block grant to states, funded in the first year at 95 percent of the aggregate amount of the individual programs. Programs consolidated into the block grant include food stamps, the supplemental feeding program for women, infants, and children (WIC), and the school lunch and breakfast programs, among others. Under the block grant, states will distribute food assistance to economically disadvantaged individuals more freely.

To further reduce welfare spending, welfare assistance (AFDC, SSI, food stamps, housing and host of other public assistance) is denied to non-citizens, except refugees over 75 years of age, those lawfully admitted to the U.S., or those who have resided in the U.S. for at least five years. Emergency medical assistance will continue to be provided to non-citizens.

State Flexibility

The bill allows states to create their own work programs and determine who participates in them. States can also opt out of the AFDC program and convert their AFDC payments into a fixed annual block grant and have the option to provide new residents AFDC benefits comparable to the level provided in the state in which they previously resided. To help combat illiteracy, states may reduce AFDC payments by up to $75 per month to mothers under the age of twenty-one who have not completed high school or earned their high school "equivalency". Payments may also be reduced if a dependent child does not maintain minimum school attendance.

Other Provisions

State adoption agencies are encouraged to decrease the amount of time a child must wait to be adopted (today, the average child waits approximately 2.8 years). Specifically, the bill prohibits states from discriminating on the basis of race, color or national origin when placing children for adoption.

Also, AFDC beneficiaries who the state identifies as addicted to drugs or alcohol must enroll in an addiction treatment program and participate in random drug testing in order to continue receiving welfare benefits.

Estimated Savings

The bill is estimated to result in net savings of approximately $40 billion over five years. The denial of welfare to non-citizens saves about $22 billion, the cap on welfare spending saves about $18 billion, the nutrition block grant saves about $11 billion, and the requirement for paternity establishment saves about $2 billion. The costs included in the bill are $9.9 billion for the work program and approximately $2 billion for miscellaneous state options.

Supreme Court Decision in *Saenz v. Roe*

In Saenz, Director, California Department of Social Services et al. v. Roe et. al., *the Supreme Court ruled on May 17, 1999, that a provision in PRWORA allowing states to pay differential welfare benefits to new residents violated the Fourteenth Amendment's equal protection clause by infringing on recipients' right to travel. The following are selected excerpts from the Court decision.*

SAENZ, DIRECTOR,
CALIFORNIA DEPARTMENT OF SOCIAL SERVICES, et al.
v.
ROE, et al.,
ON BEHALF OF THEMSELVES AND ALL OTHERS SIMILARLY SITUATED

CERTIORARI TO THE UNITED STATES COURT OF APPEALS
FOR THE NINTH CIRCUIT

No. 98-97. Argued January 13, 1999-Decided May 17, 1999

California, which has the sixth highest welfare benefit levels in the country, sought to amend its Aid to Families with Dependent Children (AFDC) program in 1992 by limiting new residents, for the first year they live in the State, to the benefits they would have received in the State of their prior residence. Cal. Welf. & Inst. Code Ann.§11450.03. Although the Secretary of Health and Human Services approved the change—a requirement for it to go into effect—the Federal District Court enjoined its implementation, finding that, under *Shapiro v. Thompson*, 394 U.S. 618, and *Zobel v. Williams*, 457 U.S. 55, it penalized "the decision of new residents to migrate to [California] and be treated [equally] with existing residents," *Green v. Anderson*, 811 F. Supp. 516, 521. After the Ninth Circuit invalidated the Secretary's approval of §11450.03 in a separate proceeding, this Court ordered *Green* to be dismissed. The provision thus remained inoperative until after Congress enacted the Personal Responsibility and Work Opportunity Reconciliation Act of 1996 (PRWORA), which replaced AFDC with Temporary Assistance to Needy Families (TANF). PRWORA expressly authorizes any State receiving a TANF grant to pay the benefit amount of another State's TANF program to residents who have lived in the State for less than 12 months. Since the Secretary no longer needed to approve §11450.03, California announced that enforcement would begin on April 1, 1997. On that date, respondents filed this class action, challenging the constitutionality of §11450.03's durational residency requirement and PRWORA's approval of that requirement. In issuing a preliminary injunction, the District Court found that PRWORA's existence did not affect its analysis in *Green*. Without reaching the merits, the Ninth Circuit affirmed the injunction.

Held:

1. Section 11450.03 violates Section 1 of the Fourteenth Amendment.

(a) In assessing laws denying welfare benefits to newly arrived residents, this Court held in *Shapiro* that a State cannot enact durational residency requirements in order to inhibit the migration of needy persons into the State, and that a classification that has the effect of imposing a penalty on the right to travel violates the Equal Protection Clause absent a compelling governmental interest.

(b) The right to travel embraces three different components: the right to enter and leave another State; the right to be treated as a welcome visitor while temporarily present in another State; and, for those travelers who elect to become permanent residents, the right to be treated like other citizens of that State.

(c) The right of newly arrived citizens to the same privileges and immunities enjoyed by other citizens of their new State—the third aspect of the right to travel—is at issue here. That right is protected by the new arrival's status as both a state citizen and a United States citizen, and it is plainly identified in the Fourteenth Amendment's Privileges or Immunities Clause, see *Slaughter-House Cases*, 16 Wall. 36, 80. That newly arrived citizens have both state and federal capacities adds special force to their claim that they have the same rights as others who share their citizenship.

(d) Since the right to travel embraces a citizen's right to be treated equally in her new State of residence, a discriminatory classification is itself a penalty. California's classifications are defined entirely by the period of residency and the location of the disfavored class members' prior residences. Within the category of new residents, those who lived in another country or in a State that had higher benefits than California are treated like lifetime residents; and within the broad subcategory of new arrivals who are treated less favorably, there are 45 smaller classes whose benefit levels are determined by the law of their former States. California's legitimate interest in saving money does not justify this discriminatory scheme. The Fourteenth Amendment's Citizenship Clause expressly equates citizenship with residence, *Zobel,* 457 U.S., at 69, and does not tolerate a hierarchy of subclasses of similarly situated citizens based on the location of their prior residences.

2. PRWORA's approval of durational residency requirements does not resuscitate §11450.03. This Court has consistently held that Congress may not authorize the States to violate the Fourteenth Amendment. Moreover, the protection afforded to a citizen by that Amendment's Citizenship Clause limits the powers of the National Government as well as the States. Congress' Article I powers to legislate are limited not only by the scope of the Framers' affirmative delegation, but also by the principle that the powers may not be exercised in a way that violates other specific provisions of the Constitution. See *Williams v. Rhodes,* 393 U.S. 23, 29.

134 F.3d 1400, affirmed.

Stevens, J., delivered the opinion of the Court, in which O'Connor, Scalia, Kennedy, Souter, Ginsburg, and Breyer, JJ., joined. Rehnquist, C. J., filed a dissenting opinion, in which Thomas, J., joined. Thomas, J., filed a dissenting opinion, in which Rehnquist, C. J., joined.

Index

Note: *t* next to page number refers to tables, and *n* refers to notes.